Singular Stars

✳ JUDY MARTIN'S
BOOK OF LONE STAR QUILTS

CROSLEY-GRIFFITH PUBLISHING COMPANY

Wintry Lone Star, page 23

San Francisco Lone Star, page 26

New Orleans Lone Star, page 29

Sea Breeze, page 58

Midnight Lone Star, page 117

Colorado Lone Star, page 134

Traditional Lone Star, page 54

Spiral Radiant Star, page 62

Skewed Nine-Patch, page 77

Shiloh, page 83

Galileo's Star, page 90

Harvest Lone Star, page 97

Crosley-Griffith Publishing Company, Inc.
www.judymartin.com   (800) 642-5615
Photography by Mittera Creative Services, Des Moines, IA
Printed by Colorfx, Des Moines, IA

Contents

Harvest Lone Star (Bordered), page 98

Supernova, page 105

Star of Wonder, page 119

Appalachian Spring, page 138

Queen of Diamonds, page 145

Wave on Wave, page 152

Acknowledgments

Special thanks to Chris Hulin, Margy Sieck, and Marilyn Deppe for making quilts from my designs; to Lana Corcoran, Deb Treusch, Jane Bazyn, and Lee Smith for quilting the quilts; to Jan Krentz for permission to adapt her Spiral Lone Star design; to Will Bennett for the cover design and for book design suggestions; to Kate Bennett for clerical assistance, and to Steve Bennett, Chris Hulin, and Margy Sieck for proofreading.

Singular Stars Will Help You Master Unique & Beautiful Lone Star Quilts with Minimal Fuss

Who Has Time For Anything Less?

Why make a Lone Star quilt?

The Lone Star has a reputation for being (Dare I say it?) hard. Let me tell you a little story: I came to quilt making after I had been sewing all of my clothes for five years. The sense of satisfaction I got from completing my first (and very simple) quilt was so much more than I ever derived from making a dress or a jacket. The moment I finished that quilt I was already planning my next quilt! Once I had a taste for quilt making, I never went back to dressmaking.

Because not many beginners would choose a Lone Star for their first quilt, I assume you already know the joy of quilt making. I mention this anecdote because I think that you will find that the same elevation of satisfaction awaits you when you take the leap from making a quilt to making a **Lone Star** quilt. There is simply no comparison: the feeling you get from making an heirloom Lone Star quilt beats hands down what you may have felt making most other quilts. A Lone Star rewards you with its beauty, with the praise it garners, the pride you feel, and with the satisfaction you feel in meeting a challenge, mastering new skills, and gaining confidence in your abilities.

Okay. So you want to make a Lone Star. It's still hard, right? Don't let its reputation intimidate you. Let's look at what may have contributed to the notion of its being difficult and see how we can improve the process and the product. (Here's a hint: There's a book for that!)

More Math for Me = No Math for You (+ Better Patterns All Around)

Let's address the elephant in the room: that pesky Lone Star math. I have a confession to make: I like math. Don't worry; this means you don't have to. By doing lots of math (in the passenger seat of the car on a cross-country trip), I discovered a set of numbers with nearly magical properties for Lone Star quilts. By simply making the blocks in the sizes I list, you will be able to cut all of the strips and rows and background squares and triangles using nice numbers on your regular rotary ruler, and everything will fit together precisely, with perfect diamonds and all. I have found magical numbers for small, medium, and large Lone Stars, as well as Broken Stars and other arrangements. Some of the numbers relate to others, meaning you

can make my Broken Star from small blocks and add the pieced border from my Lone Star made from large blocks, and it will fit perfectly.

So Much to See, So Little to Draw

A second, related, factor is that Lone Stars do not lend themselves to drawing on graph paper. However, with 183 illustrated examples here, do you really need to draw your Lone Star? With my magical numbers, the cutting and sewing is much easier than the drawing! If you have an uncontrollable urge to draw your quilt, on my website I provide Lone Star graph paper for free download at judymartin.com/LSgraph.cfm

Y-Seams? What Y-Seams?

Traditionally, Lone Star construction involves the dreaded Y-seam, also known as a set-in seam. This may be the single, biggest deterrent to making Lone Star quilts. You will be happy to learn that you can make nearly all of the quilts in this book with nary a Y-seam. I present these patterns with a choice of background patches so you can make the quilts with or without Y-seams. However, you will find that when your cutting and sewing are accurate, Y-seams are no big deal. My how-to chapter gives you tips for perfecting your seam allowances as well as for tackling Y-seams, should you desire to do so.

Calm Advice for Joint Jitters

Lone Stars have some tricky joints. I think you will find that your joints will get better and better as you make your quilt. I know mine did. I also found that if my joints missed here and there, I only needed to rip out a half-inch or so at the joint in question, and my second try was nearly always good enough. On page 15, I share my best tips for mastering the joints. If they still worry you, I suggest you start your Lone Star adventure with the Sea Breeze quilt on page 58. I designed this quilt to almost entirely eliminate the need to match joints.

Singular Stars: What's in Store for You?

This book will have you looking at Lone Star quilts in a whole new way. The book's comprehensive approach to strip-pieced Lone Stars will give you new confidence to make Lone Stars; its innovative designs will provide ample inspiration; and the accurate patterns and how-to information will guide you every step of the way as you create your own singular star quilt.

For a start, I present photographs and complete patterns for the 18 quilts my friends and I made for the book. But wait: there's more! The book includes 73 surprisingly different looking variations of these quilts, made using the same blocks and strip sets, with yardage figures when they differ from the yardage presented in the main pattern. Besides the sewn quilts and variations, there are four chapters packed with Lone Stars. In all, *Singular Stars* has patterns for 26 queen- or king-sized Lone Stars, 33 simple, little Lone Stars, and 120 variations, complete with yardage figures.

One pattern is for a traditional Lone Star because a Lone Star book would not be complete without it.

One pattern is a 16-pointed variation of Jan Krentz's brilliant Spiral Lone Star (used with permission). I also designed a new pieced border for the quilt.

Other than these two, the quilts are never-before-published Lone Star designs based on original diamond-shaped blocks. Some of these designs depart from the traditional simply with coloring, taking the basic pattern beyond octagonal rings of color.

THE SAME SHAPES, NEW COLORINGS
The "Gradated Lone Star Mix & Match" chapter (page 32) starts with little Lone Stars having blocks

with a traditional outline and unique colorings that use gradated fabric selections or ombre fabrics for new looks. These are subtly shaded, shimmering geometric compositions, each a new interpretation of the Lone Star in a simple wall quilt.

At the end of the chapter, I present Grand Lone Stars made by mixing and matching the blocks from the small stars in sets of four per star point. If you like, you can take this mixing and matching further on your own to make countless more.

The gradated patterns include yardage figures, exploded block diagrams, pressing arrows, shared quilt assembly diagrams, and abbreviated instructions.

The Spiral Radiant Star shown at left is made from 8 block types, with each one advancing the color placement up one row from the previous block. In the "Spiral-Block Mix & Match" chapter (page 67), I recombine these blocks in various configurations of 4 per star point to create brilliant explosions of color that suggest flickering flames and exuberant blooms as much as they bring to mind the traditional Lone Star that provides the basic outline for these quilts.

I give 7 complete patterns and show 21 variations, with yardage and complete patterns for each. I also show you how you can turn 7 patterns into dozens and dozens of different quilts simply by rotating the blocks, much as you would for a Log Cabin quilt.

My previous book covered Log Cabin quilts, so I found myself looking for ways to achieve the setting possibilities inherent in a Log Cabin in my Lone Star book, as well. By mixing and matching 4 diamond-shaped blocks per star point, I multiplied the possibilities for rotating and rearranging blocks to achieve new looks in the gradated and spiral-block chapters as well as in the Supernova and Star of Wonder patterns.

ROTATE BLOCKS FOR NEW LOOKS

In Supernova (page 105) and Star of Wonder (page 119), I introduce a couple of additional strip widths and row widths to make four asymmetrical block types for each quilt. You can make the eight blocks of each type, according to the pattern directions, and then play with rotating them to make a stunning array of variations. I show a dozen unique and surprisingly different versions of each of these quilts, all using the exact same blocks and yardage figures!

NEW SHAPES ADD NEW EXCITEMENT

My Appalachian Spring, Wave on Wave, and Queen of Diamonds patterns vary the strip widths and the row widths to form dazzling undulating curves and scallops in large Lone Stars.

MIX-AND-MATCH FUN

Mixing and matching is a major theme of this book. Because of their related sizes, you can incorporate satellite stars from the Queen of Diamonds pattern (page 145) into any of the 84½" Lone Stars.

Several of the pieced borders can be applied to a variety of quilts, as well.

Shiloh (page 83) is a unique color variation that makes a star within a star. The small block is useful for little Lone Stars or for large quilts in Broken Star, Unfolding Star, Grand Lone Star, or four-Lone Star arrangements. I list yardage separately for the backgrounds in each of these arrangements. This allows you to easily mix and match gradated blocks, spiral blocks, or any of the 8¾"-wide blocks in the book with the sets presented with Shiloh.

LET'S GET STARTED ON YOUR LONE STAR

You'll find plenty of inspiration within these pages, and plenty of information, too, if you take the time to read it. Let me stress: If you read just 2 pages, make them the "Pattern Pointers" on pages 8–9. If you skip them, you might miss some of the useful information to be gleaned from the pattern diagrams. With *Singular Stars* as your guide, you will soon be ready to make your own Lone Star. In fact, the hardest part will be deciding which Lone Star you want to make first!

The Language of Singular Stars
A Brief Glossary

Analogous Colors: two or more colors that are neighbors on the color wheel, such as blue and blue-green.

Arm: my term for the diamond-shaped unit that makes up one-eighth of the star. This is usually a block, but some of my quilts are made with each arm composed of 4 small blocks.

Assembly-Line Strategies: an efficient approach to patchwork that has you repeat the same step for multiple blocks or units before proceeding with the next step for each block or unit.

Block: the diamond-shaped construction unit made from rows of diamonds (or sometimes parallelograms).

Chain Piecing: an efficient sewing method that has you leave the work under the needle after sewing a seam, stitch through thin air for a couple of stitches, and proceed with the next seam. This leaves a chain of thread between units that you snip later.

Cloth Template: a rotary cutting guide for a patch having hard-to-measure or oversized dimensions or an unusual shape. You measure, mark, and rotary cut the cloth template from unwanted or inexpensive (but not wiggly or stretchy) fabric. To use it, smooth it over one or more layers of the fabric you wish to cut, and align your rotary ruler with its edges, one at a time, to cut along the ruler's edge.

Diamond: my term for a sub-unit of the block. In strip piecing you will cut no diamonds. However, upon its completion, the block appears to be made from diamonds, and I may refer to these as diamonds.

Finger-Pressing: creasing the seam allowances to one side by running your thumbnail over the seamline from the front of the work.

Gradated: having a series of blended hues or values.

Grand Lone Star: a Lone Star with 4 blocks per arm.

Hue: the color of a fabric, regardless of how light or dark it is.

Opposing Seams (also called nesting seams): a sewing joint where seam allowances of two previously seamed segments are pressed in opposite directions so that they align with one another to help you match joints and distribute bulk.

Oversized Pressing Board: a large plywood board covered with cotton batting and fabric. This can be placed over your ironing board or over a bookcase or cabinet of appropriate height. Instructions for making one are on page 11.

Point Trimming: cutting off the excess seam allowance at the point of a triangle or diamond before sewing. The trim helps you align patches precisely for stitching.

Pressing Lid: a flannel-covered board placed over freshly steam-pressed patchwork. This improves pressing outcomes by holding in the heat for a few minutes. You can easily make your own pressing lid. (See page 12.) A pressing lid also makes a useful lapboard or portable staging area for laying out block parts prior to piecing them.

Rotate Blocks: turn the blocks 180° so that the tips that had been closer to the center of the quilt are now the tips farther from the center.

Row: one of several units used to construct the block. In strip piecing, the row is the resulting unit when you cut a strip set into pieces of a specific width parallel to the angled end.

Satellite Stars: small stars in the background of a Lone Star or other set. These can be seen in the Queen of Diamonds quilt on page 145.

Set or **Setting:** the arrangement of diamond-shaped blocks to form a star or other configuration. Lone Star, Broken Star, Radiant Star and Unfolding Star are examples of classic sets.

Strip Set: a construction unit made by sewing several strips together along their long sides.

Tips: my term for the pointy ends of the block; the outer tips are the pointy ends that are furthest from the center of the quilt.

Value: how light or dark a color or printed fabric appears. The value of a fabric may be relative to its neighbors. For example, the pastel prints of a depression-era quilt are dark compared to the muslin background.

Y-Seam (also called a set-in seam): a sewing joint requiring you to stop stitching at the end of the seamline (¼" in from the raw edge) at the corner; remove the work from under the needle; move the seam allowances aside; and resume stitching the subsequent seam at the precise point where you stopped stitching earlier. I recommend backtacking at the corner to secure a Y-seam. Some quilters prefer to avoid Y-seams. Most of my patterns give you a choice of background patches for use with or without Y-seams.

Pattern Pointers

2 Pages You Must Read to Get the Most from My Patterns

Read these 2 pages and you may find that you can just look at pictures for the rest of the book. My pattern diagrams have lots of information in them that you might never know about if you skip this section.

Check your seam allowance using my test on page 10 before you embark on a Lone Star quilt.

Cut a little, sew a little: I list strip totals at the beginning of each pattern. That does not mean you must cut out all strips before you begin sewing. Cut a little, then sew a little if you prefer working that way.

Cutting diamonds or cutting diamond rows from strip sets is not so different from cutting squares or Nine-Patch rows. The measurement given is the distance between two parallel sides of the strip or row. For true diamonds, you cut strips and rows the same size. You do not need to measure along the side of the strip and make a mark. To cut a 2¼"-wide row from a strip set, you simply place the 2¼" line over the angled end of the strip and cut along the ruler's edge.

Color numbers: Some of my patterns have several shades of a color. I have numbered the colors in the yardage charts, strip piecing diagrams, and in blocks where needed so you can tell the colors apart.

A number in a black or white circle in a quilt assembly diagram indicates sewing sequence. Sew the seam labeled "1" first; sew the seam labeled "2" next, and so on. When there are multiples of a number sequence, the quilt has similar units in different quadrants of the quilt. Make these assembly-line style, sewing all of the #1 seams before proceeding to all the #2 seams.

Pressing arrows: Diagrams show which direction to press seam allowances: press toward the pointy end of the little "v" at each seam.

Do not resize blocks. My block sizes are magical. If you resize the blocks, they will lose their magical properties. That means you must not add rows of diamonds to the block, and you must not change the sizes of the strips, rows, or diamonds unless these changes do not alter the block size.

Do not resize pieced borders. The same goes for my pieced borders. If you change the size or number of repeats in the pieced border, or if you change the width of the inner border, you will lose the patterns' magical properties. The one exception is the spiral-block border on page 65. You can change the number of repeats in that border because the block size is magical.

Lengthwise grain: I suggest you cut all of your Lone Star strips on the lengthwise grain. My patterns call for strip-piecing strips 18" long, cut parallel to the selvage. There is a very real difference in stretchiness between the lengthwise and crosswise grains. A Lone Star block will have bias for two sides; it is better to have lengthwise grain than crosswise for the remaining two sides.

Strip ends: I have you cut one end of a strip at a 45° angle, as shown in the yardage chart. I also have you trim this point as described on page 14. This helps you join strips without guesswork or waste.

Strip sets and rows are labeled with letters at the beginning of the alphabet; blocks use letters from the end of the alphabet or extend into lower case letters.

Chain piecing and assembly-line sewing: The diagrams may suggest that you sew one thing to another, then add a third thing. This does not mean that you must finish one unit before starting another one just like it. I encourage you to piece assembly-line style, repeating one step as many times as necessary before proceeding to the next step. I am all for chain piecing and assembly-line strategies.

Yardage figures allow a little extra for shrinkage if you prewash fabric. They also include a small amount extra for the occasional cutting error. They do not allow enough extra for recutting a big background square that you accidentally cut too small (a good reason for using my cloth rotary cutting template method).

Borders are lengthwise and seamless (except for the ombre borders in New Orleans Lone Star). Border lengths are exact with seam allowances included. They are sized exactly for miters at the corners, unless otherwise noted. If you prefer abutted borders, you can trim them down for that instead of mitering them.

Background patch dimensions include seam allowances. Cut the largest patches first.

No trimming down or squaring up. Listed dimensions do not include extra for trimming down or squaring up. If your seam allowance is right, you won't need to trim down or square up.

Block, quilt, and star sizes are finished sizes, without seam allowances.

Binding figures are for doubled binding cut 2" wide on the lengthwise grain.

Backing dimensions allow for ¼" seams between panels and 8" of extra length and width for mounting on longarm quilting machines.

More about the math: If you like math, you will find an explanation of what is magical about my patterns on my web site at judymartin.com/magic.cfm

The Yardage Charts

At the top of the yardage chart, I list the star size and quilt size (including borders). The length and width are the same in all cases. I also list the block width, measuring the distance between two parallel sides. All of these dimensions are finished sizes, not including seam allowances. I also list the types and quantities of blocks here.

The yardage chart identifies the fabrics in the quilt with a colored box and a number to help you distinguish similar shades. Within a color family, the darkest shade has the lowest number.

Next I list the yardage requirement for each fabric. This includes 5% for shrinkage in case you wish to prewash your fabric, as I do. If the pattern calls for 1 yard for cutting strips for strip piecing, and your preshunk fabric measures 34", cut 2 lengths of 17" instead of 1 length of 18" and 1 length of 16".

Strip quantities are listed next. All strips are cut 18" long. Strip widths and strip end cuts vary. I list quantites separately for each type from each fabric.

Strip ends can be regular: ⬡ or reversed: ◹ , as indicated by the icon at the right of the chart. If you cut strips from folded fabric, you will get regular and reversed strip ends in equal quantities. If you do not need them in equal quantities, unfold the fabric before you cut the ends off the strips.

Most fabrics will be cut into strips for strip piecing. Some fabrics are needed for background patches or borders. When a fabric is to be used for background or borders as well as strips for strip piecing, cut the large border strips or background patches first. Then cut the remaining fabric into 18" lengths for cutting strips.

Everything can be rotary cut in these patterns, even when I provide a template. I do so only for pieced borders having uncommon shapes or sizes that may not be in your rotary cutting repertoire. In these cases, I give illustrated instructions for rotary cutting them and trimming points to help you align patches for sewing.

The yardage charts list binding and backing requirements. The binding is narrow, doubled, and cut on the lengthwise grain. See page 22 for complete binding instructions. The backing yardage is for fabric 42"–45" wide. I allow 8" extra length and width for mounting the quilt on a longarm quilting machine.

The Strip Piecing Diagrams

The strip piecing diagrams show strips sewn together to make a strip set. They show the sequence of fabrics, with color numbers at the right end of the strip to help you distinguish similar shades.

Just to the right of the strip set, strips are labeled with their cut width. All strips are 18" long and cut on the lengthwise grain. At the left end of the strip set,

you can see how each strip end is cut at a 45° angle. The strip set diagram shows the rows that you will cut from the strip set. The row on the left is slightly separated from the strip set to show that it is already cut off.

Within this first row the "v" icons point in the direction you should press the seam allowances.

Below the leftmost row is the width you should cut the rows. This is the cut width of the row from the raw edge on one side of the row to the raw edge on the opposite side of the row. Lay your rotary ruler's ruling matching the listed row width precisely on the angled edge of the strip; also align the 45° line of your ruler with a raw edge or seamline of the strip set. Cut along the edge of your ruler.

Additional diagonal lines on the strip set outline rows not yet cut. Below the strip set, I tell you how many strip sets of that type you should make. I also tell you the total number of rows you will need to cut. Sometimes, it is possible to cut more rows from a strip set than I show. You do not need to cut more than I show. For example, a strip set may be long enough to cut 6 rows; you need 8 rows; I show 4 rows because you need to cut 4 rows from each of 2 strip sets to result in the 8 rows required.

The Block Diagrams

The block diagram may be presented before or after the associated strip-set diagram. In the block diagram, you will find pressing arrows to indicate which direction to press the seams used to join the rows. Above or in the block diagram are letters indicating what strip set each row was cut from.

The Gradated Block Diagrams

In the case of the gradated Lone Stars on pages 32–53, I show only a block diagram; I do not show the strip sets. It is easy to see the strip sets when you look at the block's rows. See figures 1 and 2 on page 33. Each row is cut from a different strip set. The color sequence for each row is the same as the color sequence for its strip set. The strip ends are all the same in this chapter, with no reverses. The strip widths are all the same, as well: cut 2¼" wide. The strip set looks just like the row, except the strip set is wide enough to cut 4 rows. I give in the gradated block drawings some of the information I would have presented in the strip sets. These block drawings have color numbers; they also have pressing arrows for the strip sets' seams as well as the block's seams. The letters above the block diagram represent both the strip set and the row cut from the strip set. Next to the block drawing, I list how many strip sets to make of each type and how many total rows to cut. On the other side of the block, I list how many blocks of this type the quilt requires.

By showing you how to see the strip sets in the block, I can present 2–3 patterns per page instead of 1 pattern in 3 pages. This means more patterns for your money!

9

How to Make a Lone Star Quilt

BEFORE YOU BEGIN YOUR LONE STAR

Selecting Fabric for Your Lone Star

My personal preference is for Lone Stars with colors that blend in some areas and contrast with each other in certain places. I like a strong contrast of visual texture and value where the diamond blocks touch the background. As the large background patches are ideal for showcasing beautiful quilting, I often use a solid background to allow the quilting to shine.

Within the diamond blocks, I recommend avoiding directional prints (like stripes) if you are making some of the Lone Stars with parallelograms as well as diamonds. The strip-pieced units can look out of balance when the stripes go every which way. The blocks with fewer strip sets, such as Star of Wonder, will look less balanced than those like Galileo's Star and/or Supernova, that always have the long sides of the parallelograms on the straight grain.

Before you cut into your fabric, I suggest arranging your fabrics in a row, following the sequence you plan to use. Overlap them so you see a couple of inches of each one. In a second row, place the background fabric,

touching each of the other fabrics. Take a photo to judge how the fabrics work together. You may want to convert the photo to black and white to help you see the contrasts.

Mastering the Perfect Scant ¼" Seam Allowance

I usually recommend making a sample block before you cut out the rest of the quilt. With the strip piecing involved here, I suggest verifying the accuracy of your scant ¼" seam allowances. This is not a matter of measuring your seam allowance. Seam allowances often look pretty good and line up with a ruler pretty well. However, if your seams start to jog as you get farther along, a very slight correction may help you achieve the results you desire.

Take my seam allowance test. The proper scant ¼" seam allowance will go a long way toward taking the frustration out of making a Lone Star (or any quilt). From leftover fabric, cut 9 squares of 1½" and 1 rectangle 1½" x 9½". Sew the squares end to end. Finger-press and press seams to one side. Lay the squares over the rectangle. They should be the same size. Pin them together along one long side, aligning the two pieces at the top. Do not ease. Pin and stitch the seam. If the squares come up shorter than the rectangle, your seam allowance is too deep. If your squares overhang the rectangle, your seams are too shallow.

Three seam allowance tests: 1) rectangle overhangs on right, seams too deep; 2) squares overhang on right, seams too shallow; 3) no overhang, seams perfect.

How do you correct your seam allowance? Let's say, for the sake of simplicity, that your squares are ½" shorter than the rectangle. (This is an extreme example. Your seam allowances will be better than this!) You will have sewn eight seams affecting 16 seam allowances. Take the ½" shortage and divide it by 16 seam allowances. Your seam is too deep by $^1/_{32}$". More realistically, your squares might be ⅛" short, meaning each seam allowance is too deep by ⅛" ÷ 16 = $^1/_{128}$". That is not a very big error, but if you correct it, all your sewing will go more easily. The line below is $^1/_{128}$" wide:

That is about a thread's width. Your adjustment will be small, but it will make a big difference in your patchwork. If you can move your sewing machine needle to the left just a tick, that might do the trick. If you use an etched or tape guide on your throatplate, place another piece of tape to the left of your tape or line, with just a glint of space between them. Remove the old tape guide, if you had one, and put a new one directly to the right of the tape you just placed. The two tapes should touch all along their edges. Remove the tape on the left. The new tape guide should serve you well. I use black electrical tape, which lasts longer and gets less gummy than masking tape.

Black electrical tape on throatplate for use as a seam gauge.

Making an Oversized Pressing & Blocking Surface

Nearly 25 years ago, when I had my current sewing room built above my garage, I made myself an oversized ironing board. As I had the space for it, I assembled a sturdy Inter Metro wire shelving unit for its base. The shelf unit is 36" high, 18" deep, and 48" long.

Oversized pressing board mounted on a shelf unit.

I store my ironing supplies and stacks of fabric on the shelves. For the pressing surface, I had the lumber yard cut a 4-foot x 8-foot x ¾" sheet of plywood into one piece 30" x 60". If you have the space, you can make your surface wider to keep big quilts from dragging on the floor, but I found the 60" length was about as far as my iron's cord would reach. I had the plywood remnants cut into 18" squares for pressing lids/lap boards/ portable work stations (see page 12).

I cut two 1" x 2" x 8-foot furring boards into a total of two 4-foot lengths and two 18" lengths. I placed the 30" x 60" plywood face down on the floor, and I centered the top of the shelf unit on top of the plywood. I arranged the 1" x 2" boards to hug the shelf top, and drilled and screwed them to the plywood, making sure the screws would not go all the way through the plywood. You can cover your pressing board with snazzy fabric, or you can make it strictly utilitarian with a plain cover. In any case, start with 2 yards of 40"- 45"-wide 100% cotton fabric and some 100% cotton batting without scrim. Cut the batting into 2 pieces 33" x 63". Prewash the fabric in warm water and tumble dry it. Lay the batting on the floor in 2 layers. Center the plywood over it, face down with the 1" x 2" boards up. Starting at the center of each side, pull the batting around to the back of the board and secure it using a staple gun. Staple every few inches around the perimeter. Cut away the excess at the corners so the batting does not overlap. Cut the fabric to measure 36" x 66". Lay it face down on the floor. Center the plywood, face down, over it. Pull the fabric around to the back of the plywood, and use a staple gun to secure it, as you did with the batting. Be careful to avoid the staples already in the board. Place the pressing board over the shelf unit with the 1"x 2" boards hugging the shelf unit.

If you have covered your pressing board with pretty fabric, you may want to cover a second board with plain fabric on which you can draw lines for blocking. Use the same method I describe above for the oversized pressing board. However, you won't need the 1" x 2" boards. Besides the ¾" plywood cut 30" x 48", you will need 1 piece of cotton batting cut 33" x 51" and 1⅝ yards of heavy duty white flannel. (You may be able to find this at a drapery and upholstery fabric store.) Prewash the flannel in warm water and tumble dry on medium high heat. Cut it 38" x 56". Staple the batting, then the flannel, to the board as described above. To use your blocking board, place it on your oversized pressing board or on a table. Use a permanent marker to measure and mark an outline of the block, row, or other unit, including seam allowances. (For one of the 8¾" blocks in this book, mark a diamond 9¼" wide.) I was making numerous quilts for the book, so I outlined diamond blocks in 12⅞" and 18" widths, as well. Below is my blocking board with outlines for diamond blocks of 3 sizes. I also outlined a single row and a 2-row unit 3¼" wide for use with the Traditional Lone Star pattern. (This width is 2 times the 1⅞" cut size of each row minus ½" for the seam already sewn.) It is helpful to extend the lines a little beyond the shape to allow you to see some indication of the outline when the block or unit is on top of it. Here is my blocking board with outlines:

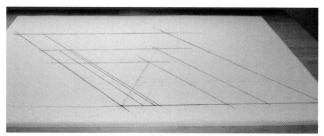

Blocking board with block and row outlines.

To use the blocking board, press your block or unit from the back, then flip it over to press the front. Align the unit with the outline, as shown below. Press straight down with a steam iron. For the absolute best results, cover with a pressing lid until it cools.

Blocking rows to an outline on a flannel blocking board.

Making and Using a Pressing Lid

A pressing lid is my own term for a piece of plywood covered with flannel. I made several from the leftovers from making my oversized pressing board and blocking board. These are handy for laying out strips, patches, and units before making them into blocks for a Lone Star or other quilt. They are also useful as a lap board when I am sitting in front of the TV. Best of all, they can be used as a pressing aid. If you are familiar with a tailor's clapper, this uses the same principle. I used pressing lids for all the Lone Stars in this book, and I have never before pressed so perfectly. You have to try this!

To make 2 pressing lids, buy ¾ yard of heavy white flannel 40"- 45" wide, preshrink it, and cut it into two 20" squares. Cut two 18" x 18" x ¾" pieces of plywood

(the top side should be smooth; the bottom doesn't have to be). Lay one square of flannel face down on a work surface. Center the plywood square, smooth side down, over the flannel. Wrap the flannel around the edges to the back of the board. Starting in the center of each side, use a staple gun to secure it tightly in place. Staple every inch or two. Fold it to distribute the bulk at the corners. Cut off the excess fabric.

Two pressing lids face down over a large block.

To use the pressing lids, steam press your blocks or units on your ironing board, blocking board, or oversized pressing board. Press the backs of several small units or one large one, then press their fronts. Immediately cover the work with a pressing lid, flannel side down. Leave the lid in place long enough for the work to cool. The boards hold the heat and keep the work perfectly flat, with the seam allowances making depressions in the surface of the ironing board.

In assembling the diamond blocks into stars, I sometimes direct you to press in ways that seem counterintuitive, but they really do work using this system. You can easily press seam allowances toward the bulk using this method, and seam allowances will stay put for quilting. I carefully considered the pressing arrows to allow seams to oppose where they might not otherwise and to distribute the bulk evenly.

When I assembly-line piece, I press several small units, cover them with a pressing lid, and go on to press more units on another area of my oversized pressing board. I cover these with a second lid, and I remove the work from under the first one so I can reuse it. Depending on how fast you work and how big your pressing surface is, you might want a third pressing lid to keep things moving.

Preparation for Sewing

For machine sewing, set your stitch length at about ten stitches per inch. If you have shortened your stitch for paper piecing at some point, don't forget to reset your machine to a longer stitch.

Use a size 10 or 11 sewing machine needle for cottons of the weight typically used for quilts. It's a good idea to change your needle after every large quilt project. My favorite thread is Aurifil 50-weight, a silky-smooth 100% cotton thread that is fine enough for me to thread in spite of my aging eyes. Choose a neutral thread color. I use beige for quilts with a golden cast and silvery gray for quilts that have a cool cast. I don't generally change thread color as I piece the quilt top. I do change thread color to match the fabric across the center of a Lone Star, as when I don't the thread always manages to show there. I also change thread to match when joining binding strips, long border strips, or backing panels.

I suggest winding several bobbins in advance so you won't lose your momentum when your bobbin runs out, and you won't need to rethread your machine nearly so often.

Pin Pointers

Pinning is essential to sewing success whenever seams are long or have joints to match. If you find yourself needing to trim off the hanging end of a row, that is an indication that your machine does not feed the top and bottom fabric evenly. You shouldn't be trimming anything down in these Lone Stars; pin to avoid the overhang. I always pin borders, bindings, lining panels, and block rows at every joint and no more than four inches apart. I pin even short seams if they have joints. I historically have stitched over the pins, though I have broken some needles that way on occasion. Now, more and more often, I remove the pins as I come to them.

If you are having trouble with the joints of your patchwork, it just might be because of your pins. Pins that are too thick, too long, or have a large head may make too much of a hump in the seam line. I prefer pins for patchwork that are very fine (0.5 mm) and pretty short (1¼" or so).

Chain Piecing

Chain piecing allows you to stitch one seam after another without cutting the thread. You can stitch as fast or as slowly as you like. You can backtack at both ends of each seam. You simply join two patches in a seam, stitching from edge to edge. You come to a stop and leave the presser foot down. Insert another pair of patches under the tip of the presser foot. Don't cut the thread. You can stitch through thin air for a couple of stitches if you need to. Chain piecing conserves thread and makes it unnecessary to trim off threads later.

Units will be connected by a twist of thread. When you complete a step, use thread snips to cut units apart. If your sewing machine has an automatic thread-cutting function, you may be able to step on a pedal

to snip threads between units as you chain piece. If you want to use your automatic thread cutter and your thread pulls out of the needle, try different threads until you find one that works with your sewing machine.

Assembly-line Strategies

With assembly-line piecing, you chain piece all of one unit before proceeding to the next one. This can be very efficient, as you only have to think once about what goes next, which way to turn patches, which side to stitch, and so on. If you use this method, be careful or you might repeat a mistake many times before you realize it!

I get impatient with assembly-line work because I am always eager to see results. I usually repeat a step just enough to make one or two strip sets or blocks. After I complete those, I may go back to the beginning and make more or I may start yet another block or strip set.

MAKING A LONE STAR
Cutting Strips on the Lengthwise Grain

Lone Stars, even strip-pieced ones, involve bias on half of the edges and straight grain on the other half. Crosswise grain is much stretchier than lengthwise, so I recommend cutting your strips, as well as borders, lengthwise for stability. (Actually, I cut everything for all my quilts on the lengthwise grain for stability.) My patterns call for strips cut 18" long. They are perfect for fat quarters and half-yard cuts of fabric. In order to cut the 18"-long strips for strip piecing, longer yardages can be cut down to 18" lengths after cutting borders, background patches, or long binding strips. You don't have to throw out everything you've learned about rotary cutting to start using lengthwise strips today. You will need to trim off the selvage before you cut lengthwise strips parallel to the selvage. Everything else is the same as for crosswise strips except the grain and the length of your strips.

Cutting Strip Ends

If you fold the fabric to cut through layers, unfold it before you cut off the strip ends at a 45° angle unless you need strips and their reverses in equal quantities. (Many of the quilts require regular strips only, with no reverses.) If your pattern calls for few or no reverses, you can stack single layers of different fabrics requiring the same strip widths. Below are 2 strips with ends cut.

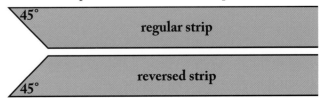

Most of the plain borders in this book are mitered. If you wish to avoid Y-seams (set-in seams), you can attach these borders to the 4 diagonal quadrants of the star before you join the quarters to make half stars. Doing so, allows you to avoid Y-seams in the border as well as avoiding Y-seams within the star. If you use Y-seams where the background meets the diamond blocks, you use the same skill to miter the borders.

I like to cut the ends off my border strips at a 45° angle before I pin and stitch the border to the quilt. I simply cut the border the exact length listed, then cut off the ends at a 45° angle. Make sure that you cut the triangles off the inner edge of the border on both ends as shown here:

| 45° | ∨ inner edge of border ∨ | 45° |

Trimming Points of Strips

Trimming points helps you align strips for stitching. Do not trim the point of the top strip in a regular strip set or the bottom strip of a reversed strip set, as these points will be trimmed later (and differently) as rows. For Lone Star strips you will want to trim the point off at a right angle to the short end of the strip. You can make your own Point Trimmer tool by downloading the file from judymartin.com/LSPT.cfm and following the directions in the file. If you have my Point Trimmer tool, you can use it to get the same result. Place the strip face up on your cutting mat. Align the 2 sides of the 45° angle of the tool with the sides at the point of the fabric strip. The point of the strip will extend about ⅜" beyond the Point Trimmer. Cut off the extending fabric along the edge of the tool. For reversed strips, place fabric face down; trim the point as you would for a regular strip.

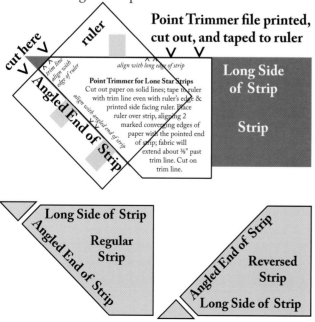

Sewing Strips Together

Refer to the strip set diagram in the pattern for fabric sequence. For a regular strip set, place the first strip face to face over the second strip. (The first strip is the top strip in the strip set diagram.) Align the trimmed point of the second strip with the wide angle of the first strip as shown. Press the strips together with a dry iron and/or pin the strips every 3"–4". Stitch with a scant ¼" seam, starting at the wide angle of the first strip and ending at the square end of the first strip. The square end of the second strip will extend beyond the first strip. Angle your stitches off the edge of the seam allowance at the end of the first strip. This allows

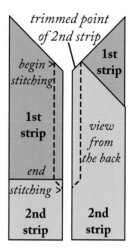

you to chain piece without wasting the time and thread it takes to stitch to the end of the second strip.

Continue in this fashion, adding strips in the order shown for a strip set. If you like, stitch duplicate units in succession if multiple strip sets are needed.

After each seam, leave the strips face to face and press to set the seam allowance. Then open the work and finger press the seam allowance to one side, following the pressing arrows in the strip set diagram. Finally, steam press the seam in the direction you finger pressed it, being careful to avoid tucks. I have several pressing lids 18" square: big enough to put over multiple small units. I press several units in succession. When I am ready to cover them with a pressing lid, I quickly go over each one again in order to heat them again just before I drop the pressing lid over the batch of them.

Continue adding strips to the strip sets in this manner. Finger press and steam press after each seam.

Cutting Rows from the Strip Set

When the strip set is completed and pressed, trim a sliver off the angled end, if necessary, at a perfect 45° angle. The width you need to cut rows is listed below the first row in the strip set diagram. Lay the rule line for the row width over the angled end of the strip. Also align the 45° angle of your ruler with a seam or raw edge of the strip set. This is shown below for a 2¼"-

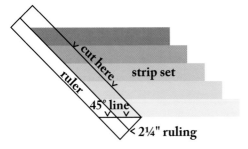

wide strip. The 2¼" ruling is aligned with the angled end of the strip set. Cut along the ruler's edge to make a row. For large strip sets, slide the ruler as necessary,

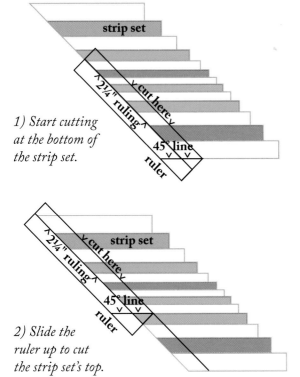

1) Start cutting at the bottom of the strip set.

2) Slide the ruler up to cut the strip set's top.

realigning the 45° angle with a seamline within the strip set or the raw edge at the top. Repeat for each additional row. True up the 45° angle at the end of the strip set after cutting one or two rows, if necessary.

Trimming Points of Rows

Trimming points helps you align rows for stitching. It will also help you make joints that match. To trim the 2 points of a row, you want the trims to be at a right angle to the short ends of the row. You can use my Point Trimmer if you have one. If not, download the file from judymartin.com/LSPT.cfm and follow the directions in the file. The point of the row will extend ⅜" beyond the tool. Cut off the extending fabric even with the edge of the tool. Repeat at the opposite end of the row.

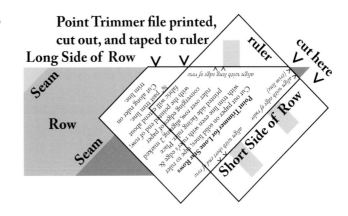

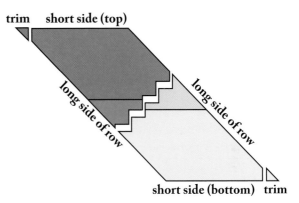

Sewing Rows Together

Place the first (leftmost in the block diagram) and second rows face to face with the second row on top. Align the trimmed end of the point of the second row with the wide angle of the first row; pin. At the opposite end of the rows, align the wide angle of the second row with the trimmed point of the first row. Pin at this end. In between, pin at each joint as described in the next paragraph, and stitch with a scant ¼" seam allowance. Check your joints. If one or more joints do not match to your satisfaction, use your seam ripper to remove the stitches for a half inch or so at the joint in question. See the next topic for ways to improve your joints. When you are happy with the joints, press seam allowances as shown in the block diagram. Continue adding rows, pressing after each seam.

Strategies for Matching Joints

Generally, patchwork seam allowances are pressed to one side rather than being pressed open. This keeps the batting from seeping through the spaces between the stitches. It also forms ridges that will help you align opposing (or nesting) seams perfectly at joints. Hold the joint between your thumb and forefinger and slide the two halves until they stop at the ridge formed by the seam allowances. At this point, the joint matches perfectly. Pin at a slight angle across both sets of seam allowances, and stitch.

If you can make a pinwheel block, you should have no trouble with the joint at the center of the star. I did find that the center joint looked better if I used thread that was similar in value to the diamonds at the center of the star. My pressing arrows have you press seam allowances clockwise or counter-clockwise. (It doesn't matter whether you are looking at the front or the back of the quilt when you follow my pressing arrows.) I planned the pressing to make all of the seams at the quilt center oppose nicely.

The joints between two diamond-shaped blocks should also oppose in nearly every case if you press seam allowances as I indicate in the diagrams.

The joints within the diamond block are trickier. Because the seams there cannot be opposed or nested, it can be a little harder to perfectly align the joints side to side as well as at the precise depth of the seam allowance. An accurate seam allowance gives you the best chance for joints that match. Trimming points with my Point Trimmer also helps here. This gets you off on the right foot by helping you align the trimmed pointy end of one strip with the wide angle of the adjacent strip. (The trimmed edge will have the same angle and will align precisely with the end of the neighboring patch.) Pinning definitely helps, especially for your first Lone Star.

Pin the ends of the strips first, then pin at each joint. Trust your sewing. If one row seems longer between joints than the other, you may have stretched the bias. After pinning (and before stitching the seam), touch the looser segment with the tip of your steam iron. The segment should now fit easily.

When I first started, I found it helpful to set one of those little metal seam gauges to match my seam allowance. I would use the gauge to find the place where my next seam should intersect each seam in the row. With practice, I got to the point where I could "eyeball" it. Either way, stick a pin through the point where the seam in the row intersects the seam depth. Insert a pin at this point in one row, and on

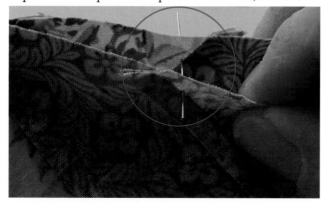

into the intersection in the second row. Pull the pin all the way through until its head is up against the first row and the second row is tight against the first row. Hold this position, insert another pin just barely to the right of this point to keep the rows in place for stitching; pull out the first pin. Repeat at every seam in the row. Stitch the seam, pausing to pull out each pin right after stitching a joint but before you hit the pin. When you finish the seam, check your joints.

Whether your joints are good enough is nobody's business but your own. I found the more I sewed, the better my joints got. Apparently, I could tolerate just so much ripping and restitching. As my sewing improved, I raised my standards. My friend, Chris, found she did not even need to pin her joints, though I continued to do so. To each her own. I found that I almost always got the errant joint perfect on the second try. I do not recommend going for a third try because all the handling and ripping does not improve your chances.

If your joints miss here or there, you may want to use a seam ripper to remove the few stitches across the joint and ¼" to either side of the intersection. Your seam depth is visible where the needle left holes. Put a pin through the point where the holes intersect the seam in one row, then continue through the same point in the second row, as you did before. Pin just to the right of the joint with a second pin, and remove the initial pin. Stitch the short segment at the joint, backtacking to secure the seam at both ends.

If you abhor ripping out and restitching, but you are not satisfied with your joints, I have a couple of suggestions you might try: 1) Use a long stitch and sew just the ½" across each joint. Check the joints. If you miss, it's easy to pull out the stitches and try again, this time with the benefit of holes to show your seam depth. When you are satisfied with the joints, stitch the whole seam with your usual stitch length. 2) Remove the thread from your machine and "sew" down each row to make needle holes that will allow you to see the precise points where the seamline crosses the seams in the row. Rethread the machine, pin joints, and stitch the seam for real. Both of these methods require an extra step, but if they give you better results, you may find them worthwhile.

Stitching Joints That Align But Do Not Oppose

Sometimes, both seam allowances at a joint are pressed the same direction. As I prepared the pressing arrows in the block diagrams, I tried to avoid this wherever possible, but at times it is unavoidable. The easiest way to achieve a perfect joint in this case is to flip the top seam to oppose the bottom seam. Feel the ridge, and pin right beside the joint but not through the top seam allowance. Flip the top seam allowance back the way it was pressed. Insert a second pin, this time through both seam allowances. Remove the first pin before stitching.

Playing with Block Arrangements

When you make a big Lone Star from 32 small blocks, I call the resulting star a "Grand Lone Star." Supernova, Star of Wonder, Shiloh, the Spiral-Block Lone Stars, and the big Lone Stars at the end of the Gradated Lone Stars chapter are examples of Grand Lone Stars that I designed to play well. By that I mean that you can completely change the look of the quilt simply with the placement and rotation of the finished blocks. (Think Log Cabin.) This is seriously fun!

The Grand Lone Stars are made with four small blocks in each arm of the star. You can place a given block in any of 4 positions in the arm; furthermore, you can place each block with one or the other of the tips toward the center. You can make all 8 arms alike or arrange 4 arms one way and 4 arms another way, alternating types. I present several arrangements for Supernova, Star of Wonder, Shiloh, and the Spiral-Block Grand Lone Stars to get you started. Be sure to take photographs as you play with the block placement and orientation. That way, you can choose a favorite arrangement and recreate it.

Be advised: it is easy to get something turned around unintentionally. Taking a photograph will make any goofs obvious. Take lots of photos as you sew to catch goofs you may be about to make as you stitch your blocks together (or goofs you have just stitched).

Rotary Cutting Background Patches by Stacking or Sliding Rulers

You can stack or slide rulers to rotary cut the background patches for the smaller Lone Stars. By stacking, I mean placing rulers side by side on the fabric so you can add more inches to your measuring. Suppose you want to cut a 13¼" square. Let's say you have 12½" x 12½" and 3½" x 24" rulers. Start by cutting off the selvage. Next place your square ruler for a crosswise cut near the right end of the fabric, aligning the square ruler with the previous cut edge. Cut along the square ruler. *Slide* the ruler, keeping it aligned with the cut you just made, to cut a few more inches. Turn the fabric around. Align the 9¾" line of the square ruler with the fabric's cut edge (3½" for the long ruler's width plus 9¾" of the square ruler equals 13¼" for our patch). *Stack* the long 3½"-wide ruler: place it next to the square ruler so that the long side of the long ruler

touches the square ruler. Cut along the other long edge of the long ruler, resulting in a 13¼"-wide patch. Similarly stack rulers to cut the fourth side parallel to the second cut to complete the square.

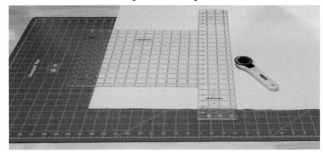

To cut large patches, stack rulers side by side.

Rotary Cutting Background Patches & Other Hard-to-Measure Patches Using Cloth Templates

The idea here is to easily and accurately rotary cut patches, such as the background squares and triangles, that are likely larger than your rotary ruler. You can rotary cut with confidence by making a template out of inexpensive stabilizer, an ugly remnant or never-used piece from your stash, or a yard of sale fabric.

To make a fabric template for the 25¼" square used in the background of many of the large Lone Star quilts, start with a large square ruler and a long ruler. Slide or stack your rulers to measure a 25¼" square and mark it on your template fabric using a sharp pencil. Double check your angles by placing your square ruler in each corner of your marked template. Double check your measurements by stacking your rulers. Make any corrections needed. Align your ruler with the lines and use your rotary cutter to cut out the template.

To use your cloth template to rotary cut the background or other patch, simply lay the cloth template in position on your fabric, align your ruler with one edge of the template, and cut along the ruler's edge. Slide your ruler as needed to cut the entire length of one side. Reposition your ruler to cut each side.

Using a cloth template to rotary cut large patches.

Avoiding Y-Seams

You are free to make any of the stars (and most of the quilts) in this book with no Y-seams. The satellite stars in Queen of Diamonds and some of the pieced borders require Y-seams. Avoiding Y-seams entails adding seams to the background to divide the quilt into eighths. The background square becomes two half-square triangles, and the background quarter-square triangle becomes two half-square triangles. To assemble a star with no Y-seams, start by stitching the background patches to the diamond blocks to make eight wedges (4 and 4 reversed). My assembly diagrams show sewing sequence in circled numbers. They also have arrows to show which direction to press the seam allowances. If you follow these carefully, your seams will nest. Rather than joining 2 wedges to make a *square* quarter of the star, in most cases, I have you join 2 wedges to make *triangular* quarter blocks. This allows you to sew borders to the quarters before the quarters are joined to each other. The result is mitered borders with no Y-seams!

Assembling a Lone Star with Y-Seams

I do not find Y-seams (also called set-in seams) difficult, and you, too, may find that you have no trouble with them. If that is the case, feel free to use the Y-seam option, which has fewer patches, fewer seams, and fewer seam allowances to cross if you plan to hand quilt your Lone Star. Traditionally, Y-seams were considered the more elegant solution, but I think now it is more a matter of personal taste.

Set-in seams or Y-seams (indicated by a colored dot in the diagrams) are nothing to fear. If you cut and stitch accurately, your set-in patches will fall into place naturally. The important thing to remember about set-in patches is that you must not stitch over the seam allowances at the joint, and you need to remove the work from under the needle, rather than just pivoting it. You will have to stitch a Y-seam in three passes, each starting at the same point ¼" in from the raw edges. In a Lone Star, the Y-seams involve two diamond blocks and one background square or triangle. I recommend sewing both diamond blocks to the background patch before sewing the diamond blocks together. Because they are the same shape, it is easier to align the diamond blocks perfectly for the final seam.

Use your little metal seam gauge to find the place to start the seam at the Y-joint. Mark with tailor's chalk or a pencil on the back side of the fabric. Pin the seam. Backtack to secure the end of the seamline, taking precisely 2 stitches forward and 2 stitches backward to secure the seam here, as it will not be crossed by another seam. Then continue forward to the raw edges at the far end of the seam line. Below are step-by-step photos showing how to sew the Y-seams for ¼ of a small Lone Star. I recommend using thread to blend with the colors of your fabric, though here I used black thread to contrast in the photos.

Backing a Winner

The backing sizes listed in my patterns allow the extra 8" of length and width required for mounting on a longarm quilting machine. Unless your quilt is very small or you are using extra-wide backing material, you will have to join two or three lengths of material to make your backing. Trim the selvages off the yard goods before cutting out the panels. Make a fresh cut at the end of the length of backing fabric to square it up. Use a square ruler or a long, wide one to make sure the corners are square. Cut each panel precisely the same length and width. Pin and stitch panels together with ¼" seam allowances. Press seam allowances to one side. Press the quilt top and backing well.

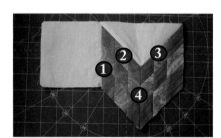

Sewing sequence, front view.

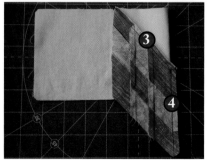

4) Sew 2 blocks together last.

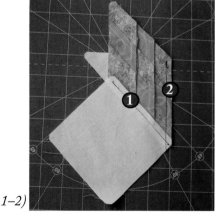

1–2)

1) Sew square to 1st block: start ¼" from the corner and continue to raw edge. 2) Sew triangle to 1st block: start ¼" from corner and continue to raw edge. 3) Sew 2nd block to triangle starting ¼" from corner. 4. Sew 2 blocks to each other, starting ¼" from corner.

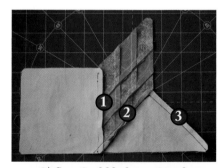

3) Sew 2nd block to triangle.

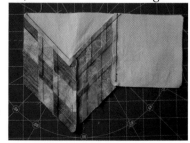

¼ Lone Star, back view.

QUILTING YOUR LONE STAR

Press your completed quilt top and pick off loose threads. You are now ready to quilt it or deliver your quilt and backing to your trusted longarm quilter. Look through this book for quilting suggestions.

If you plan to quilt the top yourself, I cannot teach you hand- or machine-quilting in the space of a few paragraphs. If you do not know how to quilt, I suggest you take a class or get a book devoted exclusively to that subject. If you are already well-versed in quilting, I suggest you study the quilting detail photographs here and in the patterns to give you some ideas.

Some suggestions for quilting the star are: quilting in the ditch around the small diamonds; outline quilting ¼" inside the diamonds (by hand) or inside the rows (by machine); outline quilting inside each ring; quilting radiating or parallel lines across the blocks; quilting a small motif inside each diamond; quilting feathers covering entire arms of the star; or quilting one or several textures, such as spirals or bubbles.

For the background squares and triangles, feathers are my go-to solution. I always try to introduce curves somewhere in the quilting, as a departure from all the angular geometry. Arcs make an attractive choice for the same reason. Concentric boxes appearing to continue behind the stars' arms are another idea. The boxes could be filled with cables, ribbons, feathers, Baptist fans, or textures.

Some of the quilting patterns used in these quilts were digitized, either from my sketches or otherwise. Some motifs were quilted freehand. Gridwork and stripes were ruler aided.

My principal quilter, Lana Corcoran, recommends starting with lines of quilting in the ditch around the star and the diamond blocks to stabilize the quilt before filling in the blocks and backgrounds with quilting details. For best results, she suggests having a similar density of quilting over the entire surface of the quilt. If you have intricate quilting in the background, you will need a similar amount of quilting in the star.

Right: Feathers grace the background and wavy lines accentuate the curves within the star in Wave on Wave. It was quilted by Lana Corcoran.

Below: Rows of diamonds are quilted ¼" inside the seamlines, and feathers fill the background in my traditional Lone Star. It was quilted by Lana Corcoran.

Below left: I designed this motif of feathers and stylized sunflowers for Galileo's Star. Half of the motif (divided diagonally) fits the background triangle. Lana Corcoran did the quilting.

Below right: Lana Corcoran quilted feathered arcs, hearts, and parallel lines in the background squares and triangles of Star of Wonder.

Next page left: Arcs, feathers, and radiating lines add interest to the background of Appalachian Spring. A center star and diagonal lines in the white areas feature in the quilting within the diamond blocks. In-the-ditch quilting adds definition. The quilting was done by Deb Treusch.

Next page top center: New Orleans Lone Star is quilted with a stylized teardrop in each diamond and intricate feathers in the background. Lana Corcoran was the quilter.

Next page bottom center: Midnight Lone Star is quilted with a rope motif within the rows of parallelograms in the star. The background quilting has a rope band, as well, though it is hard to see in a photograph. Lana Corcoran quilted this example.

Next page right: Because of the many colors, I changed Supernova's quilting motif for each change of thread color. I had Lana Corcoran quilt the yellow-to-red area ¼" inside each of the concentric rings of stars. The red-violet-to-blue-violet area is quilted in parallel lines. The blue-to-green area is quilted in curlicues. The star tips have radiating lines. Finally, the starburst has flames and curls of smoke.

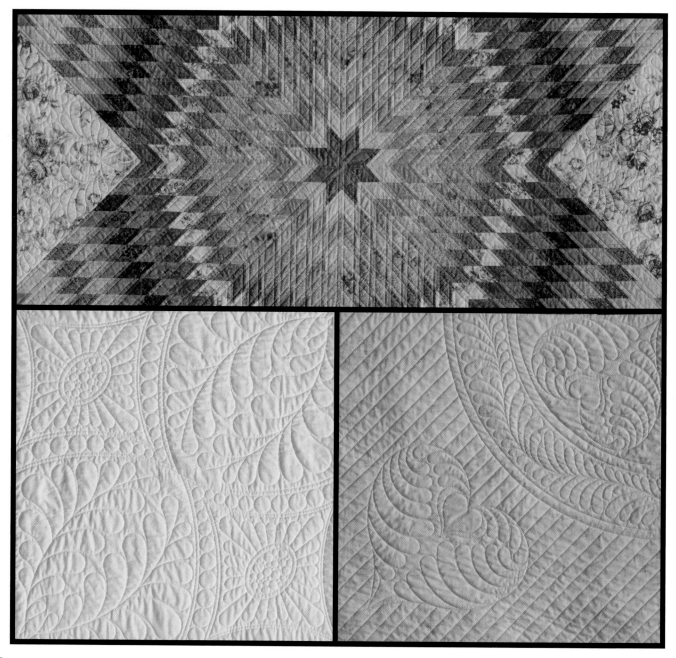

BOUND FOR GLORY

In preparation for binding, use a rotary cutter and ruler to trim the batting and backing even with the quilt top. Take special care to achieve right angles at the corners. Cut the binding fabric into straight strips (or bias) 2" wide and in sufficient quantity to go around the quilt's perimeter with several inches to spare. Trim the ends of the strips at a 45° angle, with all ends parallel to one another when the strips are all right side up. Trim the points using my Point Trimmer to help you align the strips for seaming. If you don't have one, you can download the file at judymartin.com/LSPT.cfm and follow the directions there for making a point trimmer. The trims should be at a right angle to the long edge of the strips, as shown below.

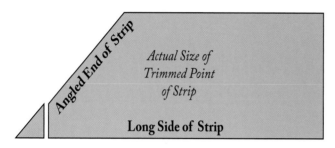

Pin and stitch the strips end to end with ¼" seam allowances to make one long strip. Press these seam allowances open. Fold the strip in half lengthwise with right sides out. Press the fold for the full length of the binding strip.

Lay the quilt face up on a flat surface. Starting on one edge of the quilt (and not near the corner), lay the folded binding strip over one edge of the quilt. Start about 4"–6" from one end of the binding. Align the raw edges of the two layers of binding with the cut edges of the quilt top, and pin through both layers of binding plus the quilt top, batting, and backing. Pin and stitch the binding to just one edge of the quilt, stopping ¼" from the raw edge at the corner of the quilt. Wrap the binding around to the back of the quilt at the corner so that it is even with the binding on the front. Crease the binding crosswise at the quilt's raw

edge. Now bring this creased edge to the front of the quilt and align the crease with the raw edge of the part you just stitched. Pin at the corner, then pin along the entire next side. Stitch from ¼" from the crease in the binding at one corner to ¼" from the raw edge at the next corner. Backtack at the ends of the seam. Repeat this process until the binding is stitched to all edges and around all corners. Stop stitching 8"–10" short of your starting point. Lay the starting end of the binding strip over the quilt top, and pin it to the edge of the quilt ¼" from the binding's starting end.

Lay the final end of the binding strip over it. With a pin, mark the point where this strip meets the pin at the end of the first strip. I always position this pin to follow the angle at the end of the first strip. This pin marks the seam line joining the two strip ends.

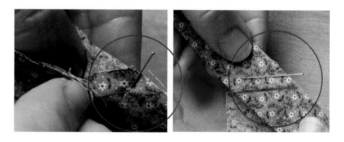

Unfold and cut off the end strip ¼" outside the pin at a 45° angle. Trim the point, as you did for the strips earlier. Pin the 2 binding strip ends together and stitch with a ¼" seam. Press the seam allowance open. Refold the binding in half lengthwise and pin it to the quilt. Stitch from the point where you left off to the starting point, backtacking at both ends.

Wrap the binding around the perimeter of the quilt to the back side as you hand stitch. Align the crease with the stitching line that attached the binding strip. Use a hem stitch or a blind ladder stitch by hand to secure the binding to the back of the quilt. At the corners, stitch to the end of the stitching line. Position the binding for the beginning of the next side. Take a stitch to secure the binding for the next side to the corner, and use your needle to tuck under the excess at the miter. Continue in this manner until the binding is hand stitched all around the quilt.

Wintry Lone Star

Quilt Size: 45¾" x 45¾"	Star Size: 42¼" sq.
Requires: 8 blocks	**Block Width:** 8¾"

Yardage & Cutting

Color	Yardage	#Strips	Cut Size	Strip End
1 ◼	1 fat qtr.	2	2¼" x 18"	◹
2 ◼	leftovers*	4	2¼" x 18"	(all)
3 ◼	1 fat qtr.	6	2¼" x 18"	
4 ◼	1 fat qtr.	8	2¼" x 18"	
5 ◼	leftovers**	10	2¼" x 18"	
6 ◼	1 fat qtr.	8	2¼" x 18"	
7 ◻	1 fat qtr.	6	2¼" x 18"	
8 ◻	1 fat qtr.	4	2¼" x 18"	
9 ◻	1 fat qtr.	2	2¼" x 18"	
10 ◻	1¼ yds.	bkgd.: 4 A, 4 B or 8 C, 8 D		
5 ◼	1½ yds.**	4 borders 2¼" x 47"		
	3¼ yds.	backing: 2 pcs. 27¼" x 54"		
2 ◼	½ yd.*	binding: 14 strips 2" x 18"		

Making Strip Sets and Cutting Rows

Start by reading the glossary, "Pattern Pointers," and "How to Make a Lone Star" chapters on pages 7–22.

Wintry Lone Star, 45¾" x 45¾". Designed by Judy Martin. Pieced by Chris Hulin. Quilted by Lana Corcoran. The quilt is made from 8 diamond blocks in an 8¾" finished width. These are arranged to form a Lone Star with your choice of background patches for assembly with or without Y-seams. Chris found the 9 values she needed for the quilt in her stash. When she ran out of a fabric, she substituted another.

Strip Piecing

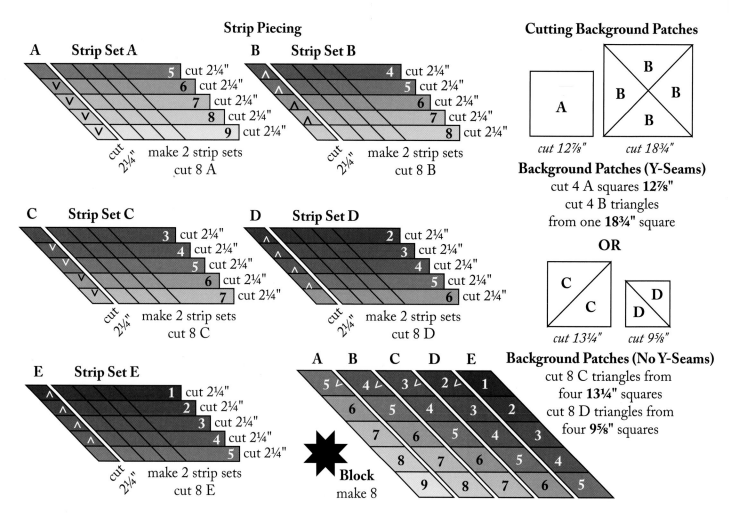

Strip Set A

A — cut 2¼"
5 cut 2¼"
6 cut 2¼"
7 cut 2¼"
8 cut 2¼"
9 cut 2¼"
make 2 strip sets
cut 8 A

Strip Set B

B — cut 2¼"
4 cut 2¼"
5 cut 2¼"
6 cut 2¼"
7 cut 2¼"
8 cut 2¼"
make 2 strip sets
cut 8 B

Strip Set C

C — cut 2¼"
3 cut 2¼"
4 cut 2¼"
5 cut 2¼"
6 cut 2¼"
7 cut 2¼"
make 2 strip sets
cut 8 C

Strip Set D

D — cut 2¼"
2 cut 2¼"
3 cut 2¼"
4 cut 2¼"
5 cut 2¼"
6 cut 2¼"
make 2 strip sets
cut 8 D

Strip Set E

E — cut 2¼"
1 cut 2¼"
2 cut 2¼"
3 cut 2¼"
4 cut 2¼"
5 cut 2¼"
make 2 strip sets
cut 8 E

Block
make 8

Cutting Background Patches

A cut 12⅞"   B cut 18¾"

Background Patches (Y-Seams)
cut 4 A squares **12⅞"**
cut 4 B triangles
from one **18¾"** square

OR

C cut 13¼"   D cut 9⅝"

Background Patches (No Y-Seams)
cut 8 C triangles from
four **13¼"** squares
cut 8 D triangles from
four **9⅝"** squares

You can cut all the strips before you sew any, or cut a little and sew a little, according to your preference. Cut the strips for a strip set, cutting off one end as indicated in the "strip end" column of the yardage chart. If you folded the fabric, unfold it before you cut off the strip ends. Trim the points as described on page 14 and shown below to help you align patches for sewing. The point should be trimmed at a right angle to the angled end of the strip. If you don't have my Point Trimmer tool, download a file to make one at judymartin.com/LSPT.cfm. Trim the points on all the strips except the top strip of a strip set.

Align the wide angle of the first strip with the point trim of the second strip. Pin and stitch the strips to each other. Finger press and steam press after each seam, following the "v" pressing arrows in the strip set diagrams. Continue pin-

ning, stitching, and pressing strips to complete a strip set. Trim a sliver off the angled end of the strip set, if necessary, at a precise 45° angle.

See the row cutting diagram below. Cut the strip set into 4 rows 2¼" wide. That is, lay the 2¼" ruling of your rotary cutting ruler over the angled end of the strip, align the 45° line with a raw edge or a seamline within the strip set, and cut along the ruler's edge. Make a second strip set to allow you to cut 8 rows in all.

Continue making strip sets and cutting rows in this fashion. When you have all the rows needed for a block, trim both points of each row at a right angle to the short end of the row as shown below.

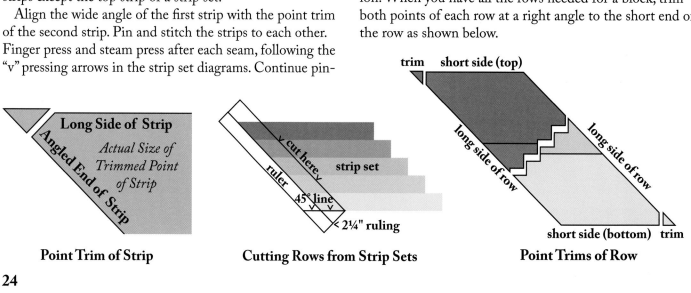

Long Side of Strip
Actual Size of Trimmed Point of Strip
Angled End of Strip

Point Trim of Strip

v cut here v
ruler
45° line
< 2¼" ruling
strip set

Cutting Rows from Strip Sets

trim   short side (top)
long side of row
long side of row
short side (bottom)   trim

Point Trims of Row

Making Blocks

Lay out the rows for a block as shown in the block diagram on the previous page. Pin rows at both ends, aligning the point trim of one row with the wide angle of the other. Also pin at each joint. See tips for matching joints on pages 15–16. Stitch all rows together, pressing after each seam as indicated in the block diagram. Make sure you press straight down and take care not to stretch the bias. Make 8 blocks.

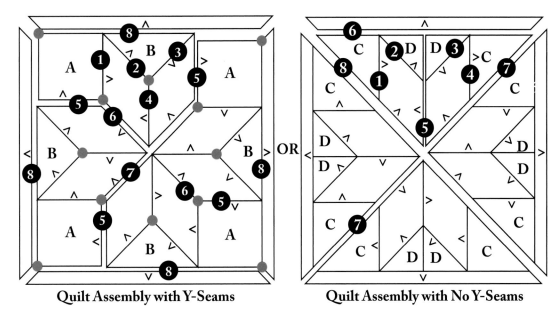

Quilt Assembly with Y-Seams   OR   **Quilt Assembly with No Y-Seams**

Assembling the Quilt

Cut out the background patches shown on the previous page. Choose background patches for use with or without Y-seams. Refer to page 17 for tips on cutting patches larger than your rotary cutting ruler.

Arrange blocks and background patches as shown in the photo or setting variation of your choice. Referring to the appropriate assembly diagram above, stitch together the blocks and patches in numerical order. Press after each seam, as indicated by the arrows. The star is made in diagonal quarters, which allows you to miter the borders without a Y-seam in the example above right.

Lana Corcoran quilted in the ditch around the star. She quilted feathers in the background and a small diamond-shaped motif in each diamond. Binding directions are on page 22.

Wintry Lone Star Setting Variations
USING THE SAME BLOCK QUANTITIES AND YARDAGE

Arrangement 2: 8 blocks with blocks turned so that dark sides touch each other at the center of each side of the quilt.

Arrangement 3: 8 blocks turned so that light sides touch each other at the center of each side of the quilt.

25

San Francisco Lone Star

Quilt Size: 42¼" x 42¼"			Star Size: 42¼" sq.	
Requires: 8 blocks			Block Width: 8¾"	

		Yardage & Cutting			**Strip**
Color	Yardage	#Strips	Cut Size		End
1 ⬛	leftovers*	4	2¼" x 18"		◻
2 ⬛	1 fat qtr.	2	2¼" x 18"		(all)
3 ⬛	1 fat qtr.	4	2¼" x 18"		
4 ⬛	1 fat qtr.	6	2¼" x 18"		
5 ⬛	½ yd.	10	2¼" x 18"		
6 ⬛	1 fat qtr.	8	2¼" x 18"		
7 ⬜	1 fat qtr.	8	2¼" x 18"		
8 ⬜	1 fat qtr.	4	2¼" x 18"		
9 ⬜	1 fat qtr.	4	2¼" x 18"		
10 ⬜	1¼ yds.	background *(see page 28)*			
	3 yds.	backing: 2 pcs. 25⅝" x 50¾"			
1 ⬛	½ yd.*	binding: 13 strips 2" x 18"			

San Francisco Lone Star, 42¼" x 42¼". Designed and pieced by Judy Martin. Quilted by Lana Corcoran. This quilt is made from 9 monochromatic fabrics in different values (darkness or lightness). They are arranged to gradate in value sequence in some places and to contrast in others. New Orleans Lone Star (page 29) is a similar quilt that utilizes just two ombre (gradated) fabrics to achieve this effect. This is a simple little Lone Star with a big graphic impact.

I cut 2"-wide binding strips from leftover strip sets and newly made strip sets from leftover fabric. In the yardage chart, I list plain black binding for a simpler solution. If you want to piece your binding from strip sets, you will need 15 rows 2" wide x 12⅞" long. Press seams open.

Making Strip Sets and Cutting Rows

Start by reading the glossary, "Pattern Pointers," and "How to Make a Lone Star" chapters on pages 7–22. You can cut all the strips before you sew any, or cut a little and sew a little, if you like. Cut the strips for a strip set, cutting off one end as indicated in the "strip end" column of

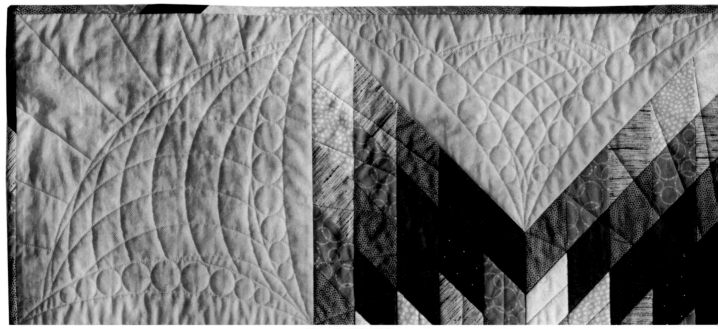

Detail of Quilting

Strip Piecing the Blocks

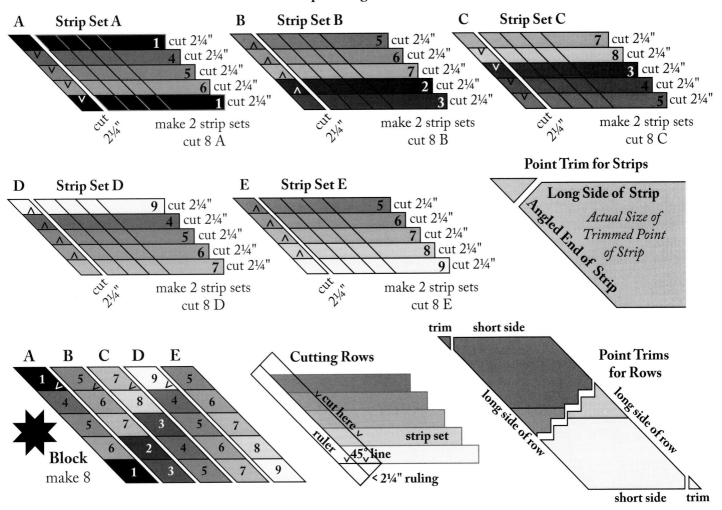

A Strip Set A
1 cut 2¼"
4 cut 2¼"
5 cut 2¼"
6 cut 2¼"
1 cut 2¼"
cut 2¼"
make 2 strip sets
cut 8 A

B Strip Set B
5 cut 2¼"
6 cut 2¼"
7 cut 2¼"
2 cut 2¼"
3 cut 2¼"
cut 2¼"
make 2 strip sets
cut 8 B

C Strip Set C
7 cut 2¼"
8 cut 2¼"
3 cut 2¼"
4 cut 2¼"
5 cut 2¼"
cut 2¼"
make 2 strip sets
cut 8 C

D Strip Set D
9 cut 2¼"
4 cut 2¼"
5 cut 2¼"
6 cut 2¼"
7 cut 2¼"
cut 2¼"
make 2 strip sets
cut 8 D

E Strip Set E
5 cut 2¼"
6 cut 2¼"
7 cut 2¼"
8 cut 2¼"
9 cut 2¼"
cut 2¼"
make 2 strip sets
cut 8 E

Point Trim for Strips
Long Side of Strip
Actual Size of Trimmed Point of Strip
Angled End of Strip

A B C D E
1 5 7 9 5
4 6 8 4 6
5 7 3 5 7
6 2 4 6 8
1 3 5 7 9
Block make 8

Cutting Rows
cut here
ruler
45° line
strip set
< 2¼" ruling

Point Trims for Rows
trim short side
long side of row
long side of row
short side trim

Making Blocks

Lay out the rows for a block as shown in the block diagram above left. Pin and stitch rows together, pressing after each seam. Read about strategies for pinning and matching joints on page 15. Make 8 blocks.

Cutting Background Patches

Cut out the background patches shown on the next page for your choice of a quilt with Y-seams or without Y-seams. Refer to page 17 for tips on cutting patches larger than your rotary cutting ruler.

Assembling the Quilt

See the quilt layouts on pages 28. Choose your favorite there or arrange blocks as shown in the photo on page 26. Referring to the appropriate assembly diagram on page 28, stitch together the blocks and patches in numerical order. Press after each seam, as indicated by the arrows in the diagram. Repeat to make four quadrants of the quilt. Join these to make half stars. Join halves to complete the star.

Lana quilted curved grids, circles, and radiating lines in the background. She quilted parallel lines in the quilt center and lines radiating from one corner of each block in the outer tips of the stars. Binding directions are on page 22.

the yardage chart. Trim the points as described on page 14 and shown above to help you align patches for sewing. The point should be trimmed at a right angle to the angled end of the strip. Don't trim the point on the top strip of a strip set. If you don't have my Point Trimmer tool, download a file to make one at judymartin.com/LSPT.cfm

Align the wide angle of the first strip with the point trim of the second strip. Pin and stitch them together. Finger press and steam press, following the "v" arrows in the strip set diagrams.

Continue pinning, stitching, and pressing strips to complete a strip set as shown. Trim a sliver off the angled end of the strip set, if necessary, at a precise 45° angle. See the row cutting figure above. Cut the strip set into rows 2¼" wide. That is, lay the 2¼" ruling of your rotary cutting ruler over the angled end of the strip, align the 45° line with the raw edge, and cut along the ruler's edge. Make a duplicate strip set to allow you to cut 8 rows in all.

Continue making strip sets and cutting rows in this fashion. When you have all the rows needed for a block, trim both points of each row at a right angle to the short end of the strip with my Point Trimmer or the one you made. The trimmed points for rows are shown above right.

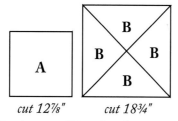

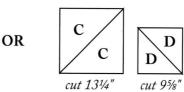

cut 12⅞"   *cut 18¾"*   OR   *cut 13¼"*   *cut 9⅝"*

Background Patches (Y-Seams)   **Background Patches (No Y-Seams)**

cut 4 A squares **12⅞"**   cut 8 C triangles from four **13¼"** squares

cut 4 B triangles from one **18¾"** square   cut 8 D triangles from four **9⅝"** squares

Assembling the Quilt

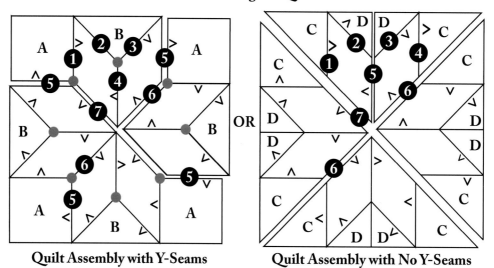

Quilt Assembly with Y-Seams   OR   **Quilt Assembly with No Y-Seams**

San Francisco Lone Star Setting Variations
USING THE SAME BLOCKS & YARDAGE

Arrangement 2: 8 blocks with the light tips of the blocks at the center.

Arrangement 3: 8 blocks with 4 blocks turned with the light tips at the center and 4 blocks turned with the dark tips at the center.

New Orleans Lone Star

Quilt Size: 45¾" x 45¾"   **Star Size:** 42¼" sq.
Requires: 8 blocks   **Block Width:** 8¾"

Yardage & Cutting

Color		Yardage	#Strips	Cut Size	Strip End
1		2¼ yds.	2	2¼" x 18"	◢
2		ombre	2	2¼" x 18"	(all)
3		fabric*	4	2¼" x 18"	
4			4	2¼" x 18"	
5			6	2¼" x 18"	
6			4	2¼" x 18"	
7			4	2¼" x 18"	
8			2	2¼" x 18"	
9			2	2¼" x 18"	
3b		2⅝ yds.	2	2¼" x 18"	
4b		ombre	2	2¼" x 18"	
5b		fabric**	4	2¼" x 18"	
6b			4	2¼" x 18"	
7b			4	2¼" x 18"	
8b			2	2¼" x 18"	
9b			2	2¼" x 18"	
		leftovers**	bkgd.: 8 C, 8 D *(see page 30)*		
		leftovers*	8 borders: cut 2¼" x 23¾"		
		3¼ yds.	backing: 2 pcs. 27¼" x 54"		
		leftovers**	binding: 6 strips 2" x 44"		

The purple ombre fabric must have a useable width of at least 40½" after trimming off selvages.

New Orleans Lone Star, 45¾" x 45¾". Designed and pieced by Judy Martin and quilted by Lana Corcoran. This Lone Star is made from 2 ombre fabrics, one in gradated purples and one in pinks. The background patches and crosswise borders are designed to avoid Y-seams and to highlight the ombre color gradations.

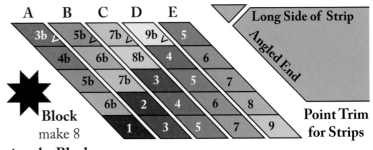

Block make 8

Strip Piecing the Blocks

Long Side of Strip **Angled End**

Point Trim for Strips

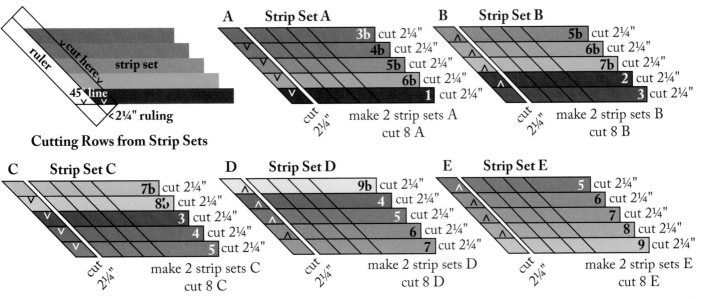

Cutting Rows from Strip Sets

ruler ∨ cut here strip set 45° line 2¼" ruling

A   Strip Set A
3b cut 2¼"
4b cut 2¼"
5b cut 2¼"
6b cut 2¼"
1 cut 2¼"
cut 2¼"
make 2 strip sets A
cut 8 A

B   Strip Set B
5b cut 2¼"
6b cut 2¼"
7b cut 2¼"
2 cut 2¼"
3 cut 2¼"
cut 2¼"
make 2 strip sets B
cut 8 B

C   Strip Set C
7b cut 2¼"
8b cut 2¼"
3 cut 2¼"
4 cut 2¼"
5 cut 2¼"
cut 2¼"
make 2 strip sets C
cut 8 C

D   Strip Set D
9b cut 2¼"
4 cut 2¼"
5 cut 2¼"
6 cut 2¼"
7 cut 2¼"
cut 2¼"
make 2 strip sets D
cut 8 D

E   Strip Set E
5 cut 2¼"
6 cut 2¼"
7 cut 2¼"
8 cut 2¼"
9 cut 2¼"
cut 2¼"
make 2 strip sets E
cut 8 E

Cutting Layouts for Ombre Fabrics

If you fold the fabric to cut through layers, do not cut ends off the strip while folded; that would result in reverse angles, which are not used for strip piecing this quilt.

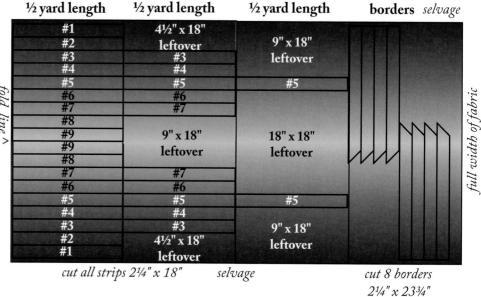

½ yard length	½ yard length	½ yard length	borders *selvage*
#1	4½" x 18"	9" x 18"	
#2	leftover	leftover	
#3	#3		
#4	#4		
#5	#5	#5	
#6	#6		
#7	#7		
#8			
#9	9" x 18"	18" x 18"	
#9	leftover	leftover	
#8			
#7	#7		
#6	#6		
#5	#5	#5	
#4	#4		
#3	#3	9" x 18"	
#2	4½" x 18"	leftover	
#1	leftover		

fold line >   cut all strips 2¼" x 18"   selvage   cut 8 borders 2¼" x 23¾"   *full width of fabric*

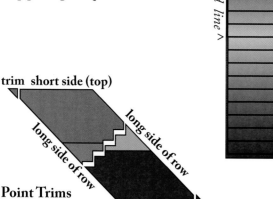

Point Trims for Rows

trim short side (top)

long side of row

long side of row

short side (bottom) trim

Note that the 2 ombre fabrics must have dark selvages and light at the center fold to go with these cutting layouts.

Note that if you prefer not to use ombre (gradated) fabric, you can use the San Francisco Lone Star pattern (page 26), which looks nearly the same. It uses 9 different fabrics for the 9 values.

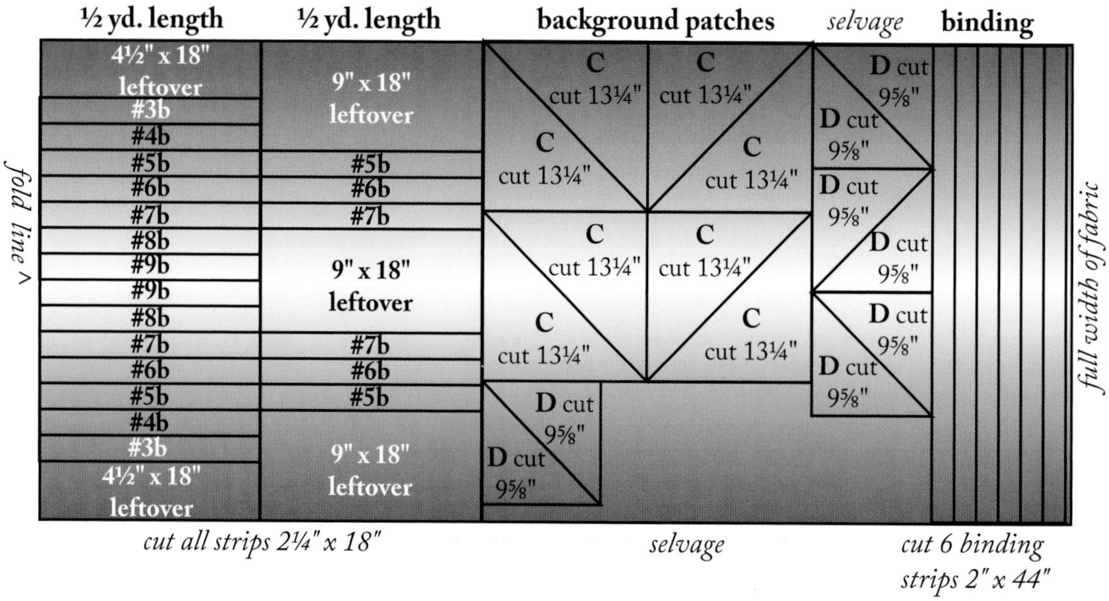

½ yd. length	½ yd. length	background patches	*selvage*	binding
4½" x 18" leftover	9" x 18" leftover	C cut 13¼" C cut 13¼"	D cut 9⅝"	
#3b				
#4b		C cut 13¼" C cut 13¼"	D cut 9⅝"	
#5b	#5b		D cut 9⅝"	
#6b	#6b			
#7b	#7b	C cut 13¼" C cut 13¼"	D cut 9⅝"	
#8b				
#9b	9" x 18"	C cut 13¼" C cut 13¼"	D cut 9⅝"	
#9b	leftover			
#8b			D cut 9⅝"	
#7b	#7b			
#6b	#6b	D cut 9⅝"	D cut 9⅝"	
#5b	#5b			
#4b				
#3b	9" x 18"	D cut 9⅝"		
4½" x 18" leftover	leftover			

fold line >   cut all strips 2¼" x 18"   selvage   cut 6 binding strips 2" x 44"   *full width of fabric*

Cutting the Strips

The value (darkness or lightness) of an ombre fabric changes across the width of the fabric. That means that in order to cut multiple strips of the same value, you need to cut them in a line parallel to the selvages. I suggest you start cutting by trimming off the selvages, then cutting off 3 half-yard lengths (purple) or 2 half-yard lengths (pink).

Referring to the cutting layouts, cut 2¼" x 18" strips, as shown, cutting the leftover areas between strips as precisely as you cut the strips. These spaces allow you to cut strips in matching values.

This pattern shows cutting layouts for ombre fabrics that are darkest on the selvages. If your ombre fabric is lightest on the selvages, you will need to cut the numbered values from different areas of the fabric. The yardage figures are for ombre fabric **with a minimum width of 40½" after you trim off the selvages.** Your fabric should also have the same colors or values along both of the selvages.

Cut strips lengthwise so each strip is one uniform value. If you do not need equal quantities of each value, you will need to cut away precisely measured blocks of unneeded values in order to cut the strips of needed values end to end at the same gradation of the fabric. For example, in the purple layout above, you need only 2 strips of values 8 and 9, but you need 4 strips of values 6 and 7. You need to cut a space 9" x 18" from the second 18" length of purple in order to cut the last #6 and #7 strips from the right values of the ombre fabric.

If you use the ombre fabric the way I did, you may notice that you are cutting the fabric apart and sewing it back together nearly the way it was. I like the seams, as they serve to demarcate the changes in value. If you are willing to experiment, you can cut crosswise strips from ombre fabric and not cut them into rows. Your blocks would simply consist of strips. In order to simulate any of the designs here, you will need the strip ends to stagger to match the values shown. This could be tricky, but you could very well come up with an awesome quilt with very little in the way of joints and half the cutting and sewing of the usual strip-pieced Lone Star.

To make the quilt as photographed, cut strips as shown in the cutting layouts. Cut off one end of each strip at a 45° angle as shown in the far right column of the yardage chart. Trim the point as shown on page 29. If you don't have a Point Trimmer, download a file to make one at: judymartin.com/LSPT.cfm

Making Strip Sets and Blocks

Read the glossary, "Pattern Pointers," and "How to Make a Lone Star" chapters on pages 7–22. Referring to the strip piecing diagrams on page 29, make 2 strip sets of each type, A–E. Press seam allowances as indicated by the "v" arrows in the diagrams.

If it needs it, trim a sliver from the angled end of the strip set at a precise 45° angle. See the row cutting figure on page 29. Align the 2¼" ruling with the angled end; align the 45° line with the raw edge or a seamline; cut along the ruler to make a row. Cut 4 rows per strip set.

Trim the points at both ends of each row as shown on page 30. Align the wide angle of one row with the trimmed point of the neighboring row. Pin and stitch rows together as shown in the block diagram on page 29,

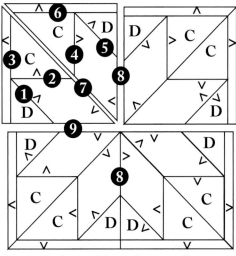

Quilt Assembly with No Y-Seams

pressing seams as indicated by the arrows. Helpful tips for matching joints are on pages 15–16. Make 8 blocks.

Assembling the Quilt

Cut 8 C and 8 D background patches as shown in the pink cutting layout. Cut 8 border strips as shown in the purple cutting layout. These are crosswise to take advantage of the ombre gradations of the fabric.

Arrange blocks, C and D patches, and border strips as shown above. Sew them together in numerical order to make ⅛ wedges; add borders to wedges. Proceed in numerical order, pressing seam allowances as indicated by the "v" notations in the diagrams. Join wedges to make square quilt quarters; join quarters to make halves; join halves to complete the quilt top.

Lana quilted in the ditch between the star and the background and between the background and border. She quilted a teardrop shape in each diamond. She quilted feathers in the background and diamonds with teardrops in the borders. Binding directions are on page 22.

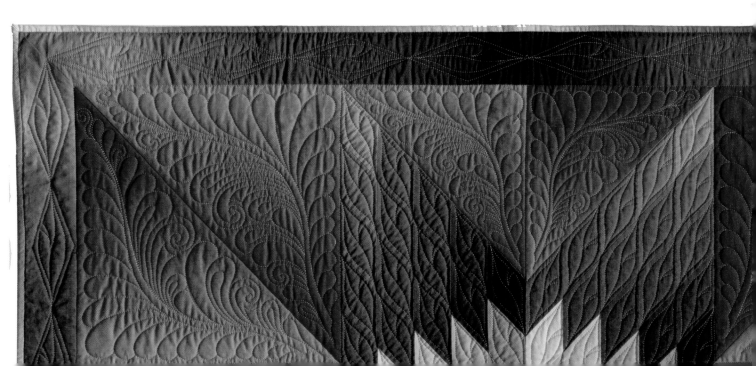

Gradated Lone Star Mix & Match

I had a decision to make for this book. I chose to present 18 sewn quilts and 69 variations with detailed instructions. In this chapter I provide abbreviated patterns for 17 simple, little Lone Stars, 8 Grand Lone Stars, and 13 variations. I wanted to share these designs with you without adding greatly to the page count and the price of the book. My compromise was to present yardage figures and block and quilt diagrams for each, but to keep the narrative to a minimum. I opted not to show strip sets because they take a lot of space. You will have to envision the strip sets from the rows in the block. I describe this at the bottom of this column, with illustrations at the top of the next page. You get 25 patterns in the space (and cost) of 7. I think you'll agree I did the right thing.

These gradated Lone Stars are all constructed using the same basic block and quilt outlines, and you can find details in my basic Lone Star instructions (starting on page 7). This may mean flipping back and forth until you internalize the information, but I felt it would be a waste of space to repeat the information for each pattern.

In this chapter I present 24 different blocks with the basic outline of a Lone Star and different color placement. (With the exception of Boulder on page 53, which is sometimes found in antique quilts, these are new blocks I designed for this book.) I provide patterns for 8 large quilts you can make by mixing and matching these blocks. You can mix and match these blocks to your heart's content. Colors are gradated and labeled 1-9, with #1 being the darkest and #9 the lightest. In each quilt, the blocks are pieced simply from strips forming 25 diamonds in 5 rows of 5.

Any of the sets (block arrangements) in the book that list 8¾"-wide blocks will work with these gradated blocks.

These quilts are the only ones in the book for which I do not show strip sets. You can find everything you need to know in the block drawing. See the block and strip set drawings at the top of the next page. The strip set is exactly the same color sequence as the block's row of the same letter. The strip set just extends farther to the right so you can cut multiple rows alike. Each block has five rows, each one lettered. Each different letter has its own color sequence and unique strip set. *In this chapter,*

all strips are cut 2¼" x 18", and all strip sets are cut into rows 2¼" wide.

Gradated Lone Stars

Most of the quilts in this chapter are made from 9 values. You can use 9 fabrics of the same hue, with each fabric a step lighter than the previous one. Alternatively, you can achieve the blended look shown, by choosing a series of analogous hues (colors) that are next to each other on the color wheel. I like to step the values as well as advance the colors when I choose this option. When all the hues on the color wheel are the same saturation, yellow is the lightest and violet the darkest color, so I suggest you build on that for a color-wheel gradation. You can start with a blackish violet. You can make the next value a slightly lighter red violet or blue violet.

It can be a challenge to shop for 9 values of one color; it is usually easier to find neighboring colors on the color wheel or find 3 values each of 3 neighboring colors. The small quilts don't take much yardage of any one color, and I found I could manage 9 values using my stash.

Printed motifs can tweak colors, affect values, or make patches cut from different areas of the print appear dissimilar. I prefer using prints that are monochromatic and read as solids from across the room. You can use true solids, if you like, though except for some of the backgrounds, my quilts are made from prints. You should remember that unless the printed motif is tightly packed, *it is the background that defines its color.* A print of half-inch red roses widely spaced on a white background behaves more like white than like red. That said, I wouldn't use such high contrast fabric for a gradated quilt. I suggest using prints with small figures; fine lines of black, white, or a neighboring hue or value of the background. I would avoid fabrics that have variable backgrounds, such as many batiks or mottled prints because different areas of the fabric will have different values.

If you want your gradated quilt to glow, use prints that read as solids, and keep the hues or values close together in adjacent areas. Look at the blocks and quilts in this chapter. I use colors in value order. If I used the same palette, but I used a sequence like 1-5-2-6-3-7-4-8, it would not blend and glow. It would look more like a checkerboard.

Note that all strips in this chapter are cut 2¼" x 18" and all strip sets are cut into rows 2¼" wide.

Right, 1) block showing rows and 2) E strip set. The block's rows tell you what the strip sets look like; simply imagine each row extended to the right. Each of the 5 rows has a unique strip set.

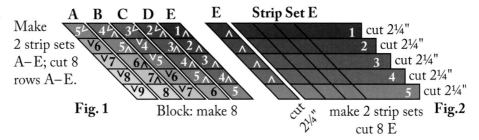

Make 2 strip sets A–E; cut 8 rows A–E.

Fig. 1   Block: make 8   cut 8 E   make 2 strip sets   **Fig. 2**

Ombre Lone Stars

Ombre fabric has different values, or sometimes different colors, blending from selvage to selvage. It is awesome for making gradated Lone Star quilts and variations. The colors are perfectly gradated, and you need just one fabric for the Lone Star blocks and a second fabric (ombre or not) for the background of the quilt.

The pattern for New Orleans Lone Star (pg. 29), shows cutting layouts for ombre fabrics. The yardage figures for that quilt are for ombre fabric having the same colors or values along both selvages.

If you wish to use ombre fabric to make a different quilt from this chapter, you will need ½ yard for every 2 strips required *of the value that has the most strips.* Round up to the next ½ yard for odd numbers of strips. For example, for Amsterdam Lone Star on page 36, you need 8 strips of the color having the most strips; you will need 8 ÷ 2 = 4 half yards, or 2 yards total of ombre fabric to strip piece the blocks. The yardage varies greatly from one quilt to the next. The next quilt on that page requires 4 yards total to strip piece the blocks. You will likely have fabric left over, especially for patterns that call for very different numbers of strips from the various values.

Making a Lone Star from This Chapter

The background should contrast with the half of the block that will touch it. The border and the binding yardages are for lengthwise borders and binding strips, and they may include extra for cutting any strips of the same value you might need for the quilt.

Follow my Lone Star instructions beginning on page 7. Remember to cut off one end of each strip at a 45° angle. Use my Point Trimmer or download a file to make your own at judymartin.com/LSPT.cfm to help you align strips and rows for stitching. Trim the points as shown on page 14.

To make strip sets, simply substitute one 2¼" x 18" strip for each diamond in the block row, as shown above. Match the hue or value of the strip to the diamond in the corresponding row.

For the little Lone Star quilts, make two strip sets to match each of the 5 rows in the block diagram. For the Grand Lone Stars, the number of strip sets of each type is listed.

Trim a sliver off the angled end of each strip set to even up the strip ends at a precise 45° angle. Cut 4 rows 2¼" wide from each strip set. Trim points of the resulting rows as shown on page 15. Arrange 5 rows in the sequence shown in the block diagram. Join in diagonal rows, matching and pinning at joints and seam ends. Press seam allowances toward the left.

Choose background patches to assemble your quilt with or without Y-seams. Cut the background patches in the dimensions below or on page 34.

Little Lone Star Background Patches

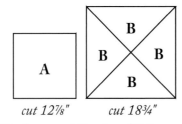

OR

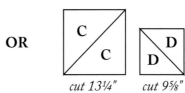

cut 12⅞"   *cut 18¾"*   *cut 13¼"*   *cut 9⅝"*

Background Patches (Y-Seams)
cut 4 A squares **12⅞"**
cut 4 B triangles from one **18¾"** square

Background Patches (No Y-Seams)
cut 8 C triangles from four **13¼"** squares
cut 8 D triangles from four **9⅝"** squares

Assemble your blocks, background, and borders in numerical order, as shown in the diagrams below. For Grand Lone Stars, start by sewing the diamond blocks in sets of 4, ending with the seam shown in red. Continue assembling the quilt in numerical order. Press seams to one side after each seam, as indicated by the arrows in the diagrams.

Quilt as desired, referring to the book's photos for ideas. Bind as shown on page 22.

Little Lone Star Quilt Assembly

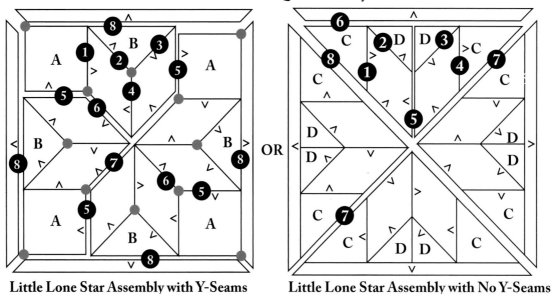

Little Lone Star Assembly with Y-Seams OR **Little Lone Star Assembly with No Y-Seams**

Grand Lone Star Background Patches and Quilt Assembly

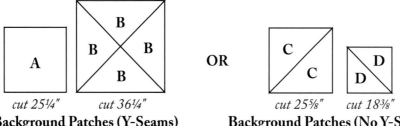

cut 25¼" *cut 36¼"* OR *cut 25⅝"* *cut 18⅜"*

Background Patches (Y-Seams)
cut 4 A squares **25¼"**
cut 4 B triangles from one **36¼"** square

Background Patches (No Y-Seams)
cut 8 C triangles from four **25⅝"** squares
cut 8 D triangles from four **18⅜"** squares

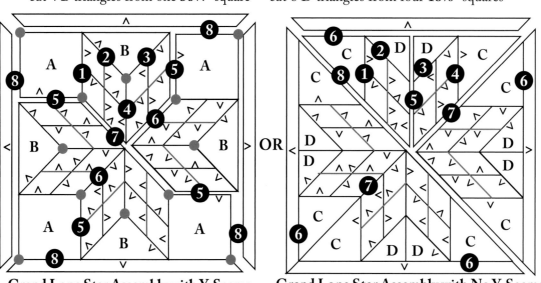

Grand Lone Star Assembly with Y-Seams OR **Grand Lone Star Assembly with No Y-Seams**

Florence Lone Star

Quilt Size: 45¾" x 45¾" **Star Size:** 42¼" sq.
Requires: 8 blocks **Block Width:** 8¾"

Yardage & Cutting

#	Value	Yardage	#Strips	Cut Size	Strip End
1	■	1 fat qtr.	4	2¼" x 18"	⬦
2	■	leftovers*	4	2¼" x 18"	(all)
3	■	1 fat qtr.	8	2¼" x 18"	
4	■	leftovers**	8	2¼" x 18"	
5	■	1 fat qtr.	8	2¼" x 18"	
6	■	1 fat qtr.	4	2¼" x 18"	
7	■	leftovers***	4	2¼" x 18"	
9	■	½ yd.	10	2¼" x 18"	
2	■	1¾ yds.*		background (see page 33)	
4	■	1½ yds.**		4 borders 2¼" x 47"	
		3¼ yds.		backing: 2 pcs. 27¼" x 54"	
7	□	½ yd.***		binding: 14 strips 2" x 18"	

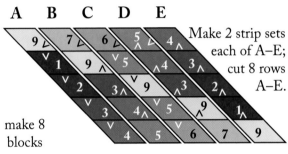

A B C D E

Make 2 strip sets each of A–E; cut 8 rows A–E.

make 8 blocks

Cut background patches and lengthwise border strips before cutting 2¼" x 18" strips from the leftovers.

Vienna Lone Star

Quilt Size: 45¾" x 45¾" **Star Size:** 42¼" sq.
Requires: 8 blocks **Block Width:** 8¾"

Yardage & Cutting

#	Value	Yardage	#Strips	Cut Size	Strip End
1	■	1 fat qtr.	4	2¼" x 18"	⬦
2	■	leftovers*	8	2¼" x 18"	(all)
3	■	½ yd.	12	2¼" x 18"	
4	■	leftovers**	16	2¼" x 18"	
5	■	1 fat qtr.	2	2¼" x 18"	
6	■	1 fat qtr.	2	2¼" x 18"	
7	■	1 fat qtr.	2	2¼" x 18"	
8	■	1 fat qtr.	2	2¼" x 18"	
9	□	1 fat qtr.	2	2¼" x 18"	
10	□	1¼ yds.		background (see page 33)	
4	■	1½ yds.**		4 borders 2¼" x 47"	
		3¼ yds.		backing: 2 pcs. 27¼" x 54"	
2	■	1 yd.*		binding: 14 strips 2" x 18"	

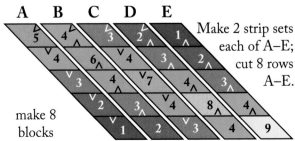

A B C D E

Make 2 strip sets each of A–E; cut 8 rows A–E.

make 8 blocks

Amsterdam Lone Star

Quilt Size: 45¾" x 45¾"   **Star Size:** 42¼" sq.
Requires: 8 blocks   **Block Width:** 8¾"

#	Value	Yardage & Cutting			Strip End
		Yardage	#Strips	Cut Size	
1		leftovers*	6	2¼" x 18"	⬯
2		1 fat qtr.	4	2¼" x 18"	(all)
3		leftovers**	8	2¼" x 18"	
4		1 fat qtr.	8	2¼" x 18"	
5		1 fat qtr.	8	2¼" x 18"	
6		1 fat qtr.	8	2¼" x 18"	
7		1 fat qtr.	4	2¼" x 18"	
8		1 fat qtr.	4	2¼" x 18"	
1		2¼ yds.*	background *(see page 33)*		
3		1½ yds.**	4 borders 2¼" x 47"		
		3¼ yds.	backing: 2 pcs. 27¼" x 54"		
1		leftovers*	binding: 14 strips 2" x 18"		

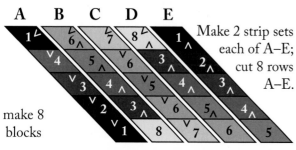

A B C D E

Make 2 strip sets each of A–E; cut 8 rows A–E.

make 8 blocks

Cut background patches and lengthwise border strips before cutting 2¼" x 18" strips from the leftovers.

Seattle Lone Star

Quilt Size: 45¾" x 45¾"   **Star Size:** 42¼" sq.
Requires: 8 blocks   **Block Width:** 8¾"

#	Value	Yardage & Cutting			Strip End
		Yardage	#Strips	Cut Size	
1		leftovers*	2	2¼" x 18"	⬯
2		leftovers**	2	2¼" x 18"	(all)
3		1 fat qtr.	2	2¼" x 18"	
4		leftovers***	2	2¼" x 18"	
5		1 fat qtr.	2	2¼" x 18"	
6		½ yd.	16	2¼" x 18"	
7		½ yd.	12	2¼" x 18"	
8		1 fat qtr.	8	2¼" x 18"	
9		1 fat qtr.	4	2¼" x 18"	
2		1¾ yds.**	background *(see page 33)*		
1		1½ yds.*	4 borders 2¼" x 47"		
		3¼ yds.	backing: 2 pcs. 27¼" x 54"		
4		½ yd.***	binding: 14 strips 2" x 18"		

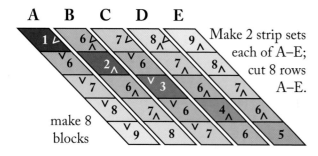

A B C D E

Make 2 strip sets each of A–E; cut 8 rows A–E.

make 8 blocks

Chamonix Lone Star

Quilt Size: 45¾" x 45¾"   **Star Size:** 42¼" sq.
Requires: 8 blocks   **Block Width:** 8¾"

Yardage & Cutting

#	Value	Yardage	#Strips	Cut Size	Strip End
1		1 fat qtr.	2	2¼" x 18"	⬯
2		1 fat qtr.	4	2¼" x 18"	(all)
3		1 fat qtr.	6	2¼" x 18"	
4		1 fat qtr.	8	2¼" x 18"	
5		leftovers*	10	2¼" x 18"	
6		1 fat qtr.	8	2¼" x 18"	
7		leftovers**	6	2¼" x 18"	
8		1 fat qtr.	4	2¼" x 18"	
9		1 fat qtr.	2	2¼" x 18"	
10		1¼ yds.	background *(see page 33)*		
5		1½ yds.*	4 borders 2¼" x 47"		
		3¼ yds.	backing: 2 pcs. 27¼" x 54"		
7		1 yd.**	binding: 14 strips 2" x 18"		

Cut lengthwise border strips before cutting 2¼" x 18" strips from the leftovers. Cut fabric #7 into 2 pieces 18" long for cutting 2¼" strips and binding.

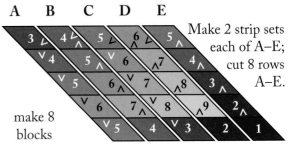

A B C D E

make 8 blocks

Make 2 strip sets each of A–E; cut 8 rows A–E.

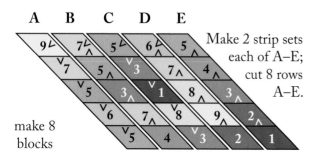

St. Louis Lone Star

Quilt Size: 45¾" x 45¾" **Star Size:** 42¼" sq.
Requires: 8 blocks **Block Width:** 8¾"

#	Value	Yardage	#Strips	Cut Size	Strip End
		Yardage & Cutting			**Strip End**
1	▪	leftovers*	4	2¼" x 18"	◸
2	▪	leftovers**	4	2¼" x 18"	(all)
3	▪	1 fat qtr.	8	2¼" x 18"	
4	▪	1 fat qtr.	4	2¼" x 18"	
5	▪	leftovers***	10	2¼" x 18"	
6	▪	1 fat qtr.	4	2¼" x 18"	
7	▪	1 fat qtr.	8	2¼" x 18"	
8	▪	1 fat qtr.	4	2¼" x 18"	
9	▪	1 fat qtr.	4	2¼" x 18"	
5	▪	1¾ yds.***		background *(see page 33)*	
2	▪	1½ yds.**		4 borders 2¼" x 47"	
		3¼ yds.		backing: 2 pcs. 27¼" x 54"	
1	▪	½ yd.*		binding: 14 strips 2" x 18"	

Cut lengthwise border strips from fabric #2 and background patches from fabric #5 before cutting 2¼" x 18" strips from the leftovers.

A B C D E

Make 2 strip sets each of A–E; cut 8 rows A–E.

make 8 blocks

Oxford Lone Star

Quilt Size: 45¾" x 45¾" **Star Size:** 42¼" sq.
Requires: 8 blocks **Block Width:** 8¾"

#	Value	Yardage	#Strips	Cut Size	Strip End
		Yardage & Cutting Chart			
1	■	leftovers*	2	2¼" x 18"	⬭
2	■	1 fat qtr.	4	2¼" x 18"	(all)
3	■	1 fat qtr.	6	2¼" x 18"	
4	■	leftovers**	8	2¼" x 18"	
5	■	½ yd.	10	2¼" x 18"	
6	■	1 fat qtr.	8	2¼" x 18"	
7	□	1 fat qtr.	6	2¼" x 18"	
8	□	1 fat qtr.	4	2¼" x 18"	
9	□	1 fat qtr.	2	2¼" x 18"	
3/9		1¾ yds.	background *(see page 33)*		
4	■	1½ yds.**	4 borders 2¼" x 47"		
		3¼ yds.	backing: 2 pcs. 27¼" x 54"		
1	■	½ yd.*	binding: 14 strips 2" x 18"		

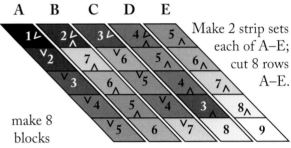

A   B   C   D   E

Make 2 strip sets each of A–E; cut 8 rows A–E.

make 8 blocks

Cut lengthwise border strips from fabric #4 and background patches from fabric #3 or 9 before cutting 2¼" x 18" strips from the leftovers.

You will want a medium or dark background if any of your blocks' outer tips are light. A light or medium background works best if any of your blocks' outer tips are dark.

If you use fabric #3 for the background, you won't need the fat quarter because you can cut the #3 strips from leftovers. If you use fabric #9 for the background, you can cut the #9 strips from leftovers.

Park City Lone Star

Quilt Size: 45¾" x 45¾" **Star Size:** 42¼" sq.
Requires: 8 blocks **Block Width:** 8¾"

#	Value	Yardage	#Strips	Cut Size	Strip End
		Yardage & Cutting			
1	■	1 fat qtr.	2	2¼" x 18"	⬡
2	■	1 fat qtr.	4	2¼" x 18"	(all)
3	■	1 fat qtr.	4	2¼" x 18"	
4	■	leftovers*	4	2¼" x 18"	
5	■	1 fat qtr.	6	2¼" x 18"	
6	■	leftovers**	8	2¼" x 18"	
7	■	½ yd.	10	2¼" x 18"	
8	■	1 fat qtr.	8	2¼" x 18"	
9	■	1 fat qtr.	4	2¼" x 18"	
10	□	1¼ yds.	background *(see page 33)*		
6	■	1½ yds.**	4 borders 2¼" x 47"		
		3¼ yds.	backing: 2 pcs. 27¼" x 54"		
4	■	½ yd.*	binding: 14 strips 2" x 18"		

Cut lengthwise border strips before cutting 2¼" x 18" strips from the leftovers.

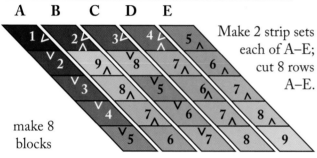

A B C D E

Make 2 strip sets each of A–E; cut 8 rows A–E.

make 8 blocks

Heidelberg Lone Star

Quilt Size: 45¾" x 45¾" **Star Size:** 42¼" sq.
Requires: 8 blocks **Block Width:** 8¾"

#	Value	Yardage	#Strips	Cut Size	Strip End
		Yardage & Cutting			
1	■	1 fat qtr.	6	2¼" x 18"	⬱
2	■	leftovers*	8	2¼" x 18"	(all)
3	■	1 fat qtr.	8	2¼" x 18"	
4	■	leftovers**	8	2¼" x 18"	
5	■	1 fat qtr.	6	2¼" x 18"	
6	■	1 fat qtr.	4	2¼" x 18"	
7	■	1 fat qtr.	4	2¼" x 18"	
8	■	1 fat qtr.	4	2¼" x 18"	
9	□	1 fat qtr.	2	2¼" x 18"	
10	□	1¼ yds.		background *(see page 33)*	
4	■	1½ yds.**		4 border 2¼" x 47"	
		3¼ yds.		backing: 2 pcs. 27¼" x 54"	
2	■	1 yd.*		binding: 14 strips 2" x 18"	

Cut lengthwise border strips before cutting 2¼" x 18" strips from the leftovers.

Make 2 strip sets each of A–E; cut 8 rows A–E.

make 8 blocks

41

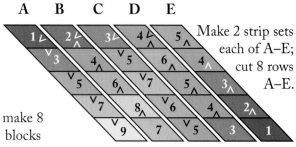

A B C D E

Make 2 strip sets
each of A–E;
cut 8 rows
A–E.

make 8
blocks

Montreal Lone Star

Quilt Size: 45¾" x 45¾" **Star Size:** 42¼" sq.
Requires: 8 blocks **Block Width:** 8¾"

#	Value	Yardage	#Strips	Cut Size	Strip End
		Yardage & Cutting			**Strip End**
1		1 fat qtr.	4	2¼" x 18"	�₂
2		leftovers*	4	2¼" x 18"	(all)
3		1 fat qtr.	8	2¼" x 18"	
4		leftovers**	8	2¼" x 18"	
5		½ yd.	10	2¼" x 18"	
6		1 fat qtr.	6	2¼" x 18"	
7		1 fat qtr.	6	2¼" x 18"	
8		1 fat qtr.	2	2¼" x 18"	
9		1 fat qtr.	2	2¼" x 18"	
10		1¼ yds.	background *(see page 33)*		
4		1½ yds.**	4 borders 2¼" x 47"		
		3¼ yds.	backing: 2 pcs. 27¼" x 54"		
2		½ yd.*	binding: 14 strips 2" x 18"		

Cut lengthwise border strips and background patches before cutting the necessary 2¼" x 18" strips from the leftovers.

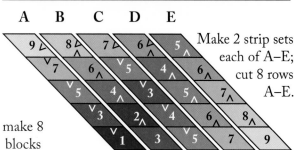

A B C D E

Make 2 strip sets
each of A–E;
cut 8 rows
A–E.

make 8
blocks

Calgary Lone Star

Quilt Size: 45¾" x 45¾" **Star Size:** 42¼" sq.
Requires: 8 blocks **Block Width:** 8¾"

#	Value	Yardage	#Strips	Cut Size	Strip End
		Yardage & Cutting			**Strip End**
1		leftovers***	2	2¼" x 18"	�₂
2		leftovers*	2	2¼" x 18"	(all)
3		1 fat qtr.	6	2¼" x 18"	
4		1 fat qtr.	6	2¼" x 18"	
5		leftovers**	10	2¼" x 18"	
6		1 fat qtr.	8	2¼" x 18"	
7		1 fat qtr.	8	2¼" x 18"	
8		1 fat qtr.	4	2¼" x 18"	
9		1 fat qtr.	4	2¼" x 18"	
2		1¾ yds.*	background *(see page 33)*		
5		1½ yds.**	4 borders 2¼" x 47"		
		3¼ yds.	backing: 2 pcs. 27¼" x 54"		
1		½ yd.***	binding: 14 strips 2" x 18"		

Honolulu Lone Star

Quilt Size: 45¾" x 45¾" **Star Size:** 42¼" sq.
Requires: 8 blocks **Block Width:** 8¾"

#	Value	Yardage	#Strips	Cut Size	Strip End
		Yardage & Cutting			**Strip End**
1		1 fat qtr.	2	2¼" x 18"	◹
2		leftovers*	4	2¼" x 18"	(all)
3		1 fat qtr.	4	2¼" x 18"	
4		1 fat qtr.	4	2¼" x 18"	
5		1 fat qtr.	8	2¼" x 18"	
6		leftovers**	8	2¼" x 18"	
7		1 fat qtr.	8	2¼" x 18"	
8		1 fat qtr.	8	2¼" x 18"	
9		1 fat qtr.	4	2¼" x 18"	
10		1¼ yds.	background *(see page 33)*		
2		1½ yds.*	4 borders 2¼" x 47"		
		3¼ yds.	backing: 2 pcs. 27¼" x 54"		
6		1 yd.**	binding: 14 strips 2" x 18"		

Cut lengthwise border strips from fabric #2 above or #3 below before cutting 2¼" x 18" strips from the leftovers.

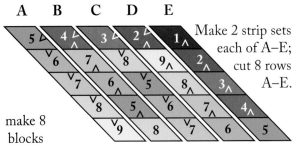

make 8 blocks

Make 2 strip sets each of A–E; cut 8 rows A–E.

Savannah Lone Star

Quilt Size: 45¾" x 45¾" **Star Size:** 42¼" sq.
Requires: 8 blocks **Block Width:** 8¾"

#	Value	Yardage	#Strips	Cut Size	Strip End
		Yardage & Cutting			**Strip End**
1		leftovers*	6	2¼" x 18"	◹
2		1 fat qtr.	8	2¼" x 18"	(all)
3		leftovers**	8	2¼" x 18"	
4		1 fat qtr.	4	2¼" x 18"	
5		1 fat qtr.	4	2¼" x 18"	
6		1 fat qtr.	4	2¼" x 18"	
7		1 fat qtr.	4	2¼" x 18"	
8		1 fat qtr.	8	2¼" x 18"	
9		1 fat qtr.	4	2¼" x 18"	
10		1¼ yds.	background *(see page 33)*		
3		1½ yds.**	4 borders 2¼" x 47"		
		3¼ yds.	backing: 2 pcs. 27¼" x 54"		
1		1 yd.*	binding: 14 strips 2" x 18"		

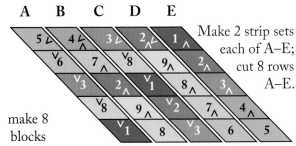

make 8 blocks

Make 2 strip sets each of A–E; cut 8 rows A–E.

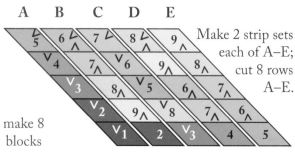

Make 2 strip sets
each of A–E;
cut 8 rows
A–E.

make 8
blocks

Loveland Lone Star

Quilt Size: 45¾" x 45¾" **Star Size:** 42¼" sq.
Requires: 8 blocks **Block Width:** 8¾"

#	Value	Yardage	#Strips	Cut Size	Strip End
1		leftovers*	2	2¼" x 18"	◹
2		1 fat qtr.	4	2¼" x 18"	(all)
3		leftovers**	4	2¼" x 18"	
4		1 fat qtr.	4	2¼" x 18"	
5		1 fat qtr.	6	2¼" x 18"	
6		1 fat qtr.	8	2¼" x 18"	
7		1 fat qtr.	8	2¼" x 18"	
8		1 fat qtr.	8	2¼" x 18"	
9		1 fat qtr.	6	2¼" x 18"	
10		1¼ yds.	background *(see page 33)*		
3		1½ yds.**	4 borders 2¼" x 47"		
		3¼ yds.	backing: 2 pcs. 27¼" x 54"		
1		½ yd.*	binding: 14 strips 2" x 18"		

Cut background patches and lengthwise border strips before cutting the necessary 2¼" x 18" strips from the leftovers.

Flagstaff Lone Star

Quilt Size: 45¾" x 45¾" **Star Size:** 42¼" sq.
Requires: 8 blocks **Block Width:** 8¾"

#	Value	Yardage	#Strips	Cut Size	Strip End
1		leftovers***	2	2¼" x 18"	◹
2		leftovers**	4	2¼" x 18"	(all)
3		leftovers*	4	2¼" x 18"	
4		1 fat qtr.	4	2¼" x 18"	
5		1 fat qtr.	4	2¼" x 18"	
6		1 fat qtr.	4	2¼" x 18"	
7		1 fat qtr.	8	2¼" x 18"	
8		½ yd.	12	2¼" x 18"	
9		1 fat qtr.	8	2¼" x 18"	
3		1¾ yds.*	background *(see page 33)*		
2		1½ yds.**	4 borders 2¼" x 47"		
		3¼ yds.	backing: 2 pcs. 27¼" x 54"		
1		½ yd.***	binding: 14 strips 2" x 18"		

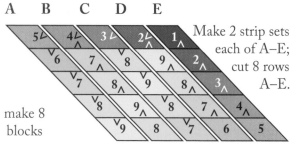

Make 2 strip sets
each of A–E;
cut 8 rows
A–E.

make 8
blocks

Paris Lone Star

#	Value	Yardage	#Strips	Cut Size	Strip End
		Yardage & Cutting			**Strip End**
1	⬛	leftovers*	10	2¼" x 18"	⬡
3	⬛	leftovers**	8	2¼" x 18"	(all)
5	⬛	1 fat qtr.	8	2¼" x 18"	
7	⬛	½ yd.	16	2¼" x 18"	
9	⬛	1 fat qtr.	8	2¼" x 18"	
10	⬜	1¼ yds.	background (see page 33)		
3	⬛	1½ yds.**	4 borders 2¼" x 47"		
		3¼ yds.	backing: 2 pcs. 27¼" x 54"		
1	⬛	1 yd.*	binding: 14 strips 2" x 18"		

Quilt Size: 45¾" x 45¾" **Star Size:** 42¼" sq.
Requires: 8 blocks **Block Width:** 8¾"

The values in the quilt above are 2 steps apart; in other quilts there are 9 closer values.

Cut lengthwise border strips before cutting 2¼" x 18" strips from the leftovers.

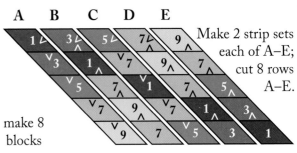

A B C D E

Make 2 strip sets each of A–E; cut 8 rows A–E.

make 8 blocks

Lillehammer Lone Star

#	Value	Yardage	#Strips	Cut Size	Strip End
		Yardage & Cutting			**Strip End**
1	⬛	1 fat qtr.	2	2¼" x 18"	⬡
2	⬛	1 fat qtr.	4	2¼" x 18"	(all)
3	⬛	leftovers*	6	2¼" x 18"	
4	⬛	1 fat qtr.	8	2¼" x 18"	
5	⬛	leftovers**	10	2¼" x 18"	
6	⬛	1 fat qtr.	8	2¼" x 18"	
7	⬛	1 fat qtr.	6	2¼" x 18"	
8	⬜	1 fat qtr.	4	2¼" x 18"	
9	⬜	1 fat qtr.	2	2¼" x 18"	
10	⬜	1¼ yds.	background (see page 33)		
5	⬛	1½ yds.**	4 borders 2¼" x 47		
		3¼ yds.	backing: 2 pcs. 27¼" x 54"		
3	⬛	1 yd.*	binding: 14 strips 2" x 18"		

Quilt Size: 45¾" x 45¾" **Star Size:** 42¼" sq.
Requires: 8 blocks **Block Width:** 8¾"

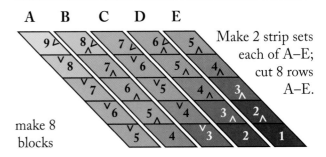

A B C D E

Make 2 strip sets each of A–E; cut 8 rows A–E.

make 8 blocks

Europa Lone Star

See the Lone Star how-to's on pages 7–22. Information about the gradated quilts and their strip sets is on pages 32–34. Note that E rows are used in 2 blocks. E is rotated in the Lillehammer block. Strip sets E and J differ only in their orientation and pressing direction.

4-block unit
make 8

A   B   C   D   E

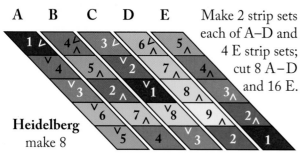

Heidelberg
make 8

Make 2 strip sets each of A–D and 4 E strip sets; cut 8 A–D and 16 E.

F   G   H   I   J

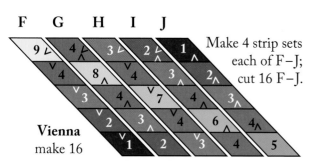

Vienna
make 16

Make 4 strip sets each of F–J; cut 16 F–J.

E   K   L   M   N

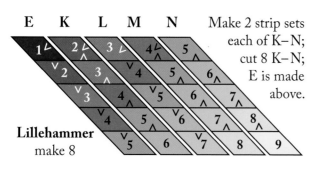

Lillehammer
make 8

Make 2 strip sets each of K–N; cut 8 K–N; E is made above.

Quilt Size: 96½" x 96½"   **Star Size:** 84½" sq.
Requires: 32 blocks   **Block Width:** 8¾"

Yardage & Cutting

#	Value	Yardage	#Strips	Cut Size	Strip End
1		leftovers*	16	2¼" x 18"	
2		leftovers**	28	2¼" x 18"	(all)
3		1½ yds.	38	2¼" x 18"	
4		1½ yds.	48	2¼" x 18"	
5		1 yd.	20	2¼" x 18"	
6		leftovers***	16	2¼" x 18"	
7		½ yd.	14	2¼" x 18"	
8		½ yd.	12	2¼" x 18"	
9		1 fat qtr.	8	2¼" x 18"	
2		4¼ yds.**	background *(see page 34)*		
1		3 yds.*	4 borders 6½" x 97¾"		
		9¼ yds.	backing: 3 pcs. 35½" x 105"		
6		1¼ yds.***	binding: 18 strips 2" x 27"		

Cut background patches from fabric #2 and lengthwise border strips from fabric #1 before cutting 2¼" x 18" strips from the leftovers.

Southern Star

See the Lone Star how-to's on pages 7–22. Information about the gradated quilts and their strip sets is on pages 32–34. Note that strip sets and rows A and J differ only in their pressing direction.

4-block unit for top quilt
make 8

Cut lengthwise border strips from fabric #1 before cutting 2¼" x 18" strips from the leftovers.

Quilt Size: 96½" x 96½"   **Star Size:** 84½" sq.
Requires: 32 blocks   **Block Width:** 8¾"

Yardage & Cutting

#	Value	Yardage	#Strips	Cut Size	Strip End
1	■	leftovers*	20	2¼" x 18"	⬦
2	■	1 yd.	32	2¼" x 18"	(all)
3	■	1 yd.	32	2¼" x 18"	
4	■	½ yd.	16	2¼" x 18"	
5	■	½ yd.	16	2¼" x 18"	
6	■	leftovers**	16	2¼" x 18"	
7	■	1 yd.	20	2¼" x 18"	
8	□	1 yd.	32	2¼" x 18"	
9	□	leftovers***	16	2¼" x 18"	
9	□	4¼ yds.***	background *(see page 34)*		
1	■	3 yds.*	4 borders 6½" x 97¾"		
		9¼ yds.	backing: 3 pcs. 35½" x 105"		
6	■	1¼ yds.**	binding: 18 strips 2" x 27"		

Same 32 Blocks Rotated Differently

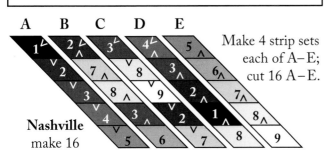

A B C D E

Make 4 strip sets
each of A–E;
cut 16 A–E.

Nashville
make 16

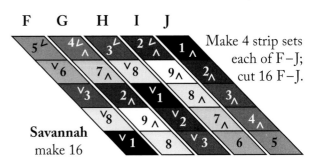

F G H I J

Make 4 strip sets
each of F–J;
cut 16 F–J.

Savannah
make 16

River City Lone Star

See the Lone Star how-to's on pages 7–22. Information about the gradated quilts and their strip sets is on pages 32–34.

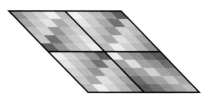

4-block unit for top quilt
make 8

Cut lengthwise border strips from fabric #9 before cutting 2¼" x 18" strips from the leftovers.

Same Blocks, Quilt Size; Different Placement

Quilt Size: 90½" x 90½"   **Star Size:** 84½" sq.
Requires: 32 blocks   **Block Width:** 8¾

#	Value	Yardage	#Strips	Cut Size	Strip End
		Yardage & Cutting			
1		½ yd.	10	2¼" x 18"	◢
2		½ yd.	14	2¼" x 18"	(all)
3		1 yd.	30	2¼" x 18"	
4		1 yd.	34	2¼" x 18"	
5		1 yd.	32	2¼" x 18"	
6		1 yd.	26	2¼" x 18"	
7		leftovers*	26	2¼" x 18"	
8		½ yd.	14	2¼" x 18"	
9		leftovers**	14	2¼" x 18"	
10		4¼ yds.	background *(see page 34)*		
9		2¾ yds.**	4 borders 3½" x 91¾"		
		8¾ yds.	backing: 3 pcs. 33½" x 99"		
7		1¾ yds.*	binding: 17 strips 2" x 27"		

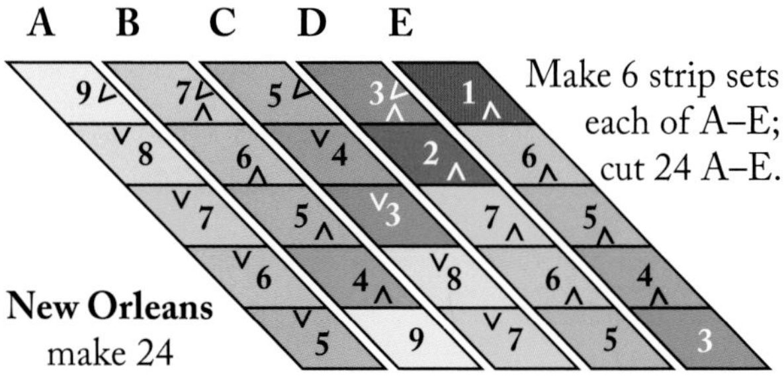

A B C D E

Make 6 strip sets each of A–E; cut 24 A–E.

New Orleans
make 24

F G H I J

Make 2 strip sets each of F–J; cut 8 F–J.

Vienna
make 8

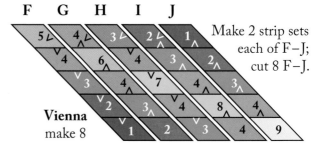

Alpine Lone Star

See the Lone Star how-to's on pages 7–22. Information about the gradated quilts and their strip sets is on pages 32–34. Note that strip sets E and J differ only in their pressing direction and orientation.

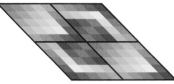

4-block unit for top quilt
make 8

Cut background patches from fabric #9 and lengthwise border strips from fabric #7 before cutting 2¼" x 18" strips from the leftovers.

Quilt Size: 96½" x 96½"   **Star Size:** 84½" sq.
Requires: 32 blocks   **Block Width:** 8¾"

#	Value	Yardage	#Strips	Cut Size	Strip End
1		½ yd.	16	2¼" x 18"	◿
2		1 yd.	32	2¼" x 18"	(all)
3		leftovers*	32	2¼" x 18"	
4		1 yd.	24	2¼" x 18"	
5		leftovers**	28	2¼" x 18"	
6		1 yd.	24	2¼" x 18"	
7		1 yd.	20	2¼" x 18"	
8		½ yd.	16	2¼" x 18"	
9		leftovers***	8	2¼" x 18"	
9		4¼ yds.***	background *(see page 34)*		
5		3 yds.**	4 borders 6½" x 97¾"		
		9¼ yds.	backing: 3 pcs. 35½" x 105"		
3		1¾ yds.*	binding: 18 strips 2" x 27"		

Yardage & Cutting

Same Blocks, Quilt Size; Different Placement

A B C D E

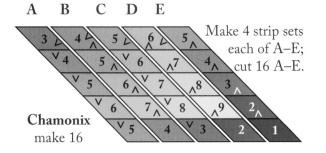

Make 4 strip sets each of A–E; cut 16 A–E.

Chamonix
make 16

F G H I J

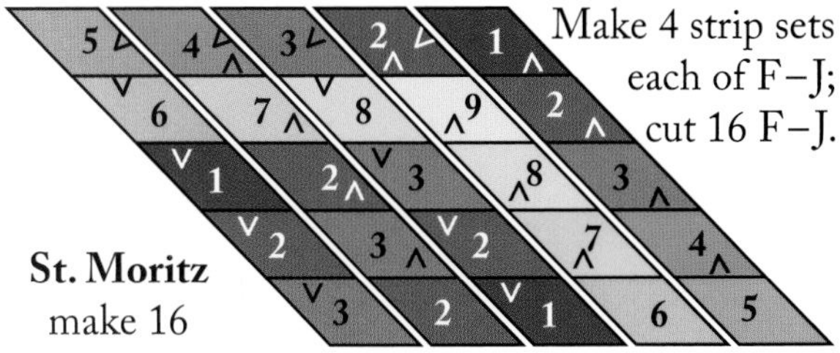

Make 4 strip sets each of F–J; cut 16 F–J.

St. Moritz
make 16

Lone Star Explosion

See the Lone Star how-to's on pages 7–22. Information about the gradated quilts and their strip sets is on pages 32–34. Note that strip sets F and O differ only in their pressing direction.

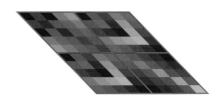

4-block unit
make 8

A   B   C   D   E

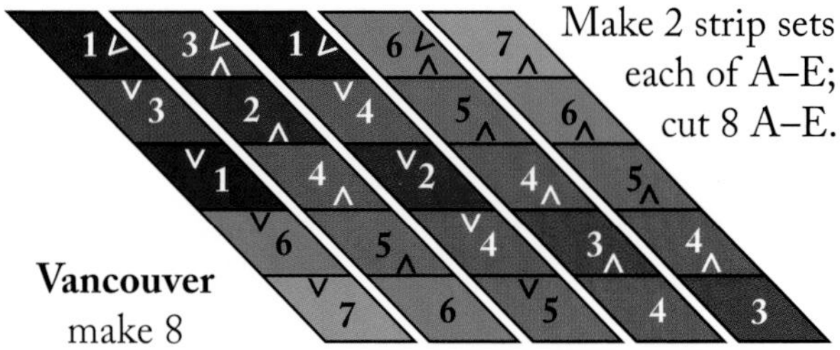

Make 2 strip sets each of A–E; cut 8 A–E.

Vancouver
make 8

F   G   H   I   J

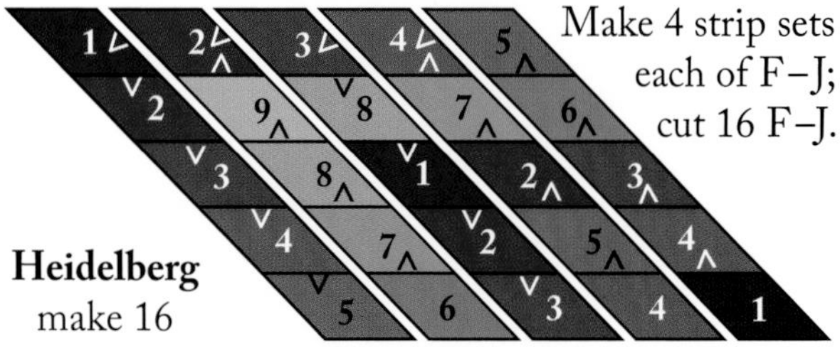

Make 4 strip sets each of F–J; cut 16 F–J.

Heidelberg
make 16

K   L   M   N   O

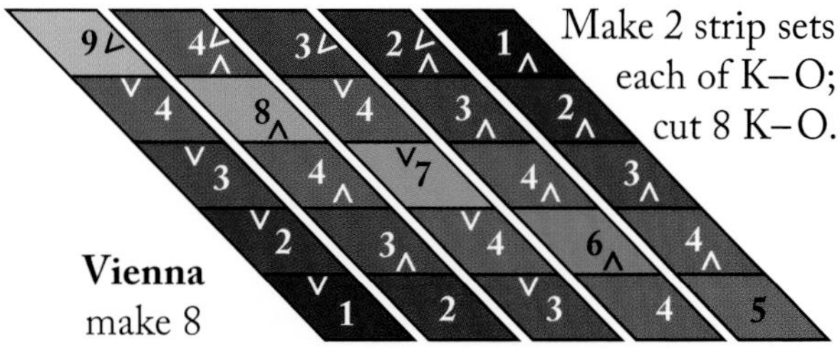

Make 2 strip sets each of K–O; cut 8 K–O.

Vienna
make 8

Cut lengthwise border strips from fabric #3 before cutting 2¼" x 18" strips from the leftovers.

Quilt Size: 90½" x 90½"	**Star Size:** 84½" sq.
Requires: 32 blocks	**Block Width:** 8¾"

#	Value	Yardage	#Strips	Cut Size	Strip End
			Yardage & Cutting		
1	■	leftovers*	22	2¼" x 18"	
2	■	1 yd.	28	2¼" x 18"	(all)
3	■	leftovers**	36	2¼" x 18"	
4	■	1½ yds.	44	2¼" x 18"	
5	■	1 yd.	22	2¼" x 18"	
6	■	1½ yds.	18	2¼" x 18"	
7	■	½ yd.	14	2¼" x 18"	
8	■	½ yd.	10	2¼" x 18"	
9	■	1 fat qtr.	6	2¼" x 18"	
10	■	4¼ yds.	background *(see page 34)*		
3	■	2¾ yds.**	4 borders 3½" x 91¾"		
		8¾ yds.	backing: 3 pcs. 33½" x 99"		
1	■	1¾ yds.*	binding: 17 strips 2" x 27"		

Sunset Lone Star

See the Lone Star how-to's on pages 7–22. Information about the gradated quilts and their strip sets is on pages 32–34. Note that E and F rows are used in 2 blocks. F is rotated in the right row of the Vienna block.

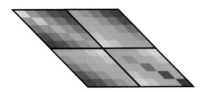

4-block unit
make 8

Cut lengthwise border strips from fabric #6 before cutting 2¼" x 18" strips from the leftovers.

Quilt Size: 96½" x 96½"   **Star Size:** 84½ sq.
Requires: 32 blocks   **Block Width:** 8¾"

#	Value	Yardage	#Strips	Cut Size	Strip End
		Yardage & Cutting			
1		½ yd.	10	2¼" x 18"	
2		1 yd.	18	2¼" x 18"	(all)
3		leftovers*	26	2¼" x 18"	
4		1 yd.	34	2¼" x 18"	
5		1 yd.	24	2¼" x 18"	
6		leftovers**	34	2¼" x 18"	
7		1 yd.	26	2¼" x 18"	
8		1 yd.	18	2¼" x 18"	
9		½ yd.	10	2¼" x 18"	
10		4¼ yds.	background *(see page 34)*		
6		3 yds.**	4 borders 6½" x 97¾"		
		9¼ yds.	backing: 3 pcs. 35½" x 105"		
3		1¾ yds.*	binding: 18 strips 2" x 27"		

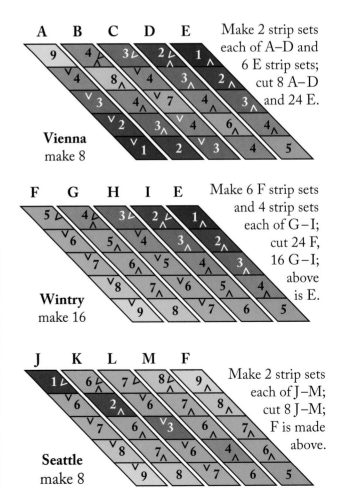

A B C D E

Vienna
make 8

Make 2 strip sets each of A–D and 6 E strip sets; cut 8 A–D and 24 E.

F G H I E

Wintry
make 16

Make 6 F strip sets and 4 strip sets each of G–I; cut 24 F, 16 G–I; above is E.

J K L M F

Seattle
make 8

Make 2 strip sets each of J–M; cut 8 J–M; F is made above.

Star Sapphire

See the Lone Star how-to's on pages 7–22. Information about the gradated quilts and their strip sets is on pages 32–34. Note that E rows are used in 2 blocks. Strip sets E and J, G and L, and H and M differ only in their orientation and pressing direction.

4-block unit
make 8

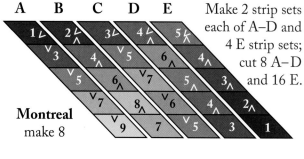

Montreal
make 8

Make 2 strip sets each of A–D and 4 E strip sets; cut 8 A–D and 16 E.

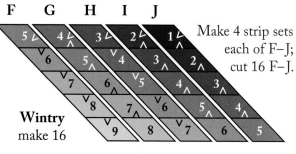

Wintry
make 16

Make 4 strip sets each of F–J; cut 16 F–J.

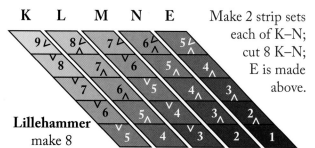

Lillehammer
make 8

Make 2 strip sets each of K–N; cut 8 K–N; E is made above.

Cut background patches from fabric #1, binding from fabric #3, and lengthwise border strips from fabric #4 before cutting 2¼" x 18" strips from the leftovers.

Quilt Size: 90½" x 90½"			**Star Size:** 84½" sq.	
Requires: 32 blocks			**Block Width:** 8¾"	
		Yardage & Cutting		**Strip**
#	**Value**	**Yardage**	**#Strips**	**Cut Size**	**End**
1		leftovers*	10	2¼" x 18"	⬡
2		½ yd.	16	2¼" x 18"	(all)
3		leftovers**	26	2¼" x 18"	
4		leftovers***	32	2¼" x 18"	
5		1½ yd.	40	2¼" x 18"	
6		1 yd.	30	2¼" x 18"	
7		1 yd.	24	2¼" x 18"	
8		½ yd.	14	2¼" x 18"	
9		1 fat qtr.	8	2¼" x 18"	
1		4¼ yds.*	background *(see page 34)*		
4		3 yds.***	4 borders 3½" x 91¾"		
		8¾ yds.	backing: 3 pcs. 33½" x 99"		
3		1½ yds.**	binding: 8 strips 2" x 54"		

Rocky Mountain Lone Star

See the Lone Star how-to's on pages 7–22. Information about the gradated quilts and their strip sets is on pages 32–34. Note that J rows are used in 3 places in 2 blocks.

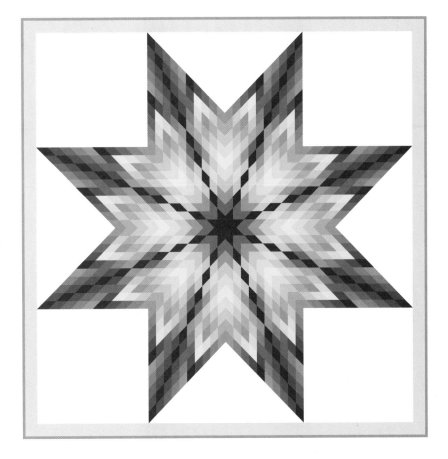

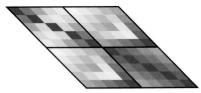

4-block unit
make 8

Cut lengthwise border strips from fabric #8 and binding strips from fabric #5 before cutting 2¼" x 18" strips from the leftovers.

			Yardage & Cutting		**Strip**
#	**Value**	**Yardage**	**#Strips**	**Cut Size**	**End**
1		1 yd.	24	2¼" x 18"	
2		1 yd.	24	2¼" x 18"	(all)
3		1 yd.	28	2¼" x 18"	
4		½ yd.	16	2¼" x 18"	
5		leftovers*	24	2¼" x 18"	
6		½ yd.	16	2¼" x 18"	
7		1½ yds.	36	2¼" x 18"	
8		leftovers**	24	2¼" x 18"	
9		1 fat qtr.	8	2¼" x 18"	
10		4¼ yds.	background *(see page 34)*		
8		2¾ yds.**	4 borders 3½" x 91¾"		
		8¾ yds.	backing: 3 pcs. 33½" x 99"		
5		1¾ yds.*	binding: 17 strips 2" x 27"		

Quilt Size: 90½" x 90½"   **Star Size:** 84½" sq.
Requires: 32 blocks   **Block Width:** 8¾"

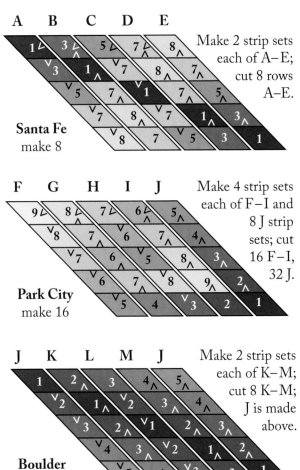

Make 2 strip sets each of A–E; cut 8 rows A–E.

Santa Fe make 8

Make 4 strip sets each of F–I and 8 J strip sets; cut 16 F–I, 32 J.

Park City make 16

Make 2 strip sets each of K–M; cut 8 K–M; J is made above.

Boulder make 8

Traditional Lone Star

Traditional Lone Star, 99⅝" x 99⅝". Pieced by Judy Martin and quilted by Lana Corcoran. Note the octagonal rings of color typical of the classic pattern. I planned this star to fit on the top surface of a queen or king bed. This quilt is embellished with a wide pieced border, also in a traditional design. If you omit the border, the quilt is a good size for a captivating wall quilt. I drew my color scheme from the background print. As I planned the rings of color, I wanted areas of blending as well as contrast. For the most part, I used two shades of a color before shifting to the next color. I was going for a shabby chic look. If you prefer a stronger contrast between the star and the background, you might choose darker values for the diamonds at the tips of the star or a lighter or less busy background fabric, such as the floral in the border triangles and outer border.

Quilt Size: 99⅝" x 99⅝" **Star Size:** 59¾" sq.
Requires: 8 Y blocks, **Block Width:** 12⅜"
32 Z border blocks

Color		Yardage	#Strips	Cut Size	Strip End
1		1½ yds.	48	1⅞" x 18"	�￢
2		½ yd.	14	1⅞" x 18"	(all)
3		1 yd.	31	1⅞" x 18"	
4		½ yd.	16	1⅞" x 18"	
5		1½ yds.	63	1⅞" x 18"	
6		½ yd.	16	1⅞" x 18"	
7		1 fat qtr.	8	1⅞" x 18"	
8		2 yds.	68	1⅞" x 18"	
9		1½ yds.	57	1⅞" x 18"	
10		1 fat qtr.	9	1⅞" x 18"	
11		1 yd.	28	1⅞" x 18"	
12		2½ yds.	background *(see page 57)*		
			4 A, 4 B or 8 C, 8D		
			+ 4 borders cut 1⅞" x 63¾"		
			+ 4 Q (2 per ◻ 8¼")		
13		5½ yds.	4 borders cut 6½" x 100⅞"		
			+ 24 R *(see page 57)*		
		9⅝ yds.	backing: 3 pcs. 36½" x 108"		
2		¾ yd.	binding: 18 strips 2" x 27"		

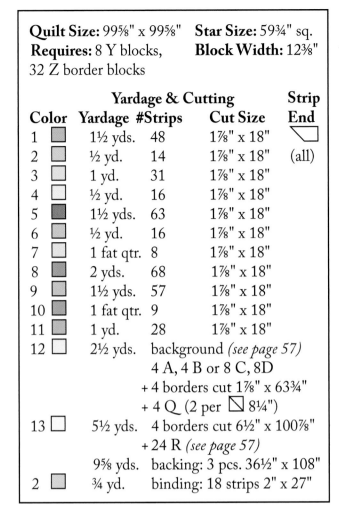

A B C D E F G H I

Block Y
make 8

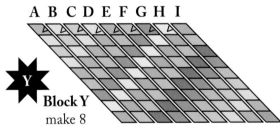

Making Strip Sets and Cutting Rows

Start by reading the glossary, "Pattern Pointers," and "How to Make a Lone Star" chapters on pages 7–22.

You can cut all the strips before you sew any, or cut a little and sew a little, according to your preference. Cut the strips for a strip set, cutting off one end as indicated in the "strip end" column of the yardage chart. If you folded the fabric, unfold it before you cut off the strip ends so that all of the strips have the same end.

Trim the points as described on page 14 and shown on page 56 to help you align patches for sewing. The point should be trimmed at a right angle to the angled end of the strip. Don't trim the point on the top strip of a strip set. If you don't have my Point Trimmer tool, download a file to make one at judymartin.com/LSPT.cfm

Align the trimmed point of one strip with the wide angle of the neighboring strip. Pin and stitch the first strip to the

second strip. Add the third strip. Finger press and steam press after each seam, following the "v" pressing arrows in the strip set diagrams. Continue pinning and stitching strips together to complete a strip set as shown. Measure your strip set down the middle from the raw edge at the top to the raw edge at the bottom. It should measure 12⅞". If it does not, adjust your seam guide and correct your seams before proceeding.

When you have your seam allowance right, trim a sliver off the angled end of the strip set, if necessary, at a precise 45° angle. See the row cutting diagram on page 56. Cut the strip set into rows 1⅞" wide. That is, lay the 1⅞" ruling of your rotary cutting ruler over the angled end of the strip and cut along the ruler's edge. For strip sets A–I, make a duplicate strip set to allow you to cut 4 more rows like the first 4. For strip sets for the pieced border, make 7 strip sets of each type. When you have all the rows needed for a block, trim both points of each row A–I as shown on page 56. Trim just the top point of rows J–O and P patches.

Making Blocks

Lay out the rows for a Y or Z block as shown in the block diagram at left or on the next page. Align the trimmed point of the second row with the wide angle of the first row, and pin there. Also pin at each joint. Strategies for matching joints are on page 15. Stitch rows together, pressing after each seam in the direction indicated with an arrow in the block diagram. After adding the P patch to the Z border block, align the ¼" ruling of your rotary ruler with the outer tips of the dark blue diamonds. Cut off the excess brown, leaving a ¼" seam allowance. Make 8 Y blocks and 32 Z border blocks.

Assembling the Pieced Border

Make a cloth rotary cutting template for R as shown on page 57. Use it to cut 24 R from fabric #13, as shown. The strip will be a little too wide, so align your ruler with the short side of the template to trim off a sliver there. Trim points of R patches and Z blocks by downloading a file for making a Point Trimmer especially for that shape at judymartin.com/cdef.cfm. Follow the directions there. See the border in the assembly diagram on page 57. Sew an R to each of 24 Z's. Press seams toward the Z's. Join these in sets of 6 as shown on page 57, pressing seams toward R's. Sew a Q to the short side of each of 4 Z's to make a corner unit. Pin and stitch one of the remaining Z's and a corner unit to the end of each border as shown.

Assembling the Quilt

Cut out background patches shown on page 57 and outer border strips listed in the yardage chart. Choose patches for use with or without Y-seams. See page 17 for tips on cutting patches larger than your ruler.

Arrange the blocks, background patches, and borders as shown in the photo on page 54 and the quilt assembly diagram on page 57. Stitch together the blocks and patches in numerical order. Note in the left assembly diagram that you can miter the inner borders without Y-seams if you sew the diagonal seams after attaching the inner borders. Press seams to one side after each seam, as indicated by arrows in the quilt assembly diagram.

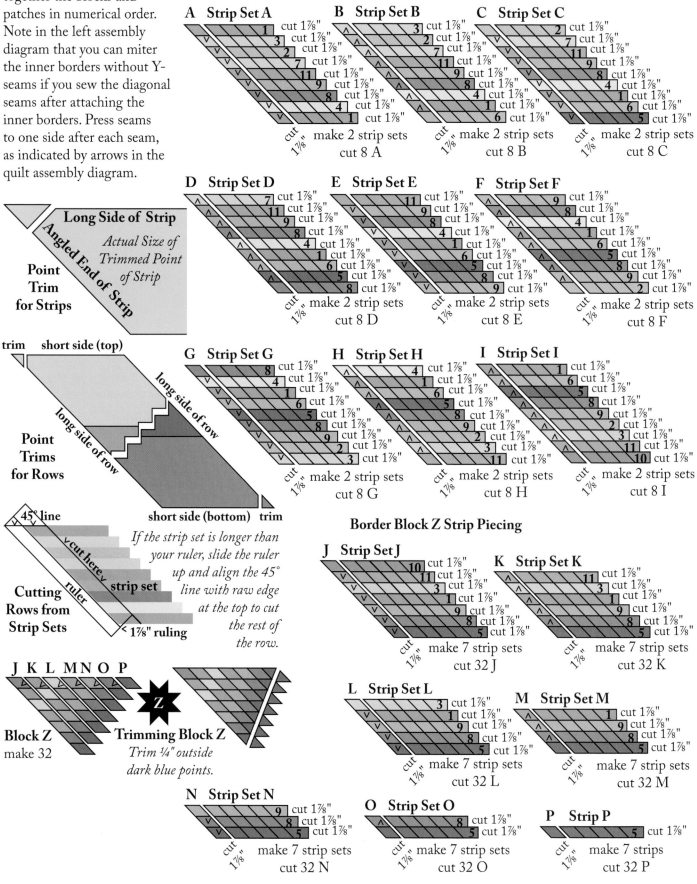

Star Block Y Strip Piecing

A Strip Set A — cut 1⅞" (×8); make 2 strip sets; cut 8 A
B Strip Set B — cut 1⅞" (×8); make 2 strip sets; cut 8 B
C Strip Set C — cut 1⅞" (×8); make 2 strip sets; cut 8 C

D Strip Set D — cut 1⅞" (×8); make 2 strip sets; cut 8 D
E Strip Set E — cut 1⅞" (×8); make 2 strip sets; cut 8 E
F Strip Set F — cut 1⅞" (×8); make 2 strip sets; cut 8 F

G Strip Set G — cut 1⅞" (×8); make 2 strip sets; cut 8 G
H Strip Set H — cut 1⅞" (×8); make 2 strip sets; cut 8 H
I Strip Set I — cut 1⅞" (×8); make 2 strip sets; cut 8 I

Border Block Z Strip Piecing

J Strip Set J — cut 1⅞" (×6); make 7 strip sets; cut 32 J
K Strip Set K — cut 1⅞" (×6); make 7 strip sets; cut 32 K

L Strip Set L — cut 1⅞" (×4); make 7 strip sets; cut 32 L
M Strip Set M — cut 1⅞" (×4); make 7 strip sets; cut 32 M

N Strip Set N — cut 1⅞" (×3); make 7 strip sets; cut 32 N
O Strip Set O — cut 1⅞" (×2); make 7 strip sets; cut 32 O
P Strip P — cut 1⅞"; make 7 strips; cut 32 P

Point Trim for Strips
Long Side of Strip
Angled End of Strip
Actual Size of Trimmed Point of Strip

Point Trims for Rows
trim — short side (top)
long side of row
long side of row
short side (bottom) — trim

Cutting Rows from Strip Sets
45° line
cut here
ruler
strip set
1⅞" ruling
If the strip set is longer than your ruler, slide the ruler up and align the 45° line with raw edge at the top to cut the rest of the row.

J K L M N O P
Block Z
make 32

Z

Trimming Block Z
Trim ¼" outside dark blue points.

Finishing the Quilt

Lana quilted in the ditch between the star and background. She quilted the rows of diamonds ¼" in from the seamlines. She quilted feathers in the background squares and triangles and in the borders and R triangles. Binding directions are on page 22.

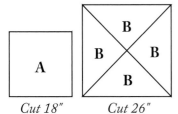

Cut 18"   *Cut 26"*

Background Patches (Y-Seams)
cut 4 A squares **18"**
cut 4 B triangles
from one **26"** square

OR

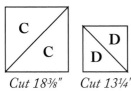

Cut 18⅜"   *Cut 13¼"*

Background Patches (No Y-Seams)
cut 8 C triangles
from four **18⅜"** squares
cut 8 D triangles
from four **13¼"** squares

ALSO
for either

Cut 8¼"

Border Corners
cut 4 Q triangles
from two **8¼"** squares

Making and Using a Cloth Rotary Cutting Template for R

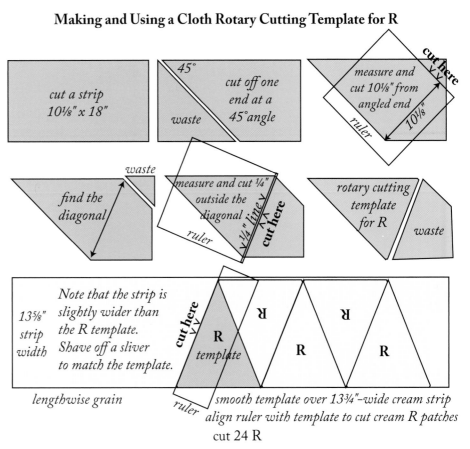

cut a strip
10⅛" x 18"

45°

waste

cut off one end at a 45° angle

measure and cut 10⅛" from angled end

cut here

10⅛"

ruler

find the diagonal

waste

measure and cut ¼" outside the diagonal

ruler

¼" line

cut here

rotary cutting template for R

waste

13⅝" strip width

Note that the strip is slightly wider than the R template. Shave off a sliver to match the template.

cut here

R template

R

R

R

R

R

lengthwise grain

ruler

smooth template over 13¾"-wide cream strip
align ruler with template to cut cream R patches
cut 24 R

Below, blue dots indicate set-in seams (Y-seams). For more information on Y-seams, see page 18. Arrows in both diagrams below indicate pressing direction.

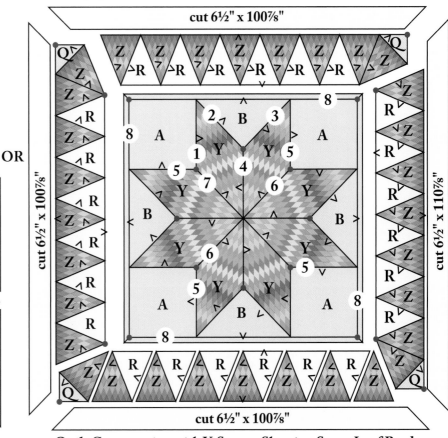

cut 6½" x 100⅞"

cut 6½" x 100⅞"

cut 6½" x 100⅞"

cut 6½" x 110⅞"

Quilt Construction with Y-Seams, Showing Sugar Loaf Borders
cut inner borders 1⅞ x 63¾"

OR

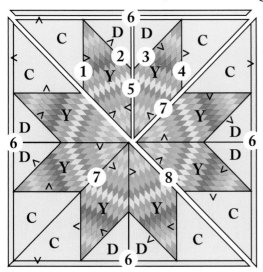

Quilt Center with No Y-Seams
Note that the pieced borders require Y-seams.

57

Sea Breeze

| Quilt Size: 42¼" x 42¼" | Star Size: 42¼" sq. |
| Requires: 8 Z blocks | Block Width: 8¾" |

		Yardage & Cutting			**Strip**
Color		**Yardage**	**#Strips**	**Cut Size**	**End**
2		1 fat qtr.	6	1¾" x 18"	▱
4		1 fat qtr.	10	1¾" x 18"	▱
5		1 fat qtr.	10	1¾" x 18"	▱
6		½ yd.	40	1" x 18"	▱
7		1 fat qtr.	8	1¾" x 18"	▱
8		1 fat qtr.	8	1¾" x 18"	▱
9		1 fat qtr.	6	1¾" x 18"	▱
10		1 fat qtr.	6	1¾" x 18"	▱
11		1 fat qtr.	4	1¾" x 18"	▱
12		leftovers*	2	1¾" x 18"	▱
13		1 fat qtr.	10	1¾" x 18"	▱
1		1¼ yds.	background *(see page 60)*		
			4 A, 4 B or 8 C, 8 D		
		3⅛ yds.	backing: 2 pcs. 25⅝" x 50¾"		
12		½ yd.*	binding: 13 strips 2" x 18"		

Sea Breeze, 42¼" x 42¼". Pieced by Marilyn Deppe from an original design by Judy Martin. Quilted by Lee Smith. The quilt is made from 8 diamond blocks in an 8¾" finished width. This is a good pattern for your first Lone Star because the strips that separate the diamond rows allow you to avoid the trickiest joints. You'll still need to take care with your seam allowances in order to fit the diamond rows to the unseamed narrow strips. Some of the variations on page 61 use 4 Z blocks and 4 Zr (reversed) blocks. Marilyn made her quilt with 8 blocks alike. If you make your quilt like the one in the photograh, you won't need to make any Zr blocks.

Marilyn cut binding strips from leftover strip sets augmented with strips cut from new strip sets made from leftover fabric. The yardage chart lists plain binding for a simpler solution. If you piece binding like Marilyn's, press seams of strip sets open. You will need 15 strips 2" x 12⅞".

For arrangements that call for 4 Z and 4 Zr blocks, cut strips in the quantity listed from folded fabric so half of the strips will have a reversed strip end: ▱. Also cut the 1"- wide strips from fabric #6 from folded fabric to yield 20 F and 20 Fr strips/patches. Make 1 strip set each of A–E and Ar–Er; cut 4 A–E and 4 Ar–Er rows.

Making Strip Sets and Cutting Rows

Start by reading the glossary, "Pattern Pointers," and "How to Make a Lone Star" chapters on pages 7–22. Test your seam allowance as described on page 10, and adjust it if necessary. This quilt will be easy if you can trust your seam allowance.

Use only the first 3 diagrams below for arrangements of 8 Z's. The last 3 diagrams are for Zr blocks.

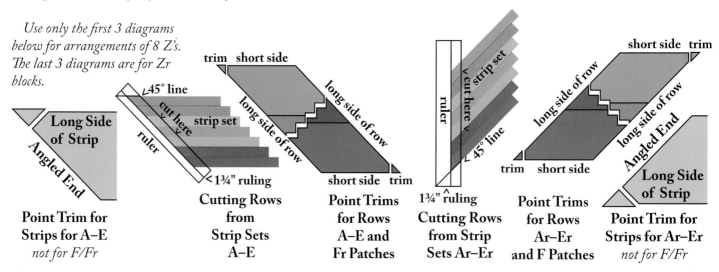

| **Point Trim for Strips for A–E** *not for F/Fr* | **Cutting Rows from Strip Sets A–E** | **Point Trims for Rows A–E and Fr Patches** | **Cutting Rows from Strip Sets Ar–Er** | **Point Trims for Rows Ar–Er and F Patches** | **Point Trim for Strips for Ar–Er** *not for F/Fr* |

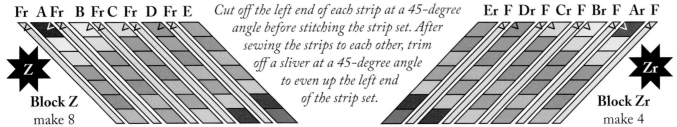

Fr A Fr B Fr C Fr D Fr E

Er F Dr F Cr F Br F Ar F

Cut off the left end of each strip at a 45-degree angle before stitching the strip set. After sewing the strips to each other, trim off a sliver at a 45-degree angle to even up the left end of the strip set.

Z

Block Z
make 8

Zr

Block Zr
make 4

This block is for all arrangements. For arrangements 3, 4, and 5 on page 61, make 4 Z and 4 Zr blocks.

This block is for arrangements 3, 4, and 5 on page 61.

Strip Piecing Z

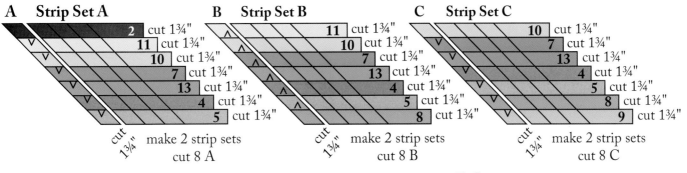

A Strip Set A

2	cut 1¾"
11	cut 1¾"
10	cut 1¾"
7	cut 1¾"
13	cut 1¾"
4	cut 1¾"
5	cut 1¾"

cut 1¾"   make 2 strip sets
cut 8 A

B Strip Set B

11	cut 1¾"
10	cut 1¾"
7	cut 1¾"
13	cut 1¾"
4	cut 1¾"
5	cut 1¾"
8	cut 1¾"

cut 1¾"   make 2 strip sets
cut 8 B

C Strip Set C

10	cut 1¾"
7	cut 1¾"
13	cut 1¾"
4	cut 1¾"
5	cut 1¾"
8	cut 1¾"
9	cut 1¾"

cut 1¾"   make 2 strip sets
cut 8 C

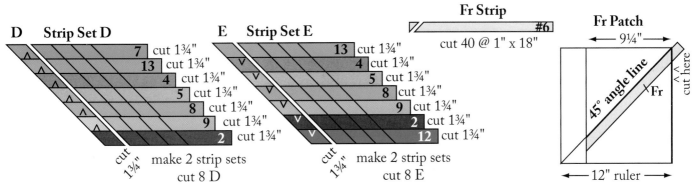

D Strip Set D

7	cut 1¾"
13	cut 1¾"
4	cut 1¾"
5	cut 1¾"
8	cut 1¾"
9	cut 1¾"
2	cut 1¾"

cut 1¾"   make 2 strip sets
cut 8 D

E Strip Set E

13	cut 1¾"
4	cut 1¾"
5	cut 1¾"
8	cut 1¾"
9	cut 1¾"
2	cut 1¾"
12	cut 1¾"

cut 1¾"   make 2 strip sets
cut 8 E

Fr Strip

#6

cut 40 @ 1" x 18"

Fr Patch

9¼"

45° angle line   Fr

cut here

12" ruler

Strip Piecing Zr

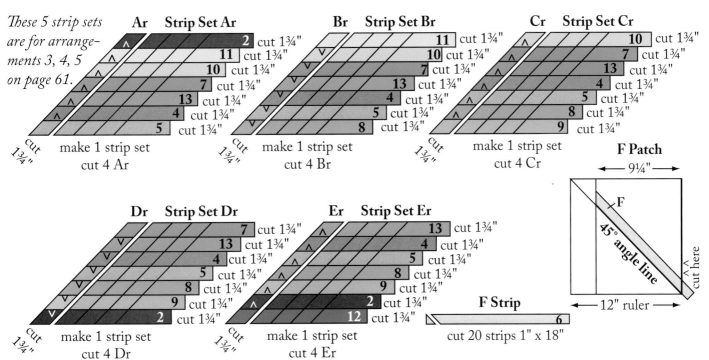

These 5 strip sets are for arrangements 3, 4, 5 on page 61.

Ar Strip Set Ar

2	cut 1¾"
11	cut 1¾"
10	cut 1¾"
7	cut 1¾"
13	cut 1¾"
4	cut 1¾"
5	cut 1¾"

cut 1¾"   make 1 strip set
cut 4 Ar

Br Strip Set Br

11	cut 1¾"
10	cut 1¾"
7	cut 1¾"
13	cut 1¾"
4	cut 1¾"
5	cut 1¾"
8	cut 1¾"

cut 1¾"   make 1 strip set
cut 4 Br

Cr Strip Set Cr

10	cut 1¾"
7	cut 1¾"
13	cut 1¾"
4	cut 1¾"
5	cut 1¾"
8	cut 1¾"
9	cut 1¾"

cut 1¾"   make 1 strip set
cut 4 Cr

F Patch

9¼"

F

45° angle line

cut here

12" ruler

Dr Strip Set Dr

7	cut 1¾"
13	cut 1¾"
4	cut 1¾"
5	cut 1¾"
8	cut 1¾"
9	cut 1¾"
2	cut 1¾"

cut 1¾"   make 1 strip set
cut 4 Dr

Er Strip Set Er

13	cut 1¾"
4	cut 1¾"
5	cut 1¾"
8	cut 1¾"
9	cut 1¾"
2	cut 1¾"
12	cut 1¾"

cut 1¾"   make 1 strip set
cut 4 Er

F Strip

6

cut 20 strips 1" x 18"

Study the setting variations on page 61 and compare them to the block arrangement in the photo on page 58. Choose a setting that uses 8 Z blocks or 4 Z and 4 Zr blocks before you begin cutting.

You can cut all the strips before you sew any, or cut a little and sew a little, according to your preference. Cut the strips for a strip set, cutting off one end as indicated in the "strip end" column of the yardage chart. Don't fold the fabric unless you are making 4 Z and 4 Zr blocks. Trim the points as described on page 14 and shown on page 58 to help you align patches for sewing. The point should be trimmed at a right angle to the angled end of the strip. Don't trim the point on the top strip of a strip set. You can download a file to make a Point Trimmer at judymartin. com/LSPT.cfm. Trim points of reversed strips face down.

Align the trimmed point of one strip with the wide angle of the neighboring strip. Pin and stitch the first strip to the second; add the third, and so on. Fingerpress and press after each seam, following the "v" pressing arrows in the strip set diagrams. Continue pinning and stitching strips together to complete a strip set as shown.

Measure your strip set from the raw edge at the top to the raw edge at the bottom. It should measure 9¼". If it does not, correct your seams before proceeding.

When you have your seam allowance right, trim a sliver off the angled end of the strip set, if necessary, at a precise 45° angle. See the row cutting diagram on page 58. Cut the strip set into rows 1¾" wide. That is, lay the 1¾" ruling of your rotary ruler over the angled end of the strip, align the 45° line with a raw edge or seamline, and cut along the ruler's edge. Cut 4 rows from the strip set. If your arrangement requires 8 Z blocks, make 2 strip sets to cut 8 rows.

Continue making strip sets and cutting rows in this fashion. When you have all the rows needed for a block, cut down the 1"-wide F/Fr strips to make F/Fr patches as shown on page 59. Trim both points of each row and F/Fr as shown on page 58. Turn reversed rows and F patches face down to use the same Point Trimmer for them.

Making Blocks

Lay out the rows and F/Fr patches for a block as shown in the block diagram on page 59. Pin and stitch rows and F/Fr patches together, aligning the point trim of one with the wide angle of the other. Press after each seam in the direction shown by the block diagram's arrows. Join these pairs to each other in a similar fashion. Make 8 Z blocks or 4 Z and 4 Zr blocks.

Finishing the Quilt

Cut out the background patches shown at the bottom of the page for your choice of a quilt with Y-seams or without Y-seams. Refer to page 17 for tips on cutting patches larger than your rotary cutting ruler.

At right, red dots indicate set-in or Y-seams. For more information on Y-seams, see page 18. Arrows indicate pressing direction. Sew in numerical order. For the Y-seamed quilt, sew A to the right side of a diamond block. Add B to its left. Add another diamond block to B. Join these 2 diamond blocks to each other. Repeat for each quarter. Join quarters to make halves, then join halves, in each case sewing the diamonds to each other last. Finally, join the A from one half to the diamond block of the other half. Repeat. Join diamond blocks of the two halves.

For the version with no Y-seams, sew the background C's and D's to diamond blocks in numerical order to make a quarter wedge of the quilt. Make 4 quarters. Join them in pairs to make half blocks. Join halves to complete the quilt top.

Assembling the Quilt

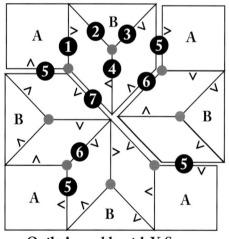

Quilt Assembly with Y-Seams

OR

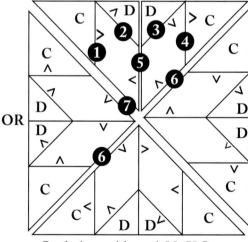

Quilt Assembly with No Y-Seams

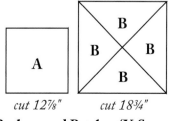

OR

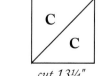

cut 12⅞" *cut 18¾"*

Background Patches (Y-Seams)
cut 4 A squares **12⅞"**
cut 4 B triangles from one **18¾"** square

cut 13¼" *cut 9⅝"*

Background Patches (No Y-Seams)
cut 8 C triangles from four **13¼"** squares
cut 8 D triangles from four **9⅝"** squares

Arrange blocks as shown in the photo or layout of your choice. Referring to the appropriate assembly diagram and instructions on page 60, stitch together the blocks and patches in numerical order. Press after each seam, as indicated by the arrows in the diagram.

Lee Smith quilted in the ditch between block rows and Fr patches. She also quilted in the ditch around the star. She quilted a feathered motif in the background.

Trim the batting and backing even with the quilt top. Binding directions are on page 22.

Sea Breeze Setting Variations

Arrangement 2: 8 Z blocks with the aqua tips in the center.

Arrangement 3: 4 Z blocks and 4 Zr (reversed) blocks alternated. Aqua tips are in the center. For this version, cut the same number of strips, but cut half with the reversed strip end. Make only one strip set each of A–E and Ar–Er.

Arrangement 4: 4 Z blocks and 4 Zr (reversed) blocks alternated. Gray tips are in the center. For this version, cut the same number of strips, but cut half with the reversed strip end. Make only one strip set each of A–E and Ar–Er.

Arrangement 5: 4 Z blocks and 4 Zr (reversed) blocks alternated. Aqua tips are in the center. For this version, cut the same number of strips, but cut half with the reversed strip end. Make only one strip set each of A–E and Ar–Er.

Spiral Radiant Star

Spiral Radiant Star, 91¾" x 91¾". Pieced by Chris Hulin from her own variation of Spiral Lone Star, a design by Jan Krentz (used with permission). The border was designed by Judy Martin. Quilted by Jane Bazyn. The quilt is made from 24 diamond blocks in an 8¾" finished width. They form a 67" square Radiant Star of 16 points surrounded by a plain border and a pieced border made from 24 additional blocks plus partial blocks in two corners. For the best spiral effect, choose fabrics that blend in places and contrast in others. In Chris's quilt, the red-violet and dark green provide contrast.

Start by reading the glossary, "Pattern Pointers," and "How to Make a Lone Star" chapters on pages 7–22.

Quilt Size: 91¾" x 91¾" **Star Size:** 67" sq.
Requires: 4 R, 4 Rr, 7 S, **Block Width:** 8¾"
7 T, 7 U, 3 V, 7 W, 7 X,
3 Y, 7 Z blocks

		Yardage & Cutting		Strip
Color	Yardage	#Strips	Cut Size	End
1 ☐	1½ yds.	40	2¼" x 18"	⬡
		2	2¼" x 18"	⬡
2 ☐	1½ yds.	39	2¼" x 18"	⬡
		1	2¼" x 18"	⬡
3 ☐	leftovers*	38	2¼" x 18"	⬡
4 ☐	1½ yds.	39	2¼" x 18"	⬡
5 ☐	1½ yds.	40	2¼" x 18"	⬡
6 ☐	1½ yds.	43	2¼" x 18"	⬡
		3	2¼" x 18"	⬡
7 ☐	1½ yds.	43	2¼" x 18"	⬡
		4	2¼" x 18"	⬡
8 ☐	1½ yds.	41	2¼" x 18"	⬡
		3	2¼" x 18"	⬡
9 ☐	3¼ yds.	background *(see pages 65–66)*		
		4 borders cut 4⅛" x 75½"		
	9 yds.	backing: 3 pcs. 33¾" x 100¼"		
3 ☐	2 yds.*	binding: 6 strips 2" x 72"		

Cut each 1½-yard length of fabric into 3 pieces 18" long by the full width of the fabric. After cutting 6 binding strips 2" wide and 2 yards long, cut the remainder of fabric #3 into 4 pieces 18" long by 28" or so in width. You will use all of these 18" pieces to cut lengthwise strips 2¼" wide x 18" long in the quantities listed above. You can layer 4 fabrics at a time for cutting. With the fabric face up and not folded, cut off one end of each strip at a 45° angle as shown at the right of the yardage chart. Trim points of strips as described on pages 14–15 and shown below right. Download a file at judymartin.com/LSPT.cfm to make a point trimmer if you do not have one.

Aligning the wide angle of one strip with the trimmed point of the next strip, join 5 appropriately colored strips to make a strip set as shown above right. Make the listed quantity of each type of strip set. Finger press, then press seam allowances as described in the captions at right and on page 64.

If necessary, trim off a sliver to even the angled edge of the strip set at a precise 45° angle. Align the 2¼" ruling of your rotary ruler with the angled edge of the strip set as shown on page 65. Also align the 45° angle line with one long edge or seamline of the strip set. Cut along the ruler's edge to make a 2¼"-wide row. Repeat to make rows in the quantity listed below each strip set.

Piecing Strip Sets and Cutting Diagonal Rows

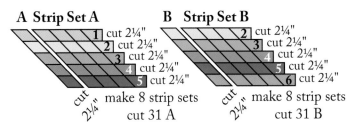

A **Strip Set A** — 1 cut 2¼", 2 cut 2¼", 3 cut 2¼", 4 cut 2¼", 5 cut 2¼" — cut 2¼" — make 8 strip sets — cut 31 A

B **Strip Set B** — 2 cut 2¼", 3 cut 2¼", 4 cut 2¼", 5 cut 2¼", 6 cut 2¼" — cut 2¼" — make 8 strip sets — cut 31 B

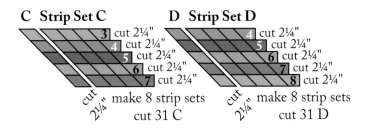

C **Strip Set C** — 3 cut 2¼", 4 cut 2¼", 5 cut 2¼", 6 cut 2¼", 7 cut 2¼" — cut 2¼" — make 8 strip sets — cut 31 C

D **Strip Set D** — 4 cut 2¼", 5 cut 2¼", 6 cut 2¼", 7 cut 2¼", 8 cut 2¼" — cut 2¼" — make 8 strip sets — cut 31 D

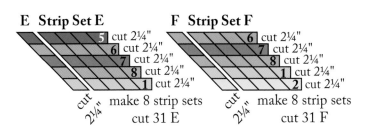

E **Strip Set E** — 5 cut 2¼", 6 cut 2¼", 7 cut 2¼", 8 cut 2¼", 1 cut 2¼" — cut 2¼" — make 8 strip sets — cut 31 E

F **Strip Set F** — 6 cut 2¼", 7 cut 2¼", 8 cut 2¼", 1 cut 2¼", 2 cut 2¼" — cut 2¼" — make 8 strip sets — cut 31 F

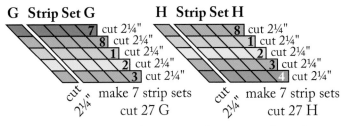

G **Strip Set G** — 7 cut 2¼", 8 cut 2¼", 1 cut 2¼", 2 cut 2¼", 3 cut 2¼" — cut 2¼" — make 7 strip sets — cut 27 G

H **Strip Set H** — 8 cut 2¼", 1 cut 2¼", 2 cut 2¼", 3 cut 2¼", 4 cut 2¼" — cut 2¼" — make 7 strip sets — cut 27 H

Note that the pressing direction in the strip sets depends on which block the cut row will be used in. To oppose (nest) seams when joining blocks to each other, it helps to press the left row down and the right row up. Within the block, it is less important which way the strip sets are pressed, though I try to minimize bulk in the seams by pressing adjacent rows in opposite directions wherever practical. I suggest pressing the seam allowances of the strip sets as follows: A, D, and G: press seams down in 3 strip sets and up in the rest; B, C, E, F, and H: press seams down in 4 strip sets and up in the rest.

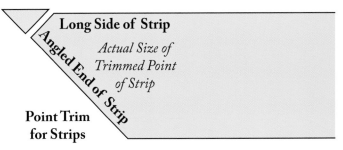

Long Side of Strip
Actual Size of Trimmed Point of Strip
Angled End of Strip
Point Trim for Strips

After cutting strip sets into rows, trim the points of rows as shown on page 65. Gather together 5 rows of the appropriate letters to make a block. Pin the first 2 rows together, aligning the trimmed point of one row with the wide angle of the other row. Pin at each end and at each joint, as described on pages 15–16. Stitch the seam and check your joints. If needed, rip out ½" at joints and restitch. Finger press and press using a pressing lid, as described on page 12. Continue in this manner, joining rows in the order

shown. Make the listed number of each type of block. Lay out your blocks as shown on the next page, being careful to orient the blocks as shown.

For the border corners, make 1 strip set each of I – K and Ir – Kr. Also cut 2¼" x 18" L and Lr strips from folded fabric. Cut 4 rows 2¼" wide from each strip set and cut 4 diamonds 2¼" wide from each L and Lr strip. Assemble rows as shown on the bottom of this page to make 4 R and 4 Rr blocks. Sew each R to an Rr. Add a T to one side to

Piecing Blocks from Diagonal Rows

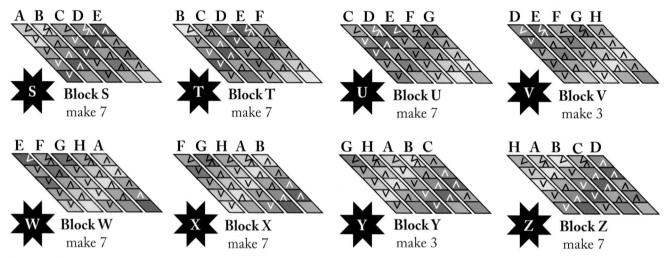

Note that the pressing direction is not especially important for the interior rows of the blocks, as no seams will oppose and nest there. If you press the strip sets as instructed on the previous page, you won't be able to exactly match the pressing in the block

diagrams above. Do not worry about the pressing except for the first and last rows. Do be sure to have the seams pressed down in the left row of each block and pressed up in the right row of each block.

Piecing Border Corner Strip Sets and Blocks R and Rr

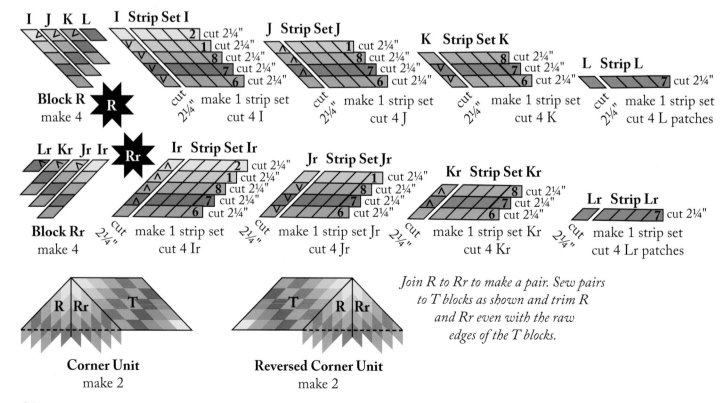

Join R to Rr to make a pair. Sew pairs to T blocks as shown and trim R and Rr even with the raw edges of the T blocks.

make 2 corner units and 2 reversed corner units as shown. Trim off the bottoms of R's and Rr's even with the raw edges of T's. Add W, Z, U, X, and S blocks to each corner unit and reversed corner unit to complete 4 pieced borders as shown below. Cut 4 light green border strips 4⅛" x 75½". Cut off both ends at a 45° angle. Pin and stitch the long edge of a light green border strip to the shorter side of each pieced border.

Assembling the Quilt

Choose whether or not you will assemble your quilt with Y-seams. Read about cloth templates for rotary cutting on page 17. A cloth template for L/Lr will help you rotary cut those shapes to nest together with no waste. Cut out the appropriate background patches as shown below and on the next page. You will need K and M patches if you want no Y-seams. You will need N and O patches for assembly with Y-seams. You will need L and Lr in either case.

Lay out the background patches with your quilt blocks and borders. Sew the blocks and background patches in numerical order to make ⅛ wedges, then quarters of the quilt. Note that in the version below with no Y-seams, you attach the borders to the quarters before the quarters are joined to make halves. In the version on the next page with Y-seams, you add borders after completing the center.

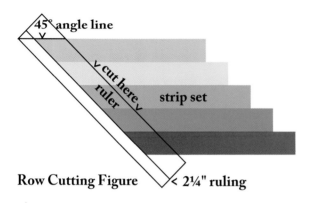

Row Cutting Figure

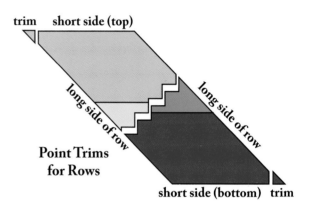

Point Trims for Rows

Background Patch Cutting
additional background patches are shown on the next page

Use K, L, Lr, and M for background with no Y-seams.

cut 9⅝"
cut 8 K triangles
from four **9⅝"** squares

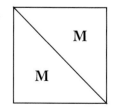

cut 16⅞"
cut 8 M triangles
from four **16⅞"** squares

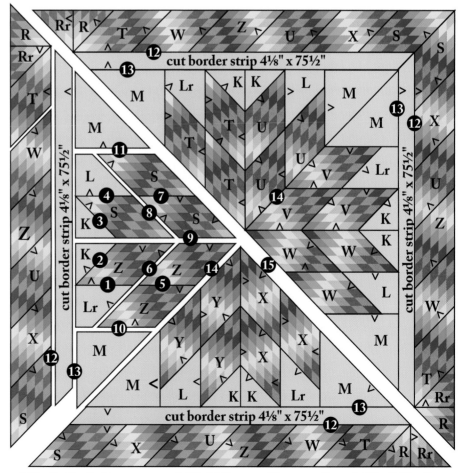

Whole Quilt Diagram with No Y-Seams, Showing Spiral-Block Border

65

Additional Background Patch Cutting

*cut a 9¼" x 13¼"
rectangle from
unwanted cloth;
cut off 1 corner at
a 45° angle; dis-
card the triangle;
use the remainder
as a rotary cutting
template for L/Lr.*

*cut a 9¼" x 17¼" rectangle; place the
cloth template at left over one corner
and align your rotary ruler with the
angled edge of the template; cut along
the ruler's edge to make 2 L's. Turn the
template over for Lr's or cut L and Lr
in equal quantities from folded fabric.*
*cut 4 L and 4 Lr
from 4 rectangles total*

**Use L, Lr,
N, and
O if you
prefer
Y-seams.**

cut 18¾"
cut 4 N triangles
from one **18¾"** square

cut 16½"
cut 4 O
squares **16½"**

At Right, Whole Quilt Diagram with Y-Seams
12 Y-seams are indicated with red dots.

Finishing the Quilt

Jane Bazyn quilted the Spiral Radiant Star in the ditch around all diamonds. She quilted curlicues in the background, continuing into the plain inner borders.

After quilting, trim the edges of the backing and batting even with the edges of the quilt top. Bind as described on page 22. For a finishing touch, stitch a label to the back.

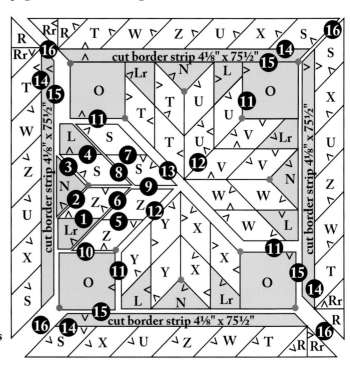

Spiral Radiant Star Color Variations

*Color Variation 2: Substitute colors as follows: Color #1
violet; #2 lime; #3 yellow; #4 yellow-orange; #5 orange; #6
red-orange; #7 red; #8 red-violet; and #9 black.*

*Color Variation 3: Substitute colors as follows: Color #1 lime;
#2 green; #3 blue-green; #4 blue; #5 blue-violet; #6 violet; #7
red-violet; #8 yellow; and #9 black.*

Spiral-Block Mix & Match

To make any of the quilts in this chapter, refer to the strip piecing diagrams on page 63 of the Spiral Radiant Star pattern, substituting the block quantities listed in this chapter. The instructions on pages 63–65 will also be helpful. Read the basic Lone Star information on pages 7–22 to learn tips for cutting, pinning, stitching, and pressing your quilt. Pay special attention to the information about cutting patches larger than your ruler on page 17.

Use the background patches and assembly diagrams and instructions that follow.

The border and binding yardages are for lengthwise borders and binding strips, and they may include extra for cutting any strips of the same color you might need for the quilt. Choose background patches to assemble your quilt with or without Y-seams. Cut them in the dimensions and quantities shown below.

After making your 32 blocks, you may wish to play with block arrangements before you assemble your quilt. On the floor or design wall, lay out blocks, 4 per arm of the star. Try rotating blocks or changing their placement. I recommend taking digital photos to help you see the effect and to help you reconstruct your favorite. A photo will also help you see mistakes in your layout.

Start the quilt assembly by joining 4 blocks in 2 rows of 2 to make a grand block, essentially a Four-Patch arm of the star. The red line in the grand block and quilt assembly diagrams is the last seam of the grand block. Make 8 grand blocks. Assemble your grand blocks, background, and borders in numerical order, as shown in the diagrams below. Press seam allowances to one side after each seam, as indicated by the arrows in the diagrams. Red dots indicate Y-seams.

If you assemble your quilt with no Y-seams, you must add the borders to the triangular quarters of the star before you join the quarters to make half stars. This will allow you to miter the borders with no Y-seams.

Quilt as desired. You will find a variety of Lone Star quilting ideas on pages 19–21. Photos throughout the book offer additional quilting ideas. Complete binding instructions are presented on page 22.

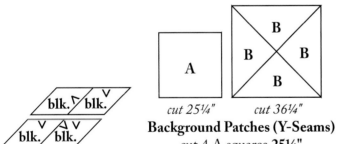

Grand Block

cut 25¼"   *cut 36¼"*
Background Patches (Y-Seams)
cut 4 A squares **25¼"**
cut 4 B triangles from one **36¼"** square

OR

cut 25⅝"   *cut 18⅜"*
Background Patches (No Y-Seams)
cut 8 C triangles from four **25⅝"** squares
cut 8 D triangles from four **18⅜"** squares

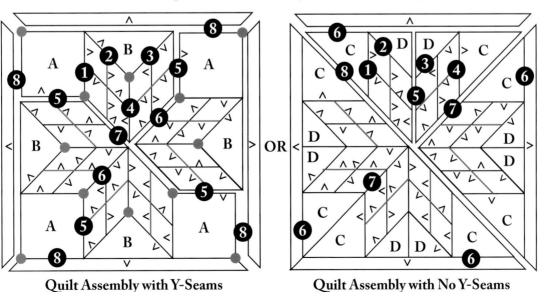

Quilt Assembly with Y-Seams   OR   **Quilt Assembly with No Y-Seams**

1

2

5

6

9

10

13

14

16 Placement
(SAME BLOCKS

1. City of Angels Lone Star (pattern on page 70) with 8 T at the center followed by 16 Y, then 8 U at the outer star tips.

2. The same star as #1 with the outer tips rotated.

5. The same star as #1 with the 16 Y blocks rotated.

6. The same star as #2 with the 16 Y blocks rotated.

9. The same star as #5 with the 8 T blocks in the center rotated.

10. The same star as #6 with the 8 T blocks in the center rotated.

13. The same star as #1 with the 8 T blocks in the center rotated.

14. The same star as #2 with the 8 T blocks in the center rotated.

Variations
AND YARDAGE)

3. The same as #1 star except switching U and T positions so the 8 U are at the center and the 8 T are the outer star tips.

4. The same star as #3 with the outer tips rotated.

7. The same star as #3 with the 16 Y blocks rotated.

8. The same star as #4 with the 16 Y blocks rotated.

11. The same star as #7 with the 8 U blocks in the center rotated.

12. The same star as #8 with the 8 U blocks in the center rotated.

15. The same star as #3 with the 8 U blocks in the center rotated.

16. The same star as #4 with the 8 U blocks in the center rotated.

By rearranging the blocks in the next six patterns you can make 16 unique quilts apiece (96 total). Recombining all 8 block types yields more than 2,400 Lone Star variations in all!

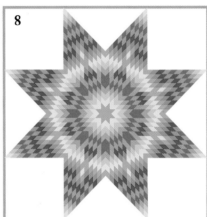

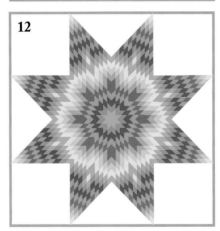

City of Angels Lone Star

Directions: Instructions and diagrams for strip sets and blocks are on pages 63–64. Instructions for assembling the quilt blocks and background patches are on page 67. Make 4 A, 6 B, 8 C, 4 D, 4 E, 4 F, 6 G, and 4 H strip sets.

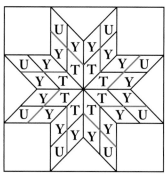

Block Placement Diagram

Same Blocks & Quilt Size; Different Placement

Quilt Size: 96½" x 96½"	Star Size: 84½" sq.
Requires: 8 T, 16 Y, 8 U blocks	Block Width: 8¾"

		Yardage & Cutting		Strip
Color	Yardage	#Strips	Cut Size	End
1 ☐	1 yd.	22	2¼" x 18"	◹
2 ☐	1 yd.	24	2¼" x 18"	(all)
3 ☐	1 yd.	28	2¼" x 18"	
4 ☐	1 yd.	26	2¼" x 18"	
5 ☐	leftovers*	26	2¼" x 18"	
6 ☐	leftovers**	26	2¼" x 18"	
7 ☐	1 yd.	26	2¼" x 18"	
8 ☐	1 yd.	22	2¼" x 18"	
9 ☐	4¼ yds.	background *(see page 67)*		
6 ☐	3 yds.**	borders: 4 @ 6½" x 97¾"		
	9¼ yds.	backing: 3 pcs. 35½" x 105"		
5 ☐	1½ yds.*	binding: 9 strips 2" x 54"		

You can cut the #5 and #6 strips from the leftover binding and border yardage. After cutting the borders and binding, cut the leftovers into 18"-long pieces from which to cut the strips for the strip sets.

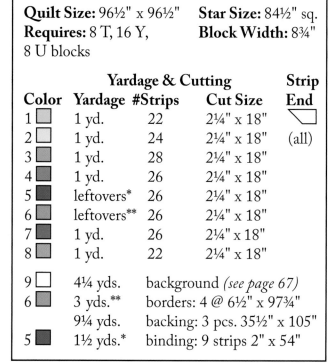

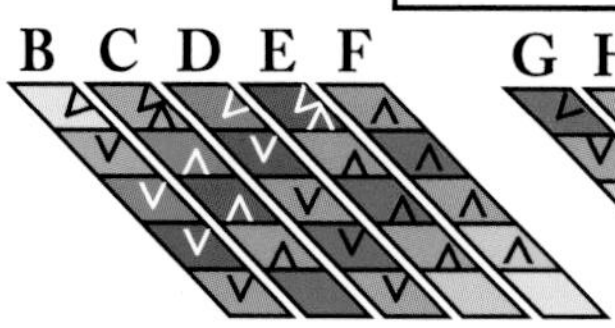

T Block
make 8

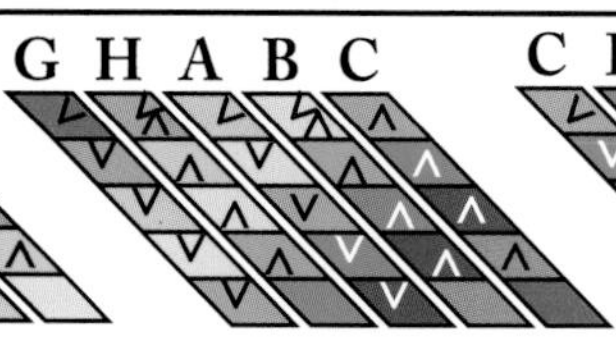

Y Block
make 16

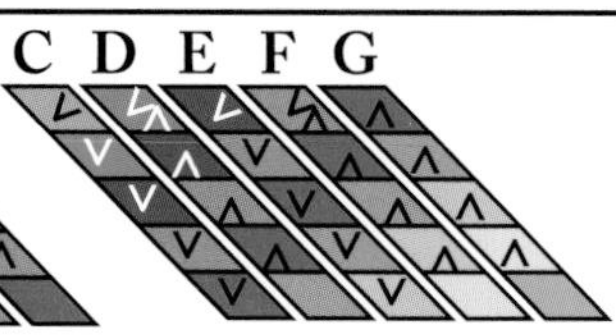

U Block
make 8

Austin Lone Star

Directions: Instructions and diagrams for strip sets and blocks are on pages 63–64. Instructions for assembling the quilt blocks and background patches are on page 67. Make 8 A, 6 B, 6 C, 6 D, 6 E, 2 F, 2 G, and 4 H strip sets.

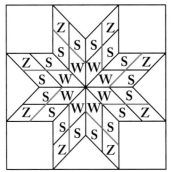

Block Placement Diagram

Quilt Size: 96½" x 96½" **Star Size:** 84½" sq.
Requires: 8 W, 16 S, **Block Width:** 8¾"
8 Z blocks

		Yardage & Cutting		Strip
Color	Yardage	#Strips	Cut Size	End
1	1 yd.	22	2¼" x 18"	
2	1 yd.	22	2¼" x 18"	(all)
3	1 yd.	26	2¼" x 18"	
4	1 yd.	30	2¼" x 18"	
5	leftovers*	32	2¼" x 18"	
6	leftovers**	26	2¼" x 18"	
7	1 yd.	22	2¼" x 18"	
8	1 yd.	20	2¼" x 18"	
9	4¼ yds.	background *(see page 67)*		
5	3 yds.*	borders: 4 @ 6½" x 97¾"		
	9¼ yds.	backing: 3 pcs. 35½" x 105"		
6	1½ yds.**	binding: 9 strips 2" x 54"		

Same Blocks & Quilt Size; Different Placement

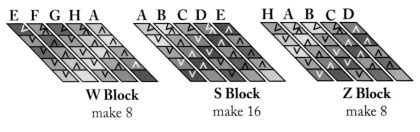

E F G H A	A B C D E	H A B C D
W Block make 8	**S Block** make 16	**Z Block** make 8

You can cut the #5 and #6 strips from the leftover yardage from the borders and binding. After cutting borders and binding, cut the leftovers into 18"-long pieces from which to cut the strips for the strip sets.

Hollywood Lone Star

Directions: Instructions and diagrams for strip sets and blocks are on pages 63–64. Instructions for assembling the quilt blocks and background patches are on page 67. Make 6 A, 6 B, 8 C, 4 D, 2 E, 2 F, 6 G, and 6 H strip sets.

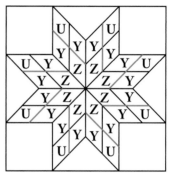

Block Placement Diagram

Same Blocks & Quilt Size; Different Placement

Quilt Size: 96½" x 96½" **Star Size:** 84½" sq.
Requires: 8 Z, 16 Y, **Block Width:** 8¾"
8 U blocks

Color	Yardage	#Strips	Yardage & Cutting Cut Size	Strip End
1	leftovers*	22	2¼" x 18"	⬡
2	1 yd.	26	2¼" x 18"	(all)
3	1 yd.	32	2¼" x 18"	
4	1 yd.	30	2¼" x 18"	
5	1 yd.	26	2¼" x 18"	
6	1 yd.	22	2¼" x 18"	
7	1 yd.	22	2¼" x 18"	
8	leftovers**	20	2¼" x 18"	
9	4¼ yds.	background *(see page 67)*		
1	3 yds.*	borders: 4 @ 6½" x 97¾"		
	9¼ yds.	backing: 3 pcs. 35½" x 105"		
8	1½ yds.**	binding: 9 strips 2" x 54"		

You can cut the #1 and #8 strips from the leftover border and binding yardage. After cutting the borders and binding, cut the leftovers into 18"-long pieces from which to cut the strips for the strip sets.

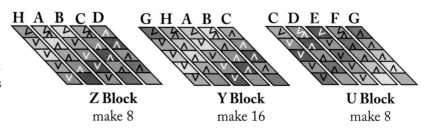

H A B C D
Z Block
make 8

G H A B C
Y Block
make 16

C D E F G
U Block
make 8

San Diego Lone Star

Directions: Instructions and diagrams for strip sets and blocks are on pages 63–64. Instructions for assembling the quilt blocks and background patches are on page 67. Make 6 A, 6 B, 6 C, 2 D, 2 E, 4 F, 8 G, and 6 H strip sets.

Block Placement Diagram

Quilt Size: 96½" x 96½" **Star Size:** 84½" sq.
Requires: 8 U, 16 Y, **Block Width:** 8¾"
8 X blocks

Yardage & Cutting

Color	Yardage	#Strips	Cut Size	Strip End
1	leftovers*	26	2¼" x 18"	
2	1 yd.	30	2¼" x 18"	(all)
3	1 yd.	32	2¼" x 18"	
4	1 yd.	26	2¼" x 18"	
5	1 yd.	22	2¼" x 18"	
6	1 yd.	20	2¼" x 18"	
7	1 yd.	22	2¼" x 18"	
8	leftovers**	22	2¼" x 18"	
9	4¼ yds.	background *(see page 67)*		
8	3 yds.**	borders: 4 @ 6½" x 97¾"		
	9¼ yds.	backing: 3 pcs. 35½" x 105"		
1	1½ yds.*	binding: 9 strips 2" x 54"		

Same Blocks & Quilt Size; Different Placement

You can cut the #1 and #8 strips from the leftover border and binding yardage. After cutting the borders and binding, cut the leftovers into 18"-long pieces from which to cut the strips for the strip sets.

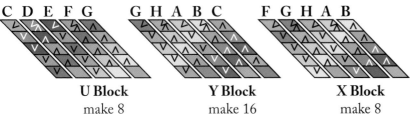

C D E F G	G H A B C	F G H A B
U Block make 8	**Y Block** make 16	**X Block** make 8

73

Palm Springs Lone Star

Directions: Instructions and diagrams for strip sets and blocks are on pages 63–64. Instructions for assembling the quilt blocks and background patches are on page 67. Make 4 A, 4 B, 8 C, 4 D, 4 E, 4 F, 8 G, and 4 H strip sets.

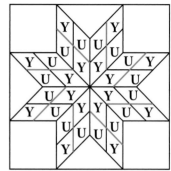

Block Placement Diagram

Quilt Size: 96½" x 96½" **Star Size:** 84½" sq.
Requires: 16 Y, 16 U **Block Width:** 8¾"
blocks

	Yardage & Cutting			**Strip**
Color	**Yardage**	**#Strips**	**Cut Size**	**End**
1	leftovers*	24	2¼" x 18"	⟍
2	1 yd.	24	2¼" x 18"	(all)
3	1 yd.	28	2¼" x 18"	
4	1 yd.	24	2¼" x 18"	
5	1 yd.	24	2¼" x 18"	
6	1 yd.	24	2¼" x 18"	
7	leftovers**	28	2¼" x 18"	
8	1 yd.	24	2¼" x 18"	
9	4¼ yds.	background *(see page 67)*		
7	3 yds.**	borders: 4 @ 6½" x 97¾"		
	9¼ yds.	backing: 3 pcs. 35½" x 105"		
1	1½ yds.*	binding: 9 strips 2" x 54"		

Same Blocks & Quilt Size; Different Placement

You can cut the color #1 and #7 strips from the leftover border and binding yardage. After cutting the borders and binding, cut the leftovers into 18"-long pieces from which to cut the strips for the strip sets.

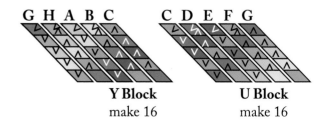

G H A B C · C D E F G
Y Block · **U Block**
make 16 · make 16

74

Las Vegas Lone Star

Directions: Instructions and diagrams for strip sets and blocks are on pages 63–64. Instructions for assembling the quilt blocks and background patches are on page 67. Make 6 A, 6 B, 6 C, 8 D, 8 E, 2 F, 2 G, and 2 H strip sets.

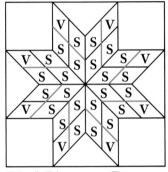

Block Placement Diagram

Quilt Size: 96½" x 96½" **Star Size:** 84½" sq.
Requires: 24 S, 8 V **Block Width:** 8¾"
blocks

Color	Yardage & Cutting			Strip End
	Yardage	#Strips	Cut Size	
1	leftovers*	20	2¼" x 18"	⟍
2	1 yd.	18	2¼" x 18"	(all)
3	1 yd.	22	2¼" x 18"	
4	1 yd.	28	2¼" x 18"	
5	1 yd.	34	2¼" x 18"	
6	1 yd.	30	2¼" x 18"	
7	leftovers**	26	2¼" x 18"	
8	1 yd.	22	2¼" x 18"	
9	4¼ yds.	background *(see page 67)*		
7	3 yds.**	borders: 4 @ 6½" x 97¾"		
	9¼ yds.	backing: 3 pcs. 35½" x 105"		
1	1½ yds.*	binding: 9 strips 2" x 54"		

Same Blocks & Quilt Size; Different Placement

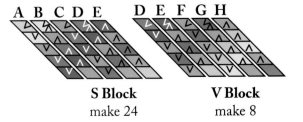

S Block
make 24

V Block
make 8

You can cut the color #1 and #7 strips from the leftover border and binding yardage. After cutting the borders and binding, cut the leftovers into 18"-long pieces from which to cut the strips for the strip sets.

Houston Lone Star

Directions: Instructions and diagrams for strip sets and blocks are on pages 63–64. Instructions for assembling the quilt blocks and background patches are on page 67. Make 4 A, 4 B, 8 C, 8 D, 4 E, 4 F, 4 G, and 4 H strip sets.

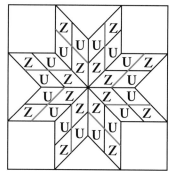

Block Placement Diagram

Same Blocks & Quilt Size; Different Placement

Quilt Size: 96½" x 96½" **Star Size:** 84½" sq.
Requires: 16 Z, 16 U **Block Width:** 8¾"
blocks

Color	Yardage	#Strips	Cut Size	Strip End
		Yardage & Cutting		
1	1 yd.	20	2¼" x 18"	(all)
2	leftovers*	20	2¼" x 18"	
3	1 yd.	24	2¼" x 18"	
4	leftovers**	28	2¼" x 18"	
5	1 yd.	28	2¼" x 18"	
6	1 yd.	28	2¼" x 18"	
7	1 yd.	28	2¼" x 18"	
8	leftovers***	24	2¼" x 18"	
2	4¼ yds.*	background *(see page 67)*		
4	3 yds.**	borders: 4 @ 6½" x 97¾"		
	9¼ yds.	backing: 3 pcs. 35½" x 105"		
8	1½ yds.***	binding: 9 strips 2" x 54"		

You can cut the #2, #4, and #8 strips from the leftover yardage from the background, borders, and binding. After cutting the background patches, borders, and binding, cut the leftovers into 18"-long pieces from which to cut the strips for the strip sets.

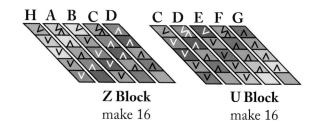

Z Block
make 16

U Block
make 16

Skewed Nine-Patch

Skewed Nine-Patch, 91½" x 91½". Designed and pieced by Judy Martin. Quilted by Lana Corcoran. The quilt is made from 312 simple diamond blocks in a 3" finished width. They are arranged to form a central 37½" square Double Broken Star surrounded by four ¾-Double Broken Star units. I colored the diamond blocks like Nine-Patches, with each block strip pieced to look like 5 dark diamonds and 4 medium ones of the same hue. I actually made my quilt smaller in order to enter it in a show that specified a maximum quilt size of 80". I resized the quilt for the book in a more useful size for a bed. This quilt size is better for rotary cutting and strip piecing. I also eliminated the many Y-seams for the pattern.

					Strip
Quilt Size: 91½" x 91½"			**Star Size:** 37½" sq.		
Requires: 64 a, 64 b,			**Block Width:** 3",		
44 c, 44 d, 48 e, 48 f,			18¾", 37½"		
12 g, 4 h, 4 i, 4 j, 4 k blks.					

Yardage & Cutting

Color	Yardage	#Strips	Cut Size	Strip End
1	1 yd.	48	1½" x 18"	◿
2	1 yd.	39	1½" x 18"	(all)
3	1 yd.	48	1½" x 18"	
4	1 yd.	39	1½" x 18"	
5	1 yd.	33	1½" x 18"	
6	1 yd.	27	1½" x 18"	
7	1 yd.	33	1½" x 18"	
8	1 yd.	27	1½" x 18"	
9	1 yd.	35	1½" x 18"	
10	1 yd.	28	1½" x 18"	
11	1 yd.	35	1½" x 18"	
12	1 yd.	28	1½" x 18"	
13	4¼ yds.	8 borders cut 8¾" x 23½"		
		4 borders cut 5¾" x 15"		
		4 S	2 per 11⅞"	◻
		24 M	2 per 6⅜"	◻
		68 O	4 per 7¼"	⊠
		88 N	2 per 3⅞"	◻
		12 Q, 12 Qr	*(see page 80)*	
		12 R, 12 Rr	*(see page 80)*	
		8 P	*(see page 80)*	
14	2¾ yds.	4 borders cut 8¾" x 61"		
		24 V	2 per 5⅛"	◻
		24 N	2 per 3⅞"	◻
		4 U	cut 1½" x 16"	▭
		8 T	cut 1½" 7¾"	▭
		4 W, 4 Wr	*(see page 81)*	
	8⅞ yds.	backing: 3 pcs. 34" x 100"		
15	2 yds.	8 bias strips cut 1½" x 56"*		
		binding: 8 bias strips 2" x 44"-56"*		
		* *(see page 82)*		

Making Strip Sets and Cutting Rows

Start by reading the glossary, "Pattern Pointers," and "How to Make a Lone Star" chapters on pages 7–22.

You can cut all the strips before you sew any, or cut a little and sew a little, according to your preference. Cut the strips for a strip set, cutting off one end at a 45° angle as indicated in the "strip end" column of the yardage chart. If you folded the fabric, unfold it before you cut off the strip ends so that all of the strips have the same end.

Blocks a–f

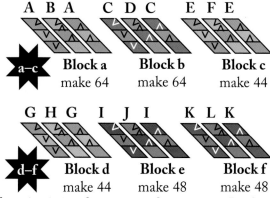

A B A   C D C   E F E

Block a make 64   Block b make 64   Block c make 44

G H G   I J I   K L K

Block d make 44   Block e make 48   Block f make 48

In the strip piecing diagrams on the next page, I indicate that you press seam allowances down in strips sets A, C, E, G, I, and K. Above, I show them pressed down on the left and up on the right ends of the blocks. You can make all of the strip sets as shown and simply rotate the right row of each block to match the block diagram.

Trim the points as described on page 14 and shown on page 79 to help you align patches for sewing. The point should be trimmed at a right angle to the angled end of the strip. Don't trim the point on the top strip of a strip set. If you don't have my Point Trimmer tool, download a file to make one at judymartin.com/LSPT.cfm

Align the wide angle of one strip with the trimmed point of the next strip. Pin and stitch strips in the order shown. Press after each seam, following the "v" pressing arrows in the strip set diagrams.

Continue pinning and stitching strips together to complete a strip set as shown. Measure your strip set straight down the middle from the raw edge at the top to the raw edge at the bottom. It should measure 3½". If it does not, adjust your seam guide and correct your seam allowances before proceeding.

When you have your seam allowance right, trim a sliver off the angled end of the strip set, if necessary, at a precise 45° angle. See the row cutting diagram on page 79. Cut the strip set into rows 1½" wide. That is, lay the 1½" ruling of your rotary cutting ruler over the angled end of the strip, align the 45° line with a raw edge, and cut along the ruler's edge. For strip sets A–L, make strip sets in the quantities listed below the strip set diagrams on page 79. You should be able to cut 7 rows from a strip set. Cut the listed number of rows of a type. When you have the rows needed for a block, trim both points of each row as shown on page 79.

Making Blocks

Lay out the rows for a block as shown above. Align the trimmed point of the second row with the wide angle of the first row, and pin there. Also pin at each joint. Strategies for matching joints are on page 15. Stitch rows together, pressing after each seam in the direction indicated in the block diagram. Add the third row to the block in the same way. Make blocks a–f in the quantities listed below the block diagrams.

Making Blocks g–i

Make a cloth rotary cutting template for R and Rr as shown on page 80. This will allow you to nest 2 R or Rr trapezoids when you cut them from white rectangles as shown.

Cut white background patches M–S as shown on the next page. When you cut the kite-shaped P's, start by cutting 2 triangles from a 5⅛" square. Leave the triangles in place and measure along the cut diagonal 5⅛" and cut to complete 2 kite-shaped P's. That is, lay the 5⅛" ruling on the lower right corner of the square; also align a rule line with the cut diagonal; cut along the ruler's edge.

Cut Q's and Qr's from folded fabric. Notice that they are not true diamonds: the strips are 3" x 20", and the rows of patches are cut 3½" wide (measured with the rule line aligned with the angled end of the strip).

See the block diagrams on the next page. Arrange blocks a–f and background patches as shown. Sew them into the units shown in the piecing diagram to the right of the lettered block diagram. Join units in numerical order to complete the g and h blocks, pressing seams as indicated by the arrows.

Decide whether you want to make the arrangement shown in the photo or the one shown at the bottom of page 82. Assemble 3 g blocks and 1 h block to make an i block, turning the g block at the center of the quilt 180° if you are making the arrangement on page 82.

Making the j and k Border Blocks

After cutting 4 blue borders as listed in the yardage chart, cut the blue patches shown at the bottom of page 80. Join c and d blocks and V and N patches to make 4 j and 4 k blocks, as shown at the bottom of page 80.

Making the Curves and Units 1–11

On tracing paper, butcher paper, or ugly fabric, map out the small W curve and the larger curved shape graphed on page 81. Fold the remainder of the blue fabric. Pin the W template to the folded fabric and use scissors to cut 4 W and 4 Wr.

See unit 1 on page 81. Align the straight edges of a W and a Wr with the raw edges of an S patch that has already been sewn to the corner of an h block. The more gradual

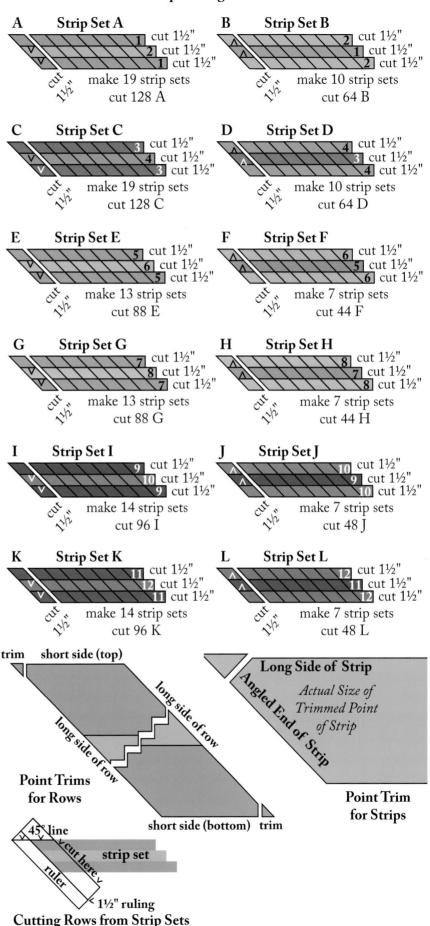

Strip Piecing Blocks a–f

A Strip Set A
1 cut 1½"
2 cut 1½"
1 cut 1½"
cut 1½"
make 19 strip sets
cut 128 A

B Strip Set B
2 cut 1½"
1 cut 1½"
2 cut 1½"
cut 1½"
make 10 strip sets
cut 64 B

C Strip Set C
3 cut 1½"
4 cut 1½"
3 cut 1½"
cut 1½"
make 19 strip sets
cut 128 C

D Strip Set D
4 cut 1½"
3 cut 1½"
4 cut 1½"
cut 1½"
make 10 strip sets
cut 64 D

E Strip Set E
5 cut 1½"
6 cut 1½"
5 cut 1½"
cut 1½"
make 13 strip sets
cut 88 E

F Strip Set F
6 cut 1½"
5 cut 1½"
6 cut 1½"
cut 1½"
make 7 strip sets
cut 44 F

G Strip Set G
7 cut 1½"
8 cut 1½"
7 cut 1½"
cut 1½"
make 13 strip sets
cut 88 G

H Strip Set H
8 cut 1½"
7 cut 1½"
8 cut 1½"
cut 1½"
make 7 strip sets
cut 44 H

I Strip Set I
9 cut 1½"
10 cut 1½"
9 cut 1½"
cut 1½"
make 14 strip sets
cut 96 I

J Strip Set J
10 cut 1½"
9 cut 1½"
10 cut 1½"
cut 1½"
make 7 strip sets
cut 48 J

K Strip Set K
11 cut 1½"
12 cut 1½"
11 cut 1½"
cut 1½"
make 14 strip sets
cut 96 K

L Strip Set L
12 cut 1½"
11 cut 1½"
12 cut 1½"
cut 1½"
make 7 strip sets
cut 48 L

trim   short side (top)

long side of row
long side of row
long side of row

Point Trims for Rows

short side (bottom) trim

Long Side of Strip
Angled End of Strip
Actual Size of Trimmed Point of Strip

Point Trim for Strips

45° line
cut here
strip set
ruler
1½" ruling

Cutting Rows from Strip Sets

curves go in the corners. Pin and machine baste close to the edges of the blue fabric. Repeat in one corner of each h block.

Next, plot the pink circles and make a template for the long curve of unit 8, as shown on page 81. Use one of the blue borders that you cut earlier. Fold it in half crosswise. Pin the large curved template to it, aligning the side of the template marked "fold" with the fold of the border. Also align the 2 straight sides of the template with raw edges of the blue border. Cut the border along the curved edge. Repeat with the other 3 borders to make 4 unit 8's. Set aside.

See the figures at the bottom left of page 81 to make unit 2. Join N-c block-O-d block-N in a row. To the bottom, add a white border cut 5¾" x 15" to complete unit 2. Make 4 unit 2's.

Sew a blue T rectangle to a j block, as shown on page 81, to make a unit 3. Make 2 unit 3's. Sew a blue T to a j block, as shown, to make unit 4. Make 2 unit 4's.

See the figures for units 5 and 6. Sew a T to the left of a k block; add U to the bottom to complete unit 5. Make 2 unit 5's. Sew a T to the right of a k block; add U to the bottom for unit 6. Make 2 unit 6's.

Sew 2 white borders 23½" long to a unit 2, as shown on page 81; this completes a unit 7. Make 4 unit 7's.

Place a face-up unit 8 over a face-up unit 7, aligning the bottom and sides of the units. Pin the straight edges together first; then

Cutting the Color #13 Background

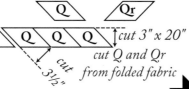

cut 6⅜"
cut 24 M triangles from 12
6⅜" squares

cut 3⅞"
cut 88 N triangles from 44
3" squares

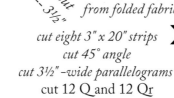

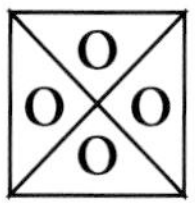

cut 7¼"
cut 68 O triangles from 17
7¼" squares

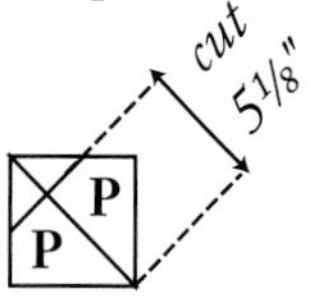

cut 5⅛"
cut 5⅛" square
cut 8 P shapes from 4
5⅛" squares

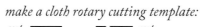

cut 3" x 20"
cut Q and Qr
from folded fabric
cut eight 3" x 20" strips
cut 45° angle
cut 3½"-wide parallelograms
cut 12 Q and 12 Qr

make a cloth rotary cutting template:

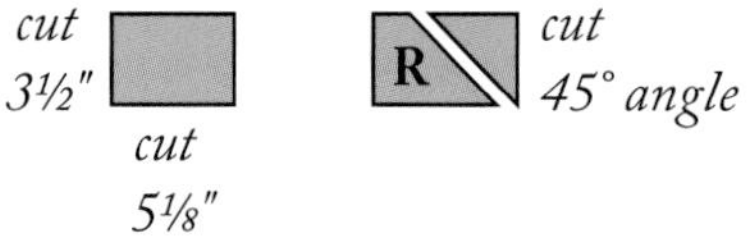

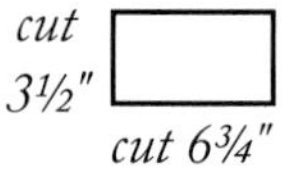

cut 3½"
cut 5⅛"

cut R
cut 45° angle

cut 3½"
cut 6¾"

cut 3½" strip
cut 12 rectangles

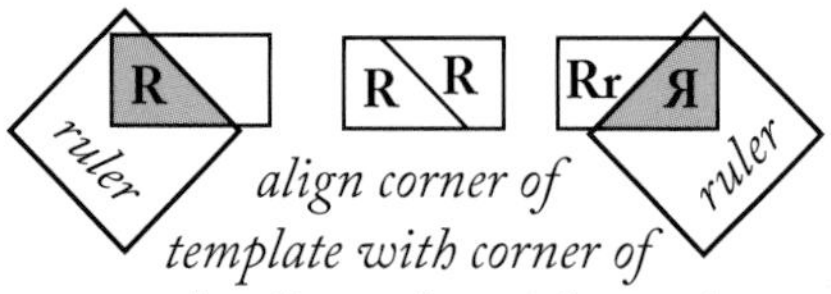

align corner of template with corner of rectangle; align ruler with template; cut rectangle into 2 R's or 2 Rr's
cut 12 R and 12 Rr

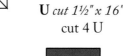

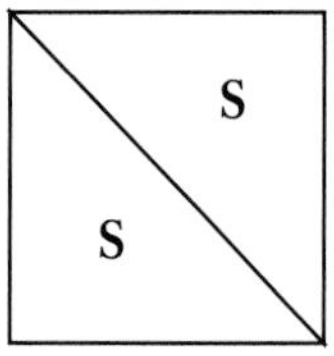

cut 11⅞"
cut 4 S from 2
11⅞" squares

Cutting the Color #14 Background

U *cut 1½" x 16"*
cut 4 U

T *cut 1½" x 7¾"*
cut 8 T

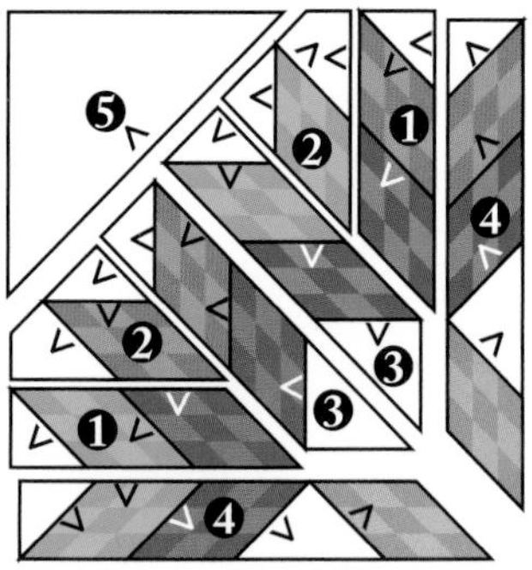

cut 3⅞"
cut 24 N triangles from 12 squares

cut 5⅛"
cut 24 V triangles from 12 squares

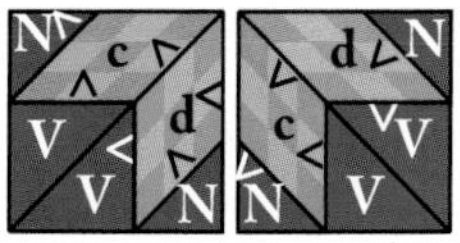

Making Blocks g–k

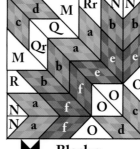

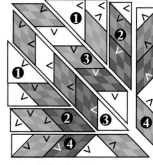

g **Block g**
make 12

Block g Piecing

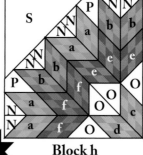

h **Block h**
make 4

Block h Piecing

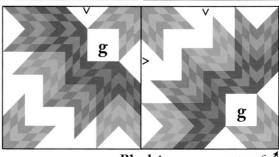

h **g**

g **g**

i **Block i**
make 4

center of quilt

j **Block j**
make 4

k

Block k
make 4

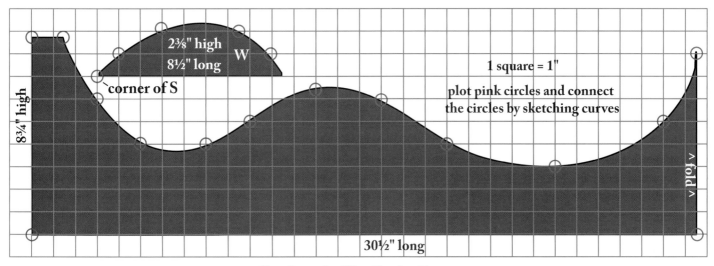

8¾" high

2⅜" high
8½" long

W

corner of S

1 square = 1"

plot pink circles and connect
the circles by sketching curves

fold

30½" long

Graphing the Blue Border Curves

Use a ruler to mark off the length and height of the templates, as listed above. Next, plot the pink circles that fall on 1" rulings (or halfway between them), counting 1" squares across and down the graph above. Sketch curves to connect the pink circles.

pin the curve. Machine baste the two units together: Stitch ¼" inside the raw edges of the blue curve using a regular stitch length. Trim away the excess white under the blue. This completes unit 9. Make 4 unit 9's, as shown below.

Stitch unit 3 to the left end of unit 9 and unit 4 to the right, to make unit 10. Make 2 unit 10's for side borders.

Stitch a unit 5 to the left end and a unit 6 to the right end of unit 9 as shown for unit 11. Make 2 unit 11's for top and bottom borders.

Attaching the Quilt Borders

Sew the i blocks to each other like a Four-Patch, pressing seams as shown in the quilt assembly diagram below. The unit 1's with the blue curves should be in the 4 corners. Notice the green lines at the flower centers in the assembly diagram. These indicate gaps in the seamline that you need for inserting the bias stem ends. With blue edges on the outside, pin and stitch unit 10's to the right and left of the quilt center. Similarly pin and stitch unit 11's to the top and bottom. Be sure to leave 2" gaps where indicated. You will stitch these gaps closed after completing the appliqué of the stems.

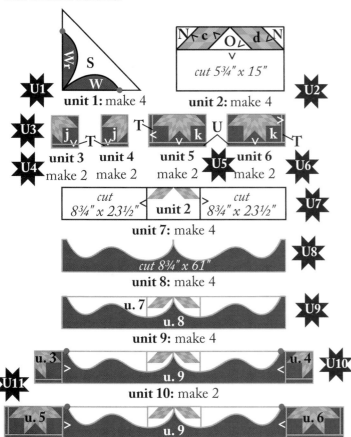

U1 — **unit 1:** make 4

U2 — **unit 2:** make 4 — *cut 5¾" x 15"*

U3 — **unit 3** make 2

U4 — **unit 4** make 2

U5 — **unit 5** make 2

U6 — **unit 6** make 2

U7 — **unit 7:** make 4 — *cut 8¾" x 23½"* **unit 2** *cut 8¾" x 23½"*

U8 — **unit 8:** make 4 — *cut 8¾" x 61"*

U9 — **unit 9:** make 4 — u. 7 / u. 8

U10 — **unit 10:** make 2 — u. 3 / u. 9 / u. 4

U11 — **unit 11:** make 2 — u. 5 / u. 9 / u. 6

Quilt Assembly with No Y-Seams, Showing Wavy Border

Bias Stems and Bias Binding Strips from Color #15

Trim off selvages from 2 yards of green fabric 44" wide. Cut off one A and one C triangle at a 45° angle from the 2 long edges.

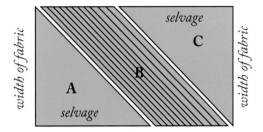

From B, cut eight seamless strips 1½" wide for appliqué stems. Also cut two strips 2" wide for binding.

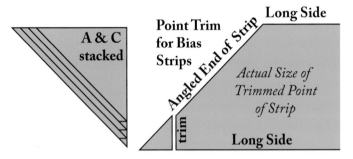

Stack the A and C triangles, aligning their long sides. Cut two layers of three 2"-wide strips along the long side of the A-C stack for binding. Cut off the end at the lower right of the diagram at a 45° angle, as shown.

Trim points of all strips as shown above. Use my Point Trimmer tool or the one you made. Sew the 2" strips to each other, end to end, and press seams open. Fold the resulting strip in half lengthwise with right sides out, and press the fold. You will use this strip to bind the quilt.

The remaining strips are for the appliqué vine that will cover the raw edges of the border curve. Lay one of the 1½"-wide strips along the curve of one half of a blue border. Add a couple of inches for seam allowances and for insurance, and cut the strip off. Cut the remaining 7 strips the same length (mine measured 49"). Fold these strips in half lengthwise, with **right sides out;** do not press. Stitch each strip with a ¼" seam allowance. Press strips so that the seam allowance is entirely hidden on the back side.

Insert one end of a binding strip into the gap you left at a flower center. Pin the bias stem to the front of the quilt, centering it over the raw edges of the blue curves. Pin the stem over half of one border. Insert the other end of the bias stem in the gap by the next flower. Hand appliqué both edges of the bias stem. Repeat for each half of each border. Note that the stems overlap at the insertion points in the centers of the flowers.

Stitch the gaps in your border seams closed, backtacking at each end. Trim away the excess stem length and the seam allowance of the bias stem at the flower centers.

Finishing the Quilt

Lana quilted in the ditch between the stars and the background. She quilted arcs and petals around the stars and flowers. In the diamond-shaped blocks, she quilted feathers, radiating lines, and curved crosshatching. She quilted feathers on either side of the bias stems. She finished with bubbles in the background. Binding directions are on page 22.

Detail of quilting in the center of Skewed Nine-Patch.

Arrangement 2: The 4 center g blocks are rotated when making the i blocks in this arrangement of 4 Double Broken Stars.

Shiloh

Shiloh, 103½" x 103½". Pieced by Margy Sieck from an original design by Judy Martin. Quilted by Lana Corcoran. The block here is colored to suggest a star within a star. The quilt is made from 32 diamond blocks in an 8¾" finished width. They are arranged to form a 42¼" square center star surrounded with four ¾-star units in an Unfolding Star set. The quilt center finishes at 84½" square. The background was designed to avoid Y-seams. Margy used three progressively darker background fabrics. If you want just one background fabric, add together the yardages and patches for all three background fabrics. A strip-pieced border of half stars, also with no Y-seams, hugs the quilt center. An outer plain border adds breathing room and keeps the pieced border seams from unraveling during quilting. The border will fit any of the 84½" square stars in the book.

Quilt Size: 103½" x 103½" **Star Size:** 84½" sq.
Requires: 32 X, 24 Y,   **Block Width:** 8¾"
4 Z blocks   **Set:** Unfolding Star

Yardage & Cutting

Color		Yardage	#Strips	Cut Size	Strip End
1	▪	1 yd.	42	1¾" x 18"	◹
2	▪	½ yd.	22	1¾" x 18"	(all)
3	▪	1½ yds.	54	1¾" x 18"	
4	▪	1 yd.	42	1¾" x 18"	
5	▪	1 yd.	28	1¾" x 18"	
6	▪	1 yd.	24	1¾" x 18"	
7	▫	1 yd.	30	1¾" x 18"	
8	▪	1½ yds.	46	1¾" x 18"	
9	▪	½ yd.	22	1¾" x 18"	
10	▪	1½ yds.	48	1¾" x 18"	
11	▪	1½ yds.	48	1¾" x 18"	

Color		Yardage	#Patches	Cut Size	Icon
12	▫	1¼ yds.	12 C	2 C per 13¼"	◹
			8 D	2 D per 9⅝"	◹
13	▫	2¾ yds.	24 C	2 C per 13¼"	◹
			16 D	2 D per 9⅝"	◹
			56 G	2 G per 3⅜"	◹
14	▫	3¾ yds.	2 borders cut 4" x 104"		
			2 borders cut 4" x 97"		
			4 binding strips 2" x 112"		
			120 F	2 F per 4½"	◹
			64 G	2 G per 3⅜"	◹
		10 yds.	backing: 3 pcs. 37¾" x 112"		

Broken Star Yardage & Cutting Changes

Color		Yardage	Patches	Cut Size	
12	▫	1¼ yds.	16 C	2 C per 13¼"	◹
			no D		

4-Lone Star Set Yardage & Cutting Changes

Color		Yardage	Patches	Cut Size	
12	▫	0 yds.	none		
13	▫	4 yds.	32 C	2 C per 13¼"	◹
			32 D	2 D per 9⅝"	◹
			56 G	2 G per 3⅜"	◹

Grand Lone Star Yardage & Cutting Changes

Color		Yardage	Patches	Cut Size	
12	▫	0 yds.	none		
13	▫	4¼ yds.	8 I	2 I per 25⅝"	◹
			8 J	2 J per 18⅜"	◹
			56 G	2 G per 3⅜"	◹

In this quilt, it is important to have the right contrasts within the block. Each block includes an inner and an outer star arm. Where the two touch (at the outer tips of the inner star arm), the contrast should be strong. It helps to have a contrast in value as well as hue. Notice how the pinks and red get darker as they approach the outer tips of the inner star arms. The greens and blues of the outer star arms get lighter in the neighboring area.

The top chart lists complete yardage for the quilt as photographed. If you prefer to make one of the setting variations on page 88–89, the only changes will be to the background. If you plan to make one of the variations, cut everything as listed for the main chart, except substitute the yardage and patch counts for color numbers 12 and 13 as noted for your chosen quilt below the main chart.

Making Strip Sets and Cutting Rows

Start by reading the glossary, "Pattern Pointers," and "How to Make a Lone Star" chapters on pages 7–22.

You can cut all the strips before you sew any, or cut a little and sew a little, according to your preference. Referring to the yardage chart and the strip set diagrams on page 85, cut 1¾" x 18" strips in the colors needed for a strip set. Cut off one end of each strip as indicated in the "strip end" column of the yardage chart. If you folded the fabric, unfold it before you cut off the strip ends. Point trimming helps you align patches for sewing. If you don't have one, make a Point Trimmer by downloading the file at judymartin.com/LSPT.cfm and following the directions there. Trim the point of a strip as shown below. You do not need to trim the point of the top strip in each strip set.

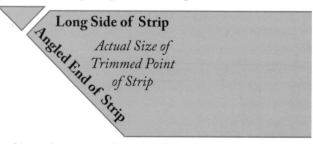

Long Side of Strip
Actual Size of Trimmed Point of Strip
Angled End of Strip

Align the trimmed point of one strip with the wide angle of the neighboring strip. Pin and stitch strips together in the order shown in the strip set diagram. Finger press and steam press after each seam, following the "v" pressing arrows in the strip set diagrams. Continue pinning and stitching strips together to complete a strip set as shown. Make 6 strip sets of each type illustrated on page 85.

Trim a sliver off the angled end of the strip set, if necessary, at a precise 45° angle. See the row cutting diagram at the bottom of the next page. Cut the rows for Shiloh the same width that you cut strips: 1¾". That is, lay the 1¾" ruling of your rotary ruler on the

Strip Piecing

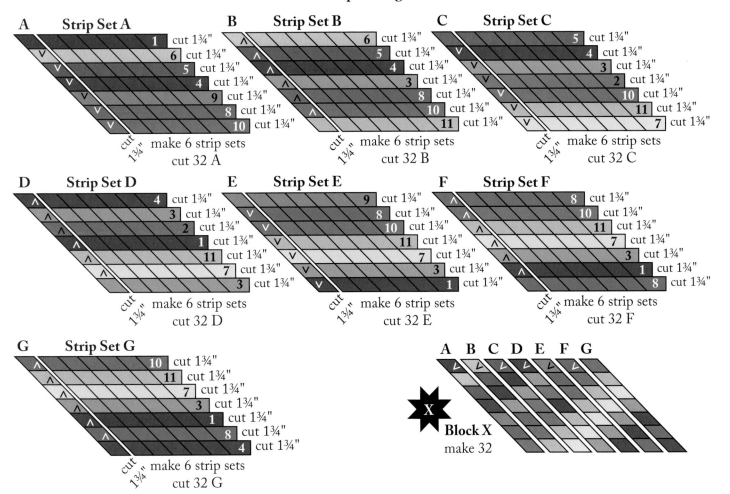

A Strip Set A
1 cut 1¾"
6 cut 1¾"
5 cut 1¾"
4 cut 1¾"
9 cut 1¾"
8 cut 1¾"
10 cut 1¾"
cut 1¾" make 6 strip sets
cut 32 A

B Strip Set B
6 cut 1¾"
5 cut 1¾"
4 cut 1¾"
3 cut 1¾"
8 cut 1¾"
10 cut 1¾"
11 cut 1¾"
cut 1¾" make 6 strip sets
cut 32 B

C Strip Set C
5 cut 1¾"
4 cut 1¾"
3 cut 1¾"
2 cut 1¾"
10 cut 1¾"
11 cut 1¾"
7 cut 1¾"
cut 1¾" make 6 strip sets
cut 32 C

D Strip Set D
4 cut 1¾"
3 cut 1¾"
2 cut 1¾"
1 cut 1¾"
11 cut 1¾"
7 cut 1¾"
3 cut 1¾"
cut 1¾" make 6 strip sets
cut 32 D

E Strip Set E
9 cut 1¾"
8 cut 1¾"
10 cut 1¾"
11 cut 1¾"
7 cut 1¾"
3 cut 1¾"
1 cut 1¾"
cut 1¾" make 6 strip sets
cut 32 E

F Strip Set F
8 cut 1¾"
10 cut 1¾"
11 cut 1¾"
7 cut 1¾"
3 cut 1¾"
1 cut 1¾"
8 cut 1¾"
cut 1¾" make 6 strip sets
cut 32 F

G Strip Set G
10 cut 1¾"
11 cut 1¾"
7 cut 1¾"
3 cut 1¾"
1 cut 1¾"
8 cut 1¾"
4 cut 1¾"
cut 1¾" make 6 strip sets
cut 32 G

A B C D E F G

X

Block X
make 32

angled end of the strip set; also align the 45° angle line of the ruler with one long side of the strip set. Cut along the edge of the ruler to make a row. You should be able to cut 6 rows from each A–G strip set. The rows are outlined on the strip set, with the first row separated slightly. Check your 45° angle after cutting a row or two, and true it up as needed. You will need 32 rows of each type A–G.

Continue making strip sets and cutting rows in this fashion. When you have all the rows needed for a block, trim both points of each row at a right angle to the short end of the row as shown below right.

Joining Rows to Make Blocks

Lay out the rows for a block as shown in the X block diagram above. Pin rows at both ends of the seamline, aligning the point trim of one row with the wide angle of the other. Also pin at each joint. To match joints, stick a pin in the place where the seamline of one row crosses the seamline you will be stitching. Continue through the same point on the second row. Review the strategies for matching joints on page 15. Stitch all rows together. After each seam, press seam allowances. Pressing direction is indicated with an arrow in the block diagram. Make 32 X blocks.

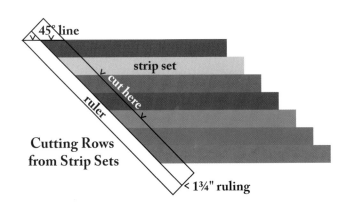

45° line
strip set
cut here
ruler

Cutting Rows from Strip Sets
< 1¾" ruling

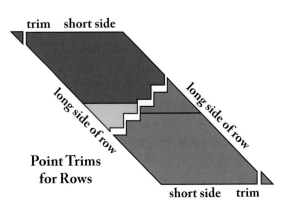

trim short side
long side of row
long side of row
Point Trims for Rows
short side trim

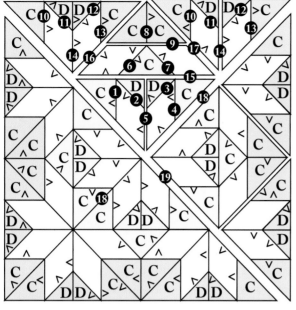

Unfolding Star Assembly with No Y-Seams

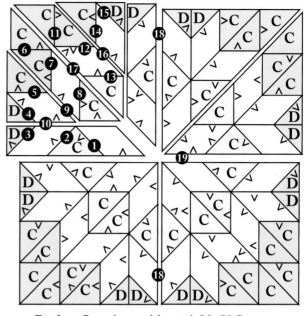

Broken Star Assembly with No Y-Seams

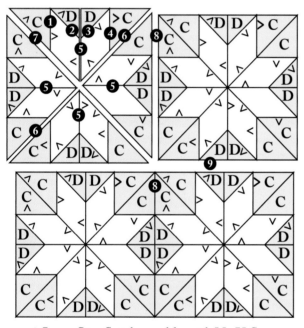

4-Lone Star Set Assembly with No Y-Seams

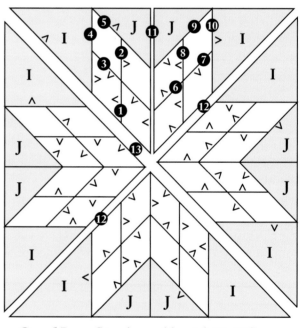

Grand Lone Star Assembly with No Y-Seams

Quilt Assembly

Lay out your 32 X blocks in the Unfolding Star, Broken Star, 4-Lone Stars, or Grand Lone Star arrangements in the photo on pages 83 or drawings on pages 88 and 89. Cut out the background patches for your arrangement in the sizes shown at the right. See page 17 for tips on rotary cutting background patches larger than your ruler. (The yardage charts list the quantities required for the various sets.) Lay out the background patches with the X blocks.

Assemble your quilt in sections, following the numbered sewing sequence shown in one of the sections in the appropriate assembly diagram above. Press seams as you go, following the arrows in the assembly diagram.

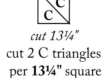

cut 13¼"
cut 2 C triangles
per **13¼"** square

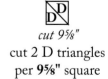

cut 9⅝"
cut 2 D triangles
per **9⅝"** square

cut 25⅝"
cut 8 I triangles
from four **25⅝"** squares

cut 18⅜"
cut 8 J triangles
from four **18⅜"** squares

After making strip sets for the X blocks, you should have 112 strips left. Sort these into dark and medium, with fabrics #1, 2, 4, 8, and 10 being dark and fabrics #3, 5, 6, 9, and 11 being medium. See the border diagram around this page. It shows the variety of half stars you can make from these leftover strips. You will be making strip sets consisting of 1 dark strip above 1 medium strip, as shown below. Pair each dark color with all mediums in 25 different combinations, as shown in the border around this page. As you make each pair into a strip set, make a second, identical strip set for a total of 50. Make 2 more strip sets each of brown-yellow, red-pink, and dark blue-medium blue, for a total of 56 strip sets.

H   Strip Set H

make 56 strip sets in matched pairs
cut 4 sets of 12 H alike (for Z)
cut 24 sets of 8 H alike (for Y)

You can cut 6 H strips from each strip set, but for the Y blocks you only need to cut 4 H from each strip set. For 24 Y's, from each of 24 pairs of strip sets cut 8 H's. For Z blocks, from each remaining pair of strip sets, cut 12 H alike.

Sew two matching H units together to make a unit 1 as shown below. Make 120 unit 1's.

H   H

Unit 1 & Piecing
make 120 unit 1's
(24 sets of 4 alike for Y)
(4 sets of 6 alike for Z)

For the border blocks, cut F and G triangles as shown at the bottom of the page. F is not a nice, easily measured size. You can cut it 4½" and trim off a sliver after completing the Y and Z blocks, or you can use the optional templates provided on the next page to rotary cut F perfectly, as described in the template.

See the border block diagrams below. Set aside the 4 sets of 6 matching unit 1's to make Z blocks later. For each Y block, use a matched set of 4 unit 1's. Sew an F and a G to unit 1, noting that half of the units have F to the right of unit 1 and half have F to the left. Note also the placement of the darker and lighter* G triangles. Sew the G-unit 1-F to the F-unit 1-G to form a square; join squares to make Y blocks.

Border Half Block Y
make 24

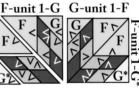

Y Piecing

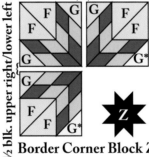

Border Corner Block Z
make 4

½ blk. upper left/lower right
½ blk. upper right/lower left

2 G triangles in each Y and Z are cut from lighter fabric #13. Light G*'s touch light G*'s in the border; dark touch dark. See Z's at left and outlined in border diagram around the page. Bracketed units make half stars for ends of top/bottom borders. The 3rd unit is for the adjacent end of side border.*

F
F
cut 4½"
cut 120 F
from 60 **4½"** squares
of color #14

G
G
cut 3⅜"
cut 56 G
from 28 **3⅜"** squares
of color #13;
cut 64 G
from 32 squares
of color #14

Use the sets of six unit 1's reserved earlier to make Z blocks in a similar fashion, noting the placement of light* G's. Do not join these squares to make half stars yet. Lay out your borders as shown around the perimeter of this page, with 3 matching Z sections at each corner. The section with 2 dark G's should be in the corner, and the lighter G triangles should be next to the light G's in the Y blocks. Sew 6 Y blocks end to end for each border. See the Z block diagram above. Join 2 of the 3 matching Z's to make a half star. Half stars are of 2 types, as indicated by brackets and notations at the top and left of the Z diagram. Make one half star for each corner. Sew these to each end of the top and bottom borders. Sew the remaining Z units to the ends of the side borders with light G's touching each other and matched ¾ stars in the 4 corners. Pin and stitch the shorter pieced borders to the sides of the quilt. Pin and stitch the longer borders to the top and bottom of the quilt. These borders are abutted to avoid Y-seams. Add the shorter 4"-wide plain border strips to the top and bottom of the quilt. Add the longer plain borders to the 2 remaining sides to complete the quilt top.

Quilting and Finishing

Lana Corcoran quilted the diamonds in the ditch. She quilted feathers in the two lighter background areas and parallel lines in the darkest background of the borders.

Bind the quilt as described on page 22. Sign and date your quilt on a label stitched to the back of the quilt.

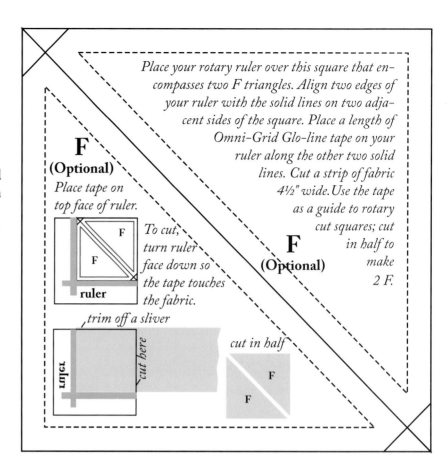

Place your rotary ruler over this square that encompasses two F triangles. Align two edges of your ruler with the solid lines on two adjacent sides of the square. Place a length of Omni-Grid Glo-line tape on your ruler along the other two solid lines. Cut a strip of fabric 4½" wide. Use the tape as a guide to rotary cut squares; cut in half to make 2 F.

F (Optional)
Place tape on top face of ruler.

To cut, turn ruler face down so the tape touches the fabric.

F (Optional)

Shiloh Setting Variations
USING THE SAME BLOCK QUANTITIES (YARDAGE ON PAGE 84)

Arrangement 2: 32 blocks in an Unfolding Star arrangement, with all blocks turned differently from the quilt made by Margy and shown in the photo on page 83.

Arrangement 3: 32 blocks in a Broken Star arrangement, with all blocks turned with the brown tip out. See changes to background yardage and cutting below the main yardage chart.

Arrangement 4: 32 blocks in a Broken Star arrangement, with only the 8 center blocks turned with the brown tip out. See changes to the background yardage and cutting below the main yardage chart.

Arrangement 5: 32 blocks in a 4-Lone Star arrangement, with all blocks turned with the brown tip out. See changes to background yardage and cutting below the main yardage chart.

Arrangement 6: 32 blocks in a Grand Lone Star arrangement, with center 8 blocks and the outermost 8 blocks turned with the brown tip toward the center. See changes to the background yardage and cutting below the main yardage chart.

Arrangement 7: 32 blocks in a Grand Lone Star arrangement, with the center 8 blocks and the outermost 8 blocks turned with the red tip toward the center. See changes to the background yardage and cutting below the main yardage chart.

Galileo's Star

Galileo's Star, 103" x 103". Pieced by Judy Martin from her original design. Quilted by Lana Corcoran. The quilt is made from 8 diamond blocks in a 17½" finished width. It is set in a standard Lone Star arrangement for an 84½" square star. The unique design looks like it has concentric feathered stars, but its construction has more in common with a Lone Star. A plain white border, a pieced border, and a plain black border complete the quilt. Galileo's Star is strip pieced a little differently from other quilts in the book. The block is made like a Nine-Patch with 3 rows of 3 strip-pieced units.

Quilt Size: 103" x 103"   **Star Size:** 84½" sq.
Requires: 8 blocks   **Block Width:** 17½"

Yardage Total for Quilt as Photographed

Due to efficiencies of cutting, the total yardage may be less than the sum of the separate yardages. Color #1: 4¼ yds.; #2: 2 yds.; #3: 2 yds.; #4: 1¾ yds; #5: 1½ yds.; #6: 1 fat qtr.; #7: 6 yds.; backing: 9⅞ yds.

Yardage & Cutting

Color	Yardage	#Strips	Cut Size	Strip End
1 ■	2 yds.	8	2¼" x 18"	
		52	1⅜" x 18"	
		41	1⅜" x 18"	
2 ■	2 yds.	12	2¼" x 18"	
		47	1⅜" x 18"	
		41	1⅜" x 18"	
3 □	2 yds.	8	2¼" x 18"	
		49	1⅜" x 18"	
		42	1⅜" x 18"	
4 ■	1 yd.	8	2¼" x 18"	
		20	1⅜" x 18"	
		20	1⅜" x 18"	
5 ■	1 yd.	18	1⅜" x 18"	
		16	1⅜" x 18"	
6 ■	1 fat qtr.	10	1⅜" x 18"	
		4	1⅜" x 18"	
7 □	5½ yds.	4 borders 4" x 92¾"	
		bkgd.: 4 A, 4 B or 8 C, 8 D	

You can use just one print for each color or multiple prints of the same color for colors #1, #4, #5, and #7. If you use just one print, start by cutting the border strips and background patches, if there are any. Then cut the remaining fabric into ½-yard lengths for 18" lengthwise strips.

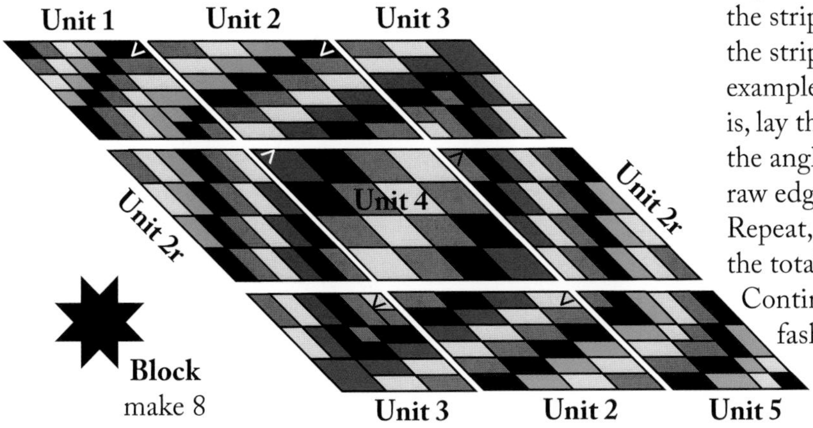

Yardage & Cutting for Borders

Color	Yardage	#Strips	Cut Size	Strip End
5 ■	1 yd.	27 (108 c)	2⅛" x 18"	

Color	Yardage	#Patches	Cut Size	
1 ■	3⅛ yds.	4 borders:	2" x 104¼"	
		+108 e	*see pg. 95*	
		+8 d	*see pg. 95*	
		+4 f	2 f per 3⅜"	
7 □	1 yd.	208 d	*see pg. 95*	

Yardage & Cutting for Backing

Color	Yardage	#Panels	Cut Size
	9⅞ yds.	3 panels	37½" x 111½"

Yardage & Cutting for Binding

Color	Yardage	#Strips	Cut Size
4 ■	¾ yd.	19	2" x 27"

Making Strip Sets and Cutting Rows

Start by reading the glossary, "How to Make a Lone Star," and "Pattern Pointers" chapters on pages 7–22. You can cut all the strips before you sew any, or cut a little and sew a little, according to your preference.

Cut the strips for a strip set, cutting off the points as indicated in the "strip end" column. Trim the points to help you align patches for sewing. Use my Point Trimmer or download a file and learn how to make your own at judymartin.com/LSPT.cfm. The point should be trimmed at a right angle to the angled end of the strip as shown on page 92. Don't trim the point on the top strip of a regular strip set or the bottom strip of a reversed strip set.

Align the wide angle of one strip with the trimmed point of the next strip. Pin and stitch strips together. Finger press and steam press after each seam, following the "v" pressing arrows in the strip sets.

Continue pinning and stitching strips together to complete the strip set as shown. Trim a sliver off the angled end, if necessary, at a precise 45° angle. Cut the strip set into rows, referring to the notation below the strip set diagram for the width of the rows. For example, for strip set A, cut A rows 1⅜" wide. That is, lay the 1⅜" ruling of your rotary cutting ruler over the angled end of the strip, align the 45° line with a raw edge or seamline, and cut along the ruler's edge. Repeat, making a duplicate strip set if indicated, to cut the total number of A rows listed below the strip set.

Continue making strip sets and cutting rows in this fashion. When you have all the rows needed for a unit, trim both points of each row as shown on page 93.

Unit 1   Unit 2   Unit 3

Unit 2r

Unit 4

Unit 2r

Block
make 8

Unit 3   Unit 2   Unit 5

Strip Piecing

Making Units from Rows

Align the trimmed point of one row with the wide angle of the neighboring row; pin and stitch. See page 15 for help with joints. Continue stitching rows together to complete the units as shown.

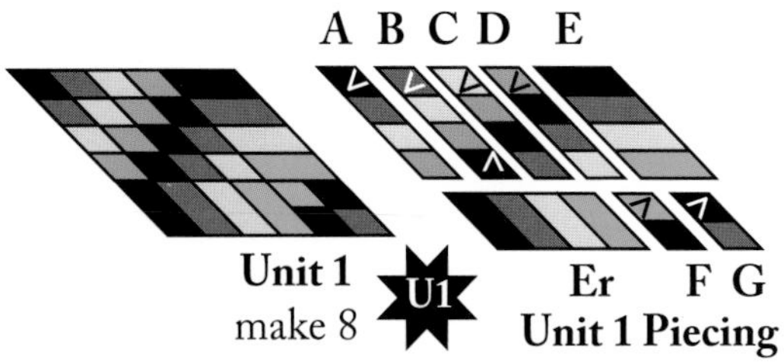

A B C D E
Unit 1
make 8
U1
Er F G
Unit 1 Piecing

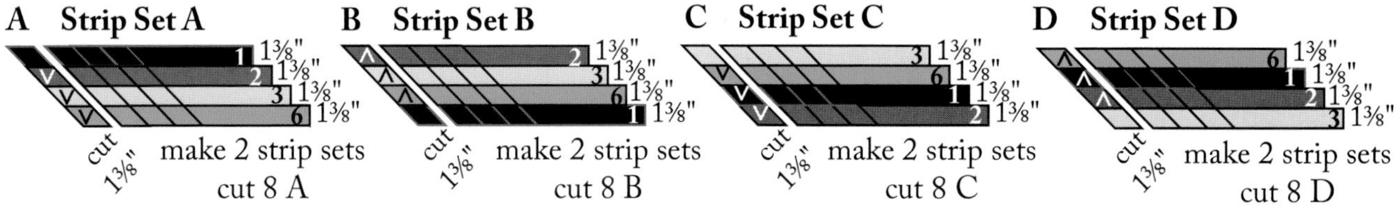

A Strip Set A
1 1⅜"
2 1⅜"
3 1⅜"
6 1⅜"
cut 1⅜"
make 2 strip sets
cut 8 A
B Strip Set B
2 1⅜"
3 1⅜"
6 1⅜"
1 1⅜"
cut 1⅜"
make 2 strip sets
cut 8 B
C Strip Set C
3 1⅜"
6 1⅜"
1 1⅜"
2 1⅜"
cut 1⅜"
make 2 strip sets
cut 8 C
D Strip Set D
6 1⅜"
1 1⅜"
2 1⅜"
3 1⅜"
cut 1⅜"
make 2 strip sets
cut 8 D

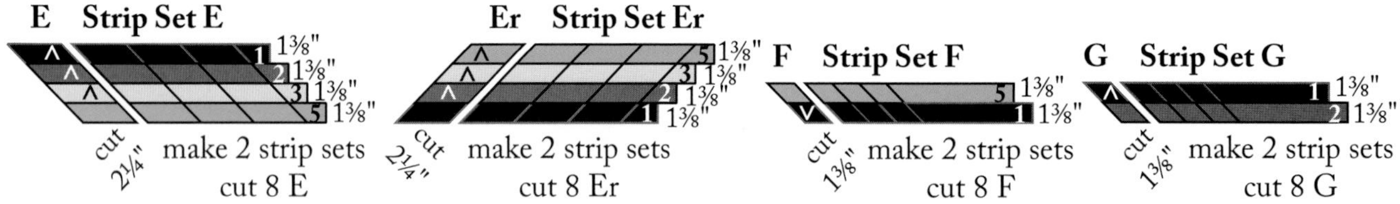

E Strip Set E
1 1⅜"
2 1⅜"
3 1⅜"
5 1⅜"
cut 2¼"
make 2 strip sets
cut 8 E
Er Strip Set Er
5 1⅜"
3 1⅜"
2 1⅜"
1 1⅜"
cut 2¼"
make 2 strip sets
cut 8 Er
F Strip Set F
5 1⅜"
1 1⅜"
cut 1⅜"
make 2 strip sets
cut 8 F
G Strip Set G
1 1⅜"
2 1⅜"
cut 1⅜"
make 2 strip sets
cut 8 G

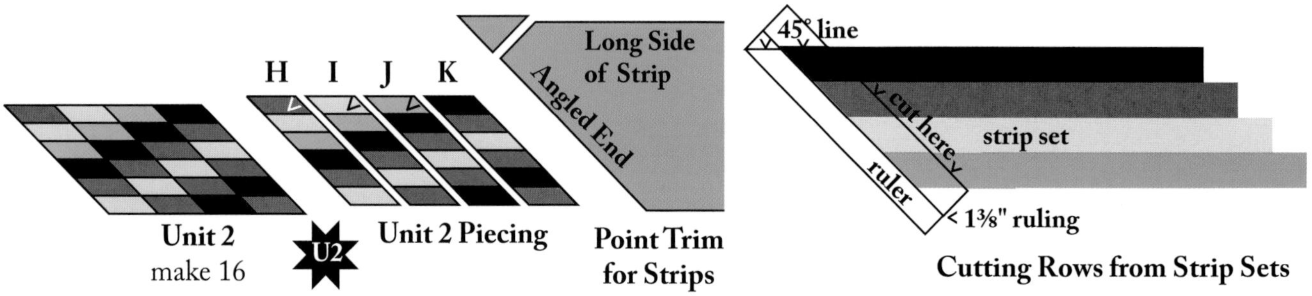

H I J K
Unit 2
make 16
U2
Unit 2 Piecing
Long Side of Strip
Angled End
Point Trim for Strips
45° line
cut here
strip set
ruler
< 1⅜" ruling
Cutting Rows from Strip Sets

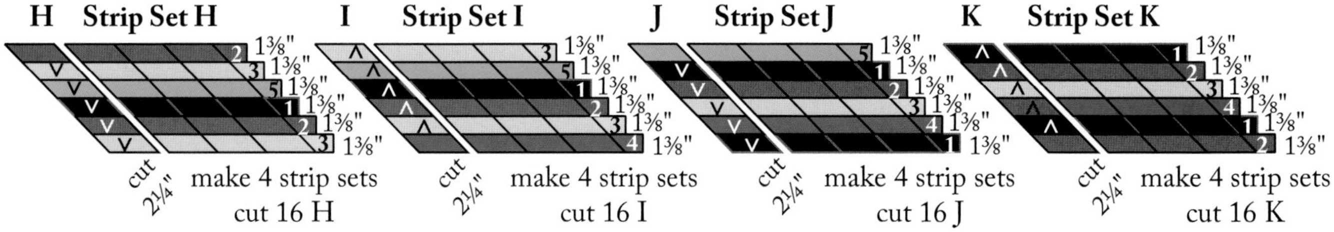

H Strip Set H
2 1⅜"
3 1⅜"
5 1⅜"
1 1⅜"
2 1⅜"
3 1⅜"
cut 2¼"
make 4 strip sets
cut 16 H
I Strip Set I
3 1⅜"
5 1⅜"
1 1⅜"
2 1⅜"
3 1⅜"
4 1⅜"
cut 2¼"
make 4 strip sets
cut 16 I
J Strip Set J
5 1⅜"
1 1⅜"
2 1⅜"
3 1⅜"
4 1⅜"
1 1⅜"
cut 2¼"
make 4 strip sets
cut 16 J
K Strip Set K
1 1⅜"
2 1⅜"
3 1⅜"
4 1⅜"
1 1⅜"
2 1⅜"
cut 2¼"
make 4 strip sets
cut 16 K

Notice that this quilt requires regular strips as well as reversed strips, distinguished by their strip ends. Reversed strips are used in strip sets and units with an "r" following the number or letter.

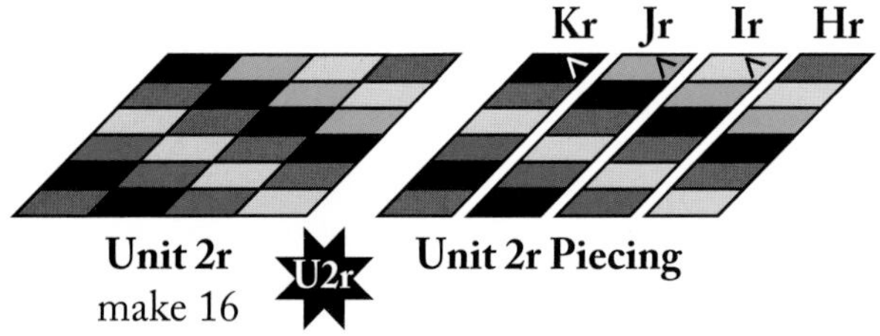

Kr Jr Ir Hr
Unit 2r
make 16
U2r
Unit 2r Piecing

Cut all strips on this page 1⅜" wide.
Cut rows 1⅜" or 2¼" wide, as listed below the strip sets.

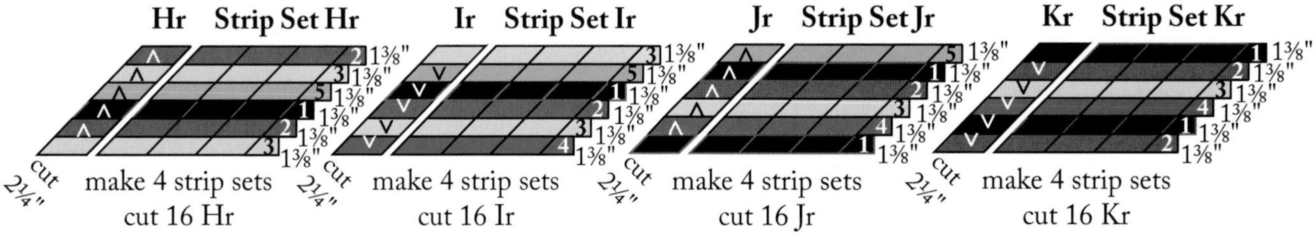

Hr Strip Set Hr
2 1⅜"
3 1⅜"
5 1⅜"
1 1⅜"
2 1⅜"
3 1⅜"
cut 2¼"
make 4 strip sets
cut 16 Hr
Ir Strip Set Ir
3 1⅜"
5 1⅜"
1 1⅜"
2 1⅜"
3 1⅜"
4 1⅜"
cut 2¼"
make 4 strip sets
cut 16 Ir
Jr Strip Set Jr
5 1⅜"
1 1⅜"
2 1⅜"
3 1⅜"
4 1⅜"
1 1⅜"
cut 2¼"
make 4 strip sets
cut 16 Jr
Kr Strip Set Kr
1 1⅜"
2 1⅜"
3 1⅜"
4 1⅜"
1 1⅜"
2 1⅜"
cut 2¼"
make 4 strip sets
cut 16 Kr

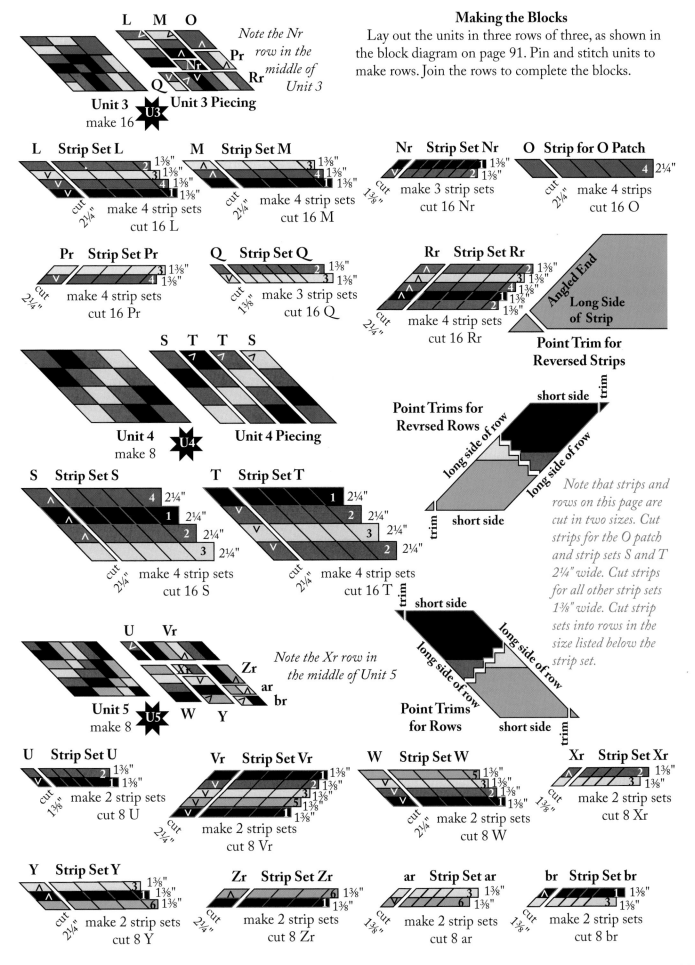

Making the Blocks

Lay out the units in three rows of three, as shown in the block diagram on page 91. Pin and stitch units to make rows. Join the rows to complete the blocks.

L M O

Note the Nr row in the middle of Unit 3

Pr

Rr

Nr

Q

Unit 3
make 16

U3

Unit 3 Piecing

L **Strip Set L**
2 1⅜"
3 1⅜"
4 1⅜"
1 1⅜"
cut 2¼"
make 4 strip sets
cut 16 L

M **Strip Set M**
3 1⅜"
3 1⅜"
1 1⅜"
cut 2¼"
make 4 strip sets
cut 16 M

Nr **Strip Set Nr**
1 1⅜"
2 1⅜"
cut 1⅜"
make 3 strip sets
cut 16 Nr

O **Strip for O Patch**
4 2¼"
cut 2¼"
make 4 strips
cut 16 O

Pr **Strip Set Pr**
3 1⅜"
4 1⅜"
cut 2¼"
make 4 strip sets
cut 16 Pr

Q **Strip Set Q**
2 1⅜"
3 1⅜"
cut 1⅜"
make 3 strip sets
cut 16 Q

Rr **Strip Set Rr**
2 1⅜"
3 1⅜"
1⅜"
1 1⅜"
2 1⅜"
cut 2¼"
make 4 strip sets
cut 16 Rr

Angled End
Long Side of Strip
Point Trim for Reversed Strips

S T T S

Unit 4
make 8

U4

Unit 4 Piecing

S **Strip Set S**
4 2¼"
1 2¼"
2 2¼"
3 2¼"
cut 2¼"
make 4 strip sets
cut 16 S

T **Strip Set T**
1 2¼"
2 2¼"
3 2¼"
2 2¼"
cut 2¼"
make 4 strip sets
cut 16 T

Point Trims for Revrsed Rows
short side — trim
long side of row
long side of row
short side — trim

Note that strips and rows on this page are cut in two sizes. Cut strips for the O patch and strip sets S and T 2¼" wide. Cut strips for all other strip sets 1⅜" wide. Cut strip sets into rows in the size listed below the strip set.

Point Trims for Rows
trim — short side
long side of row
long side of row
short side — trim

U Vr

Xr

Zr

ar
br

Note the Xr row in the middle of Unit 5

Unit 5
make 8

U5

W Y

U **Strip Set U**
2 1⅜"
1 1⅜"
cut 1⅜"
make 2 strip sets
cut 8 U

Vr **Strip Set Vr**
1 1⅜"
2 1⅜"
3 1⅜"
5 1⅜"
1 1⅜"
cut 2¼"
make 2 strip sets
cut 8 Vr

W **Strip Set W**
5 1⅜"
3 1⅜"
2 1⅜"
1 1⅜"
cut 2¼"
make 2 strip sets
cut 8 W

Xr **Strip Set Xr**
2 1⅜"
3 1⅜"
cut 1⅜"
make 2 strip sets
cut 8 Xr

Y **Strip Set Y**
3 1⅜"
1 1⅜"
6 1⅜"
cut 2¼"
make 2 strip sets
cut 8 Y

Zr **Strip Set Zr**
6 1⅜"
1 1⅜"
cut 2¼"
make 2 strip sets
cut 8 Zr

ar **Strip Set ar**
3 1⅜"
6 1⅜"
cut 1⅜"
make 2 strip sets
cut 8 ar

br **Strip Set br**
1 1⅜"
3 1⅜"
cut 1⅜"
make 2 strip sets
cut 8 br

93

Cutting Background Patches

See page 17 for tips on cutting patches larger than your ruler. Cut out the background patches shown below for your choice of a quilt with or without Y-seams.

Assembling the Quilt

Referring to the appropriate quilt assembly diagram below, stitch together the blocks and patches in numerical order. After each seam, press seam allowances in the direction indicated by the arrows in the assembly diagram. Repeat steps to make four quadrants of the quilt.

For the quilt with no Y-seams, add a white border strip to each quarter of the quilt before joining quarters to make halves of the quilt; join halves to complete the quilt center.

For the quilt with Y-seams, join quarters to make halves; join halves to complete the star. You will need to set in seams at the corners indicated with a red dot. See page 18 for more details about sewing Y-seams. Add the white borders, and stitch the border corners with a Y-seam.

Making Cloth Rotary Cutting Templates

See page 95. From an unwanted scrap of fabric, cut a strip 2⅛" x 6" or so. Cut off one end at a 45° angle. Cut off a diamond by laying the 2⅛" ruling on the angled end of the strip and cutting along the ruler. This diamond should be the same size as the turquoise c patches shown on page 95. Lay the ¼" rule line of your rotary ruler over the short diagonal of the diamond. Cut on the ruler's edge; the smaller piece is waste; the larger piece is your d template.

Make an e template in a similar fashion. Cut a strip 3¾" x 9" or so. Cut off the end at a 45° angle. Cut off a diamond 3¾" wide, measured from the angled end. Lay the ¼" rule line of your rotary ruler from corner to corner on the diamond's short diagonal. Cut on the ruler's edge to complete a cloth template for e (the larger piece). You do not need the smaller triangle.

Using Cloth Rotary Cutting Templates

To cut white d triangles, cut 18 lengthwise strips of white fabric 3⅛" x 18". Place the cloth template for d with its short side even with one long edge of the strip. Align your rotary ruler with one long edge of the cloth d template; cut. Align your ruler with the other long edge of the cloth d; cut to complete a white d. Rotate the cloth template 180° and move it down the strip to cut more d's. One long side of each subsequent d should align with the edge you just cut. Note that you will also need 8 **black** d triangles. Download a file at judymartin.com/cdef.cfm to learn how to make Point Trimmers for c, d, e, and f patches. Trim points of d's as described in the downloaded file.

Cut e patches in the same fashion. Start by cutting 13 black strips 5¼" x 24". Place the cloth template for e with its short side even with one long edge of the strip. Align

Note that the pieced border and outer border will have Y-seams even if you piece the quilt center with no Y-seams.

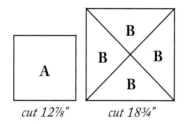

cut 12⅞"   cut 18¾"

Background Patches (Y-Seams)
cut 4 A squares **12⅞"**
cut 4 B triangles from one **18¾"** square

OR

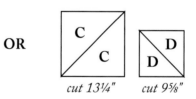

cut 13¼"   cut 9⅝"

Background Patches (No Y-Seams)
cut 8 C triangles from four **13¼"** squares
cut 8 D triangles from four **9⅝"** squares

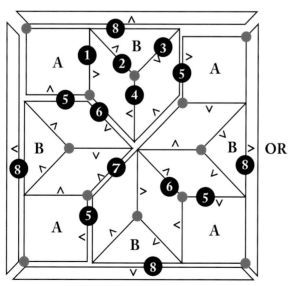

Quilt Assembly with Y-Seams

OR

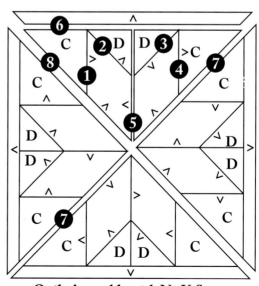

Quilt Assembly with No Y-Seams

your ruler with one long edge of the cloth template; cut. Repeat for the other long edge of the cloth template. Rotate the cloth template and move it down the strip to cut additional e patches, with each subsequent e sharing a cut side with the last e you cut. Trim the points of e's.

Making the Pieced Borders

Cut 108 c diamonds from 27 turquoise strips cut 2⅛" x 18", as shown below. Also cut 4 black f triangles for the border corners from 2 squares of 3⅜". Trim the points of c's and f's using the file you dowloaded for d point trims.

Make 104 border units and 4 corner units as shown below. Sew 26 border units together to make a border; add a corner unit to the left end, as shown below. Repeat to make 4 borders alike. Pin and stitch a pieced border to each of 4 sides of the quilt center; stitch corner miters. Next, pin and stitch a black outer border to each side of the quilt; miter the border corners with a Y-seam.

Quilt in the ditch between the star and the background. Quilt feathers in the background and parallel lines in the diamond blocks. Bind the quilt as shown on page 22.

Making a Cloth Template for d

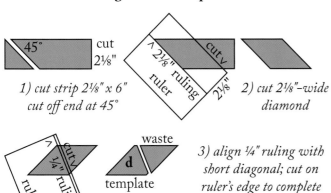

1) cut strip 2⅛" x 6" cut off end at 45°

2) cut 2⅛"-wide diamond

3) align ¼" ruling with short diagonal; cut on ruler's edge to complete the cloth d template

Making a Cloth Template for e

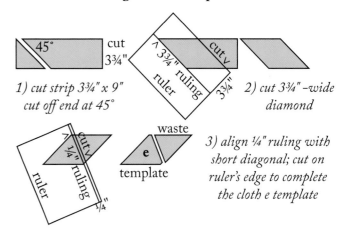

1) cut strip 3¾" x 9" cut off end at 45°

2) cut 3¾"-wide diamond

3) align ¼" ruling with short diagonal; cut on ruler's edge to complete the cloth e template

Using the Cloth Template to cut d Patches

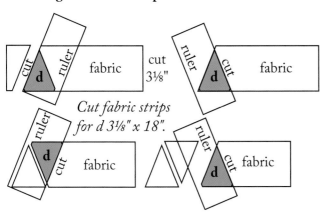

cut 3⅛"

Cut fabric strips for d 3⅛" x 18".

Using the Cloth Template to cut e Patches

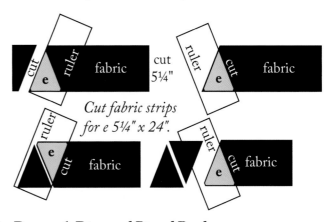

cut 5¼"

Cut fabric strips for e 5¼" x 24".

Cutting c and f Patches and Making the Dogtooth Diamond Pieced Borders

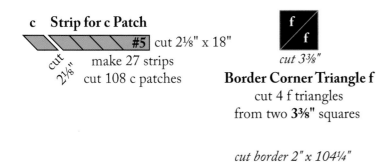

c **Strip for c Patch**

#5 cut 2⅛" x 18"

make 27 strips
cut 108 c patches

Border Corner Triangle f
cut 4 f triangles
from two **3⅜"** squares

Border Unit
make 104
join 26 for
each border

Corner Unit
make 4
sew one to the left
end of each border

cut border 2" x 104¼"

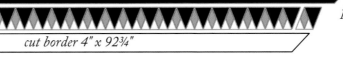

cut border 4" x 92¾"

press seam allowances to the right in the pieced borders

95

Galileo's Star Color Variations
SUBSTITUTING ONE COLOR FOR ANOTHER

Coloring 2: substitute these colors: 1 = dark brown; 2 = medium brown; 3 = light brown; 4 = dark blue; 5 = medium blue; 6 = light blue; 7 = ivory.

Coloring 3: substitute these colors: 1 = dark green; 2 = medium light green; 3 = medium green; 4 = medium dark green; 5 = brown; 6 = light yellow-green; 7 = beige.

Coloring 4: substitute these colors: 1 = medium dark blue; 2 = medium blue; 3 = very light blue; 4 = dark blue; 5 = medium light blue; 6 = light blue; 7 = cream.

Coloring 5: substitute these colors: 1 = medium blue; 2 = turquoise; 3 = light green; 4 = navy blue; 5 = aqua; 6 = medium green; 7 = white.

Harvest Lone Star

Harvest Lone Star, 84½" x 84½", designed and quilted by Judy Martin; pieced by Chris Hulin. The pattern is for an 84½" square star, though Chris made this much smaller. She used two different colorings for the blocks, with four blocks colored one way alternated with four colored the other way. Though both block types have the same outline, I call one coloring "block Y" and the other "block Z." This was the first quilt I designed for Singular Stars. I love the illusion of curves this Lone Star creates. I also love the multiple possibilities it offers when you rotate the asymmetrical blocks. In fact, this quilt was the jumping-off point for my even more variable Supernova and Star of Wonder patterns on pages 105 and 119.

Harvest Lone Star
(Bordered)

Harvest Lone Star, 88" x 88", pieced and quilted by Chris Hulin from an original design by Judy Martin. Chris made two quilts from this pattern so you can see how different the pattern looks when the blocks are rotated. This version places the Y and Z blocks in different positions and orientation from the other version. It also adds an optional pieced border. Because this border is strip pieced, it has bias edges all around the quilt.

If you don't want to deal with the possibility of stretching, either during piecing or quilting, you can simply leave the border off. In that case, use the yardage and directions for the unbordered quilt and simply arrange the blocks to match this version. You may want to play with the placement and orientation of your blocks before you sew them together. Photograph your arrangements to help you choose a favorite.

Yardage & Cutting Without Borders

Quilt Size: 84½" x 84½" **Star Size:** 84½" sq.
Requires: 4 Y, 4 Z blocks **Block Width:** 17½"

Color	Yardage	#Strips	Cut Size	Strip End
1	leftovers*	2	2¼" x 18"	◿
2	½ yd.	9	2¼" x 18"	◺
		8	2¼" x 18"	◿
3	1 yd.	13	2¼" x 18"	◺
		15	2¼" x 18"	◿
4	1 yd.	10	2¼" x 18"	◺
		8	2¼" x 18"	◿
5	1 yd	10	2¼" x 18"	◺
		8	2¼" x 18"	◿
6	½ yd.	5	2¼" x 18"	◺
		4	2¼" x 18"	◿
7	1 yd.	12	2¼" x 18"	◺
		13	2¼" x 18"	◿
8	1 yd.	13	2¼" x 18"	◺
		10	2¼" x 18"	◿
9	1 yd.	11	2¼" x 18"	◺
		9	2¼" x 18"	◿
10	1 yd.	11	2¼" x 18"	◺
		8	2¼" x 18"	◿
11	1 fat qtr.	2	2¼" x 18"	◺
		2	2¼" x 18"	◿
12	½ yd.	8	2¼" x 18"	◺
		6	2¼" x 18"	◿
13	1 fat qtr.	2	2¼" x 18"	◺
		1	2¼" x 18"	◿
14	4¼ yds.	background *(see page 102)*		
	8¼ yds.	backing: 3 pcs. 31¼" x 93"		
1	¾ yd.*	binding: 16 strips 2" x 27"		

Note that both photographed quilts use the same quantities and types of blocks. Blocks Y and Z have identical outlines and similar colors, but their color sequences differ.

Added Yardage & Cutting for Bordered Version

Quilt Size: 88" x 88" **Star Size:** 84½" sq.
Requires: 4 Y, 4 Z blocks, **Border Width:** 1¾"
4 pieced borders

Added Border Yardage & Cutting

Color	Yardage	#Strips	Cut Size	Strip End
2	+ 1 fat qtr.	+ 1	4" x 18"	◿
		+ 1	4" x 18"	◺
3	+ 0	+ 1	2⅜" x 18"	◿
		+ 1	2⅜" x 18"	◺
6	+ 0	+ 1	4" x 18"	◿
		+ 1	4" x 18"	◺
7	+ 0	+ 1	4" x 18"	◿
		+ 1	4" x 18"	◺
8	+ 0	+ 1	4" x 18"	◿
		+ 1	4" x 18"	◺
9	+ 0	+ 1	4" x 18"	◿
		+ 1	4" x 18"	◺
10	+ 0	+ 1	4" x 18"	◺
		+ 1	4" x 18"	◿
11	+ 1 fat qtr.	+ 1	4" x 18"	◺
		+ 1	4" x 18"	◿
		+ 4 f	4 per 4¾"	⊠
12	+ 0	+ 1	4" x 18"	◺
		+ 1	4" x 18"	◿

8½ yds. backing: 3 pcs. 32½" x 96½"

**The backing yardage and dimensions are listed separately for the bordered and unbordered quilts. Do not add the backing yardages together. The binding yardage and strip quantity does not change for the bordered quilt.

Add the yardage and cutting listed above for the numbered fabrics to that in the chart at left if you plan to include the pieced border. Both versions are made using the same blocks, with the blocks placed differently.

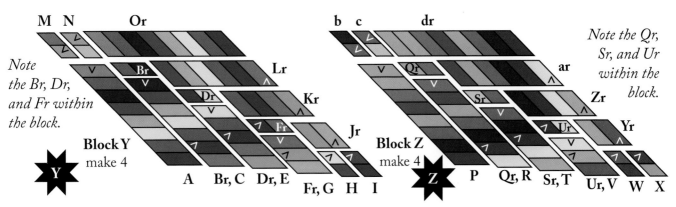

M N Or

Note the Br, Dr, and Fr within the block.

Br
Lr
Dr
Kr
Fr
Jr

Block Y make 4

A Br, C Dr, E Fr, G H I

b c dr

Qr
ar
Sr
Zr
Ur
Yr

Note the Qr, Sr, and Ur within the block.

Block Z make 4

P Qr, R Sr, T Ur, V W X

Strip Piecing Block Y

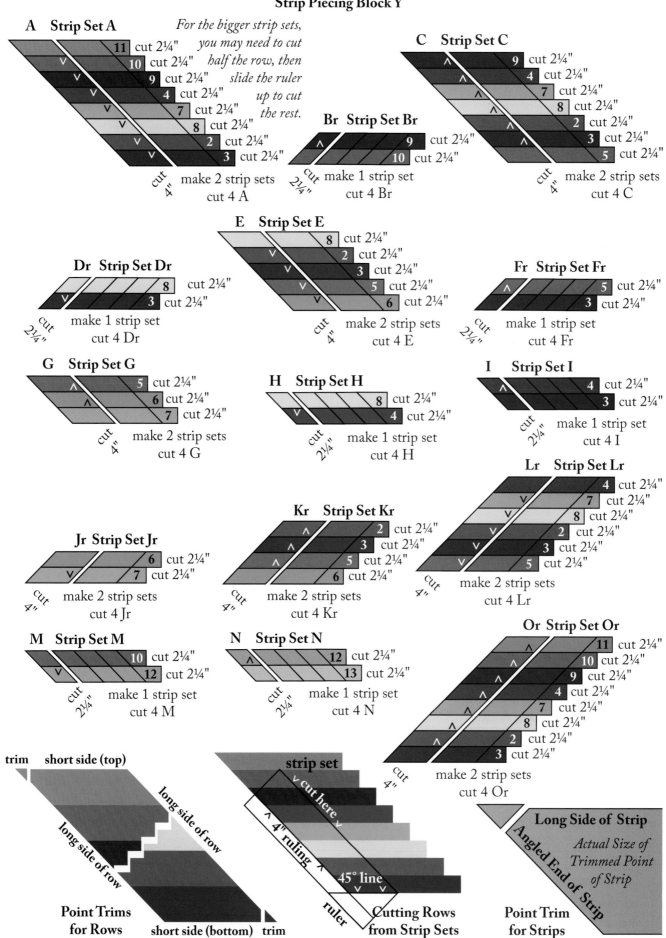

A Strip Set A

For the bigger strip sets, you may need to cut half the row, then slide the ruler up to cut the rest.

11 cut 2¼"
10 cut 2¼"
9 cut 2¼"
4 cut 2¼"
7 cut 2¼"
8 cut 2¼"
2 cut 2¼"
3 cut 2¼"
cut 4" make 2 strip sets
cut 4 A

Br Strip Set Br

9 cut 2¼"
10 cut 2¼"
cut 2¼" make 1 strip set
cut 4 Br

C Strip Set C

9 cut 2¼"
4 cut 2¼"
7 cut 2¼"
8 cut 2¼"
2 cut 2¼"
3 cut 2¼"
5 cut 2¼"
cut 4" make 2 strip sets
cut 4 C

Dr Strip Set Dr

8 cut 2¼"
3 cut 2¼"
cut 2¼" make 1 strip set
cut 4 Dr

E Strip Set E

8 cut 2¼"
2 cut 2¼"
3 cut 2¼"
5 cut 2¼"
6 cut 2¼"
cut 4" make 2 strip sets
cut 4 E

Fr Strip Set Fr

5 cut 2¼"
3 cut 2¼"
cut 2¼" make 1 strip set
cut 4 Fr

G Strip Set G

5 cut 2¼"
6 cut 2¼"
7 cut 2¼"
cut 4" make 2 strip sets
cut 4 G

H Strip Set H

8 cut 2¼"
4 cut 2¼"
cut 2¼" make 1 strip set
cut 4 H

I Strip Set I

4 cut 2¼"
3 cut 2¼"
cut 2¼" make 1 strip set
cut 4 I

Jr Strip Set Jr

6 cut 2¼"
7 cut 2¼"
cut 4" make 2 strip sets
cut 4 Jr

Kr Strip Set Kr

2 cut 2¼"
3 cut 2¼"
5 cut 2¼"
6 cut 2¼"
cut 4" make 2 strip sets
cut 4 Kr

Lr Strip Set Lr

4 cut 2¼"
7 cut 2¼"
8 cut 2¼"
2 cut 2¼"
3 cut 2¼"
5 cut 2¼"
cut 4" make 2 strip sets
cut 4 Lr

M Strip Set M

10 cut 2¼"
12 cut 2¼"
cut 2¼" make 1 strip set
cut 4 M

N Strip Set N

12 cut 2¼"
13 cut 2¼"
cut 2¼" make 1 strip set
cut 4 N

Or Strip Set Or

11 cut 2¼"
10 cut 2¼"
9 cut 2¼"
4 cut 2¼"
7 cut 2¼"
8 cut 2¼"
2 cut 2¼"
3 cut 2¼"
cut 4" make 2 strip sets
cut 4 Or

trim **short side (top)**

long side of row

long side of row

Point Trims for Rows

short side (bottom) trim

strip set

v cut here

4" ruling

45° line

ruler

Cutting Rows from Strip Sets

Long Side of Strip

Actual Size of Trimmed Point of Strip

Angled End of Strip

Point Trim for Strips

100

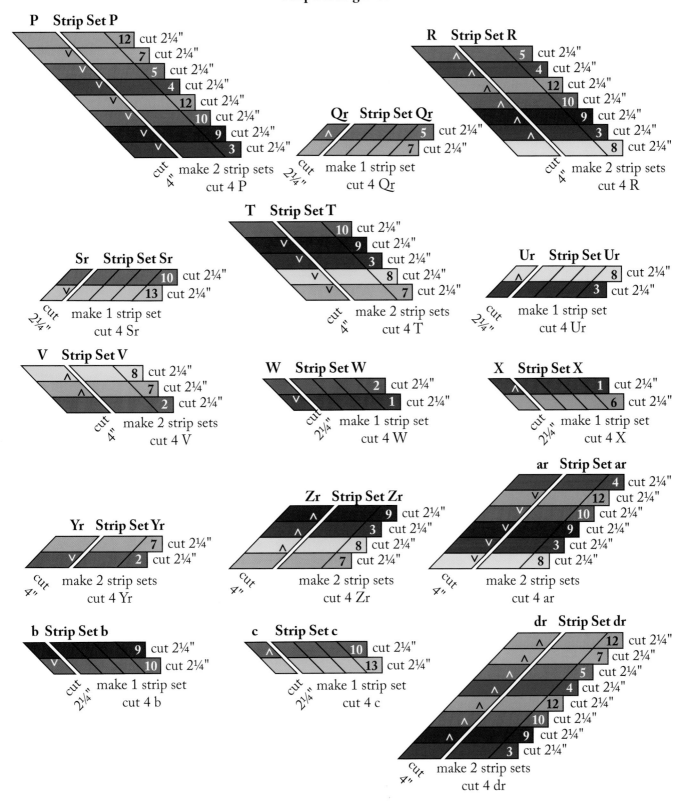

P Strip Set P

12 cut 2¼"
7 cut 2¼"
5 cut 2¼"
4 cut 2¼"
12 cut 2¼"
10 cut 2¼"
9 cut 2¼"
3 cut 2¼"
cut 4" make 2 strip sets
cut 4 P

Qr Strip Set Qr

5 cut 2¼"
7 cut 2¼"
cut 2¼" make 1 strip set
cut 4 Qr

R Strip Set R

5 cut 2¼"
4 cut 2¼"
12 cut 2¼"
10 cut 2¼"
9 cut 2¼"
3 cut 2¼"
8 cut 2¼"
cut 4" make 2 strip sets
cut 4 R

Sr Strip Set Sr

10 cut 2¼"
13 cut 2¼"
cut 2¼" make 1 strip set
cut 4 Sr

T Strip Set T

10 cut 2¼"
9 cut 2¼"
3 cut 2¼"
8 cut 2¼"
7 cut 2¼"
cut 4" make 2 strip sets
cut 4 T

Ur Strip Set Ur

8 cut 2¼"
3 cut 2¼"
cut 2¼" make 1 strip set
cut 4 Ur

V Strip Set V

8 cut 2¼"
7 cut 2¼"
2 cut 2¼"
cut 4" make 2 strip sets
cut 4 V

W Strip Set W

2 cut 2¼"
1 cut 2¼"
cut 2¼" make 1 strip set
cut 4 W

X Strip Set X

1 cut 2¼"
6 cut 2¼"
cut 2¼" make 1 strip set
cut 4 X

Yr Strip Set Yr

7 cut 2¼"
2 cut 2¼"
cut 4" make 2 strip sets
cut 4 Yr

Zr Strip Set Zr

9 cut 2¼"
3 cut 2¼"
8 cut 2¼"
7 cut 2¼"
cut 4" make 2 strip sets
cut 4 Zr

ar Strip Set ar

4 cut 2¼"
12 cut 2¼"
10 cut 2¼"
9 cut 2¼"
3 cut 2¼"
8 cut 2¼"
cut 4" make 2 strip sets
cut 4 ar

b Strip Set b

9 cut 2¼"
10 cut 2¼"
cut 2¼" make 1 strip set
cut 4 b

c Strip Set c

10 cut 2¼"
13 cut 2¼"
cut 2¼" make 1 strip set
cut 4 c

dr Strip Set dr

12 cut 2¼"
7 cut 2¼"
5 cut 2¼"
4 cut 2¼"
12 cut 2¼"
10 cut 2¼"
9 cut 2¼"
3 cut 2¼"
cut 4" make 2 strip sets
cut 4 dr

Making Strip Sets and Cutting Rows

Start by reading the glossary, "How to Make a Lone Star," and "Pattern Pointers" chapters on pages 7–22. You can cut all the strips before you sew any, or cut a little and sew a little, according to your preference.

Cut the strips for a strip set, cutting off the ends at a 45° angle, as indicated in the "strip end" column of the yardage chart. Trim the points to help you align patches for sewing. This is described on page 14 and shown on page 100. The point should be trimmed at a right angle to the angled end of the strip. Don't trim the point on the top strip of a regular strip set or the bottom strip of a reversed strip set. If you don't have my Point Trimmer tool, download a file to make one at judymartin.com/LSPT.cfm

Align the wide angle of one strip with the trimmed point of the neighboring strip. Pin and stitch strips together, pressing after each seam, following the "v" pressing arrows in the strip set diagrams. Continue pinning and stitching strips to each other to complete the strip set as shown. Trim a sliver off the angled end, if necessary, at a 45° angle.

Cut the strip set into rows, referring to the notation below the strip set diagram for the width of the rows. For example, for strip set A on page 100, cut A rows 4" wide. That is, lay the 4" ruling of your rotary cutting ruler over the angled end of the strip, align the 45° line with one of the long edges or a seamline within the strip set, and cut along the ruler's edge. Repeat, making a duplicate strip set if indicated, to cut the total number of rows listed below the strip set.

Continue making strip sets and cutting rows in this fashion. When you have all the rows needed for a block, trim both points of each row as shown on page 100.

Making Y Blocks

Lay out the rows for Block Y as shown in the block diagram on page 99. Pin and stitch rows together, pressing after each seam. The sewing order is as follows: Sew M to N; add Or. Sew Br to C, Dr to E, Fr to G, and H to I. Sew Jr to H-I. Sew Fr-G to Jr-H-I; add Kr. Sew Dr-E to the left side of this; add Lr to the top edge. Sew Br-C to the right side of A; add this to the left side of the block. Add M-N-Or to the top of the block to complete the Y block. Make 4 Y blocks.

Making Z Blocks

Lay out the rows for Block Z as shown in the block diagram on page 99. Pin and stitch rows together, pressing after each seam. The sewing order is as follows: Sew b to c; add dr. Sew Qr to R, Sr to T, Ur to V, and W to X. Sew Yr to W-X. Sew Ur-V to Yr-W-X; add Zr. Sew Sr-T to the left side of this; add ar to the top edge. Sew Qr-R to the right side of P; add this to the left side of the block. Add b-c-dr to the top to complete Z. Make 4 Z blocks.

Cutting Background Patches

Cut out the background patches shown below for your choice of a quilt with Y-seams or not. Refer to page 17 for tips on cutting patches larger than your rotary cutting ruler.

Assembling the Quilt

See the arrangements on page 104 and the photographs on pages 97 and 98; choose your favorite setting variation. Referring to your chosen arrangement and the appropriate assembly diagram below, stitch the blocks and patches together in numerical order. Press after each seam in the direction indicated by the arrows. Repeat to make 4 quarters of the quilt. Unless you are making the version with pieced borders and no Y-seams, join quarters to make 2 halves of the star; join halves to complete the quilt.

Making the Optional Pieced Border

Note that the pieced border is added to the quilt with no Y-seams when the quilt is still in quarters. See the pieced border diagram and strip sets on page 103.

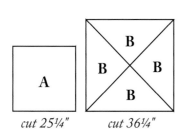

cut 25¼"   *cut 36¼"*

Background Patches (Y-Seams)
cut 4 A **25¼"** squares
cut 4 B triangles
from one **36¼"** square

OR

cut 25⅝"   *cut 18⅜"*

Background Patches (No Y-Seams)
cut 8 C from four **25⅝"** squares
cut 8 D triangles
from four **18⅜"** squares

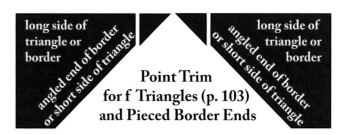

Point Trim
for f Triangles (p. 103)
and Pieced Border Ends

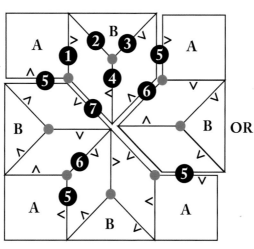

Quilt Assembly with Y-Seams

OR

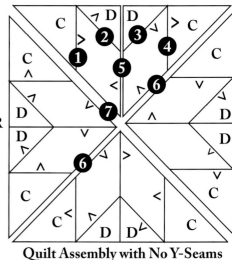

Quilt Assembly with No Y-Seams

Cut strips from folded fabric; you need just 1 strip and 1 reversed strip of each fabric #2, 3, and 6–12. Cut off strip ends through both layers to cut strips and their reverses at the same time. Join strips as shown below, pressing after each seam. Make 1 strip set e and 1 strip set er. Trim a sliver from the angled end at a precise 45° angle if that is necessary to even it. Cut 4 rows 2¼" wide from each strip set. You will need to slide the ruler to cut the full length of the row. Trim points at the green end of each ½-border row as shown on page 102.

Cut 4 f triangles from 1 square of 4¾". Trim the points as illustrated on page 102. Pin and stitch an f triangle between an e and an er ½-border row as shown below. This completes a pieced border. Make 4 pieced borders. If you are assembling your quilt without Y-seams, pin and stitch a border to each quarter of the quilt before joining quarters to make halves and joining halves to complete the quilt.

Finishing the Quilt

Chris Hulin made both of the Harvest Lone Star quilts just over 36" square. She machine quilted hers, and I hand quilted the one she gave me. We quilted in the ditch between rows in the diamond blocks and quilted parallel lines ¾" apart in the background squares and triangles. For the larger quilt in the pattern, you might want to quilt lines ⅞" apart (half the width of the narrowest strips and rows). If you are an experienced machine quilter or will be having your top quilted by one, you might choose a feathered motif or other pattern to fill the background. I show several suitable examples on pages 19–21. Bind the quilt as described on page 22.

Optional Lazy Diamonds Pieced Border

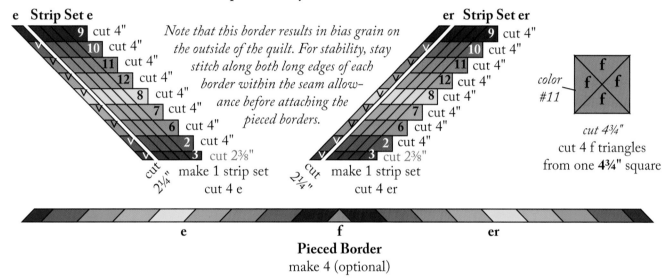

e Strip Set e

9 cut 4"
10 cut 4"
11 cut 4"
12 cut 4"
8 cut 4"
7 cut 4"
6 cut 4"
2 cut 4"
3 cut 2⅜"

cut 2¼"   make 1 strip set
cut 4 e

Note that this border results in bias grain on the outside of the quilt. For stability, stay stitch along both long edges of each border within the seam allowance before attaching the pieced borders.

er Strip Set er

9 cut 4"
10 cut 4"
11 cut 4"
12 cut 4"
8 cut 4"
7 cut 4"
6 cut 4"
2 cut 4"
3 cut 2⅜"

cut 2¼"   make 1 strip set
cut 4 er

color #11

f
f f
f

cut 4¾"
cut 4 f triangles
from one 4¾" square

e   f   er

Pieced Border
make 4 (optional)

Harvest Lone Star Variations
USING THE SAME BLOCK QUANTITIES AND YARDAGE

Arrangement 3: 4 Y blocks and 4 Z blocks; Y and Z blocks alternate and have green at the outer tips

Arrangement 4: 4 Y blocks and 4 Z blocks; Y and Z alternate; Y blocks have green at the outer tips, and Z blocks have orange at the outer tips.

Arrangement 5: 4 Y blocks and 4 Z blocks; a pair of Y blocks is at the top, another pair is at the bottom; pairs of Z blocks are at right and left sides of the star; Y have green a the outer tips; Z blocks have orange at the outer tips.

Arrangement 6: 4 Y blocks and 4 Z blocks; Y blocks have brown at the outer tips and Z blocks have green at the outer tips. A pair of Y blocks is at the top, and another pair is at the bottom; pairs of Z blocks are on the right and left sides.

Supernova

Supernova, 94½" x 94½". Designed and pieced by Judy Martin. Quilted by Lana Corcoran. The star is made from 32 diamond blocks that are arranged four per star arm. The star is tilted with a single star point centered on the top, bottom and two sides of the quilt. It is surrounded by 16 more blocks as well as 32 half blocks that form a starburst around the edges. Four black triangles and a narrow black border complete the quilt. Supernova's construction requires no Y-seams.

Supernova can be made without the 16 W-Y-Wr starburst units. Instead, use the usual orientation and background patches. It makes an 84½" square star in that case. Use the background yardage and patches for Star of Wonder on pages 120 and 122 if you prefer this option.

I designed this star to be changeable. You can change the look of the star substantially with the block placement and orientation. See the variations on pages 109–111.

Quilt Size: 94½" x 94½" **Star Size:** 91½" sq.
Requires: 16 W, 16 Wr, **Block Width:** 8¾"
8 X, 8 Xr, 24 Y, 8 Z blocks

Yardage and Cutting Chart

Color	Yardage	#Strips	Cut Size	Strip End
1	2 yds.	10	4" x 18"	
		4	4" x 18"	
		20	2¼" x 18"	
		8	2¼" x 18"	
2	2 yds.	30	2¼" x 18"	
		24	2¼" x 18"	
3	1 yd.	10	2¼" x 18"	
		10	2¼" x 18"	
4	1 yd.	12	2¼" x 18"	
		10	2¼" x 18"	
5	1 yd.	12	2¼" x 18"	
		12	2¼" x 18"	
6	1 yd.	10	2¼" x 18"	
		8	2¼" x 18"	
7	½ yd.	6	2¼" x 18"	
		8	2¼" x 18"	
8	½ yd.	6	2¼" x 18"	
		6	2¼" x 18"	
9	1 fat qtr.	6	2¼" x 18"	
10	1 yd.	18	2¼" x 18"	
		10	2¼" x 18"	
11	1 yd.	16	2¼" x 18"	
		12	2¼" x 18"	
12	1 yd.	14	2¼" x 18"	
		18	2¼" x 18"	
13	1½ yds.	28	2¼" x 18"	
		22	2¼" x 18"	
14	4 yds.	12	4" x 18"	
		12	4" x 18"	
		6	2¼" x 18"	
		6	2¼" x 18"	
		+ bkgd: 4 U	2 per 27⅝"	
		+ borders: 2 @ 2" x 95"		
			2 @ 2" x 92"	
	9¼ yds.	backing: 3 pcs. 34¾" x 103"		
2	¾ yd.	binding: 17 strips 2" x 27"		

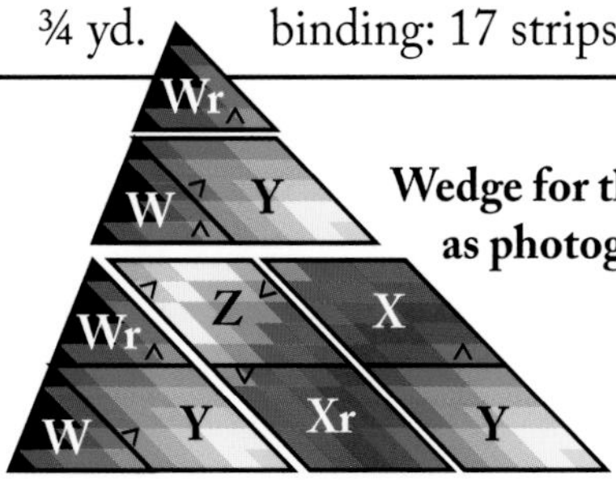

Wedge for the quilt as photographed

(Wedge diagram labels: Wr, W, Y, Wr, Z, X, W, Y, Xr, Y)

Making Strip Sets and Cutting Rows

Start by reading the glossary, "Pattern Pointers," and "How to Make a Lone Star" chapters on pages 7 – 22. Cut the strips for a strip set, cutting off one end as indicated in the "strip end" column of the yardage chart. If you folded the fabric, unfold it before you cut off the strip ends unless you are cutting X/Xr or W/Wr strips at the same time. Trimming the points of the strips as described on page 14 will help you align patches for sewing. Appropriate trims are shown at the bottom of page 107 for regular strips and reversed strips. The point should be trimmed at a right angle to the angled end of the strip. Don't trim the point on the top strip of a regular strip set or the bottom strip of a reversed strip set. If you don't have my Point Trimmer tool, download a file to make one at judymartin.com/LSPT.cfm

Lay out strips for a strip set as shown on the next 2 pages. Align the wide angle of one strip with the trimmed point of the neighboring strip. Pin and stitch the first strip to the second one. Add the third strip, and so on. Finger press and steam press after each seam, following the "v" pressing arrows in the strip set diagrams.

Continue pinning and stitching strips together to complete a strip set as shown. Measure your strip set E straight down the middle from the raw edge at the top to the raw edge at the bottom. It should measure 9¼". If it does not, correct your seams before proceeding.

When you have your seam allowance right, trim a sliver off the angled end of the strip set, if necessary, at a precise 45° angle. See the row cutting diagram on the bottom of page 107. Cut the strip sets into rows in the size listed below the strip set diagram. Rows will be 2¼" or 4" wide. That is, lay the 2¼" or 4" ruling of your rotary cutting ruler over the angled end of the strip and cut along the ruler's edge. Make multiple strip sets of each type, as indicated below the strip set diagram, to allow you to cut the number of rows needed.

Continue making strip sets and cutting rows in this fashion. When you have all the rows needed for a block, trim both points of each row as shown on page 107 for both regular and reversed rows.

Making Blocks

Lay out the rows for a block as shown in the block diagrams on page 107. Pin rows at both ends, aligning the point trim of one row with the wide angle of the other. Also pin at each joint. Strategies for matching joints are on page 15. Stitch all rows together, pressing after each seam. Referring to page 107, make 8 X, 8 Xr, 24 Y, and 8 Z blocks. Also make 16 W and 16 Wr blocks as shown on page 108.

Choose an arrangement from pages 105 and 109–111. Referring to your arrangement and the image at the left, arrange blocks for a wedge.

Strip Piecing Blocks X, Xr, Y, and Z

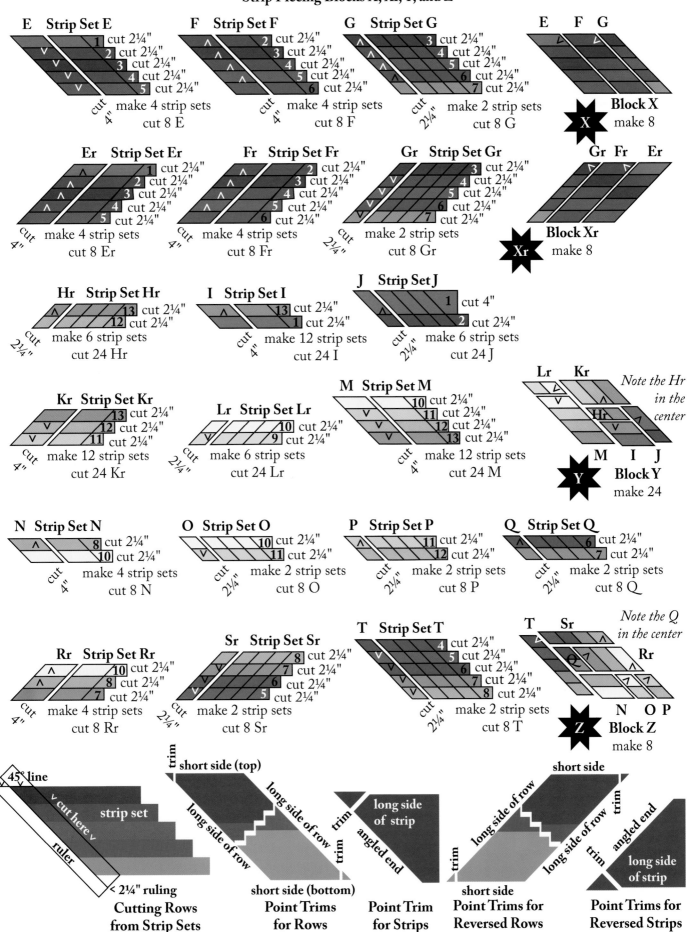

E Strip Set E
1 cut 2¼"
2 cut 2¼"
3 cut 2¼"
4 cut 2¼"
5 cut 2¼"
cut 4"
make 4 strip sets
cut 8 E

F Strip Set F
2 cut 2¼"
3 cut 2¼"
4 cut 2¼"
5 cut 2¼"
6 cut 2¼"
cut 4"
make 4 strip sets
cut 8 F

G Strip Set G
3 cut 2¼"
4 cut 2¼"
5 cut 2¼"
6 cut 2¼"
7 cut 2¼"
cut 2¼"
make 2 strip sets
cut 8 G

E F G
X **Block X**
make 8

Er Strip Set Er
1 cut 2¼"
2 cut 2¼"
3 cut 2¼"
4 cut 2¼"
5 cut 2¼"
cut 4"
make 4 strip sets
cut 8 Er

Fr Strip Set Fr
2 cut 2¼"
3 cut 2¼"
4 cut 2¼"
5 cut 2¼"
6 cut 2¼"
cut 4"
make 4 strip sets
cut 8 Fr

Gr Strip Set Gr
3 cut 2¼"
4 cut 2¼"
5 cut 2¼"
6 cut 2¼"
7 cut 2¼"
cut 2¼"
make 2 strip sets
cut 8 Gr

Gr Fr Er
Xr **Block Xr**
make 8

Hr Strip Set Hr
13 cut 2¼"
12 cut 2¼"
cut 2¼"
make 6 strip sets
cut 24 Hr

I Strip Set I
13 cut 2¼"
1 cut 2¼"
cut 4"
make 12 strip sets
cut 24 I

J Strip Set J
1 cut 4"
2 cut 2¼"
cut 2¼"
make 6 strip sets
cut 24 J

Note the Hr in the center
Lr Kr
Hr
Y **M I J Block Y**
make 24

Kr Strip Set Kr
13 cut 2¼"
12 cut 2¼"
11 cut 2¼"
cut 4"
make 12 strip sets
cut 24 Kr

Lr Strip Set Lr
10 cut 2¼"
9 cut 2¼"
cut 2¼"
make 6 strip sets
cut 24 Lr

M Strip Set M
10 cut 2¼"
11 cut 2¼"
12 cut 2¼"
13 cut 2¼"
cut 4"
make 12 strip sets
cut 24 M

N Strip Set N
8 cut 2¼"
10 cut 2¼"
cut 4"
make 4 strip sets
cut 8 N

O Strip Set O
10 cut 2¼"
11 cut 2¼"
cut 2¼"
make 2 strip sets
cut 8 O

P Strip Set P
11 cut 2¼"
12 cut 2¼"
cut 2¼"
make 2 strip sets
cut 8 P

Q Strip Set Q
6 cut 2¼"
7 cut 2¼"
cut 2¼"
make 2 strip sets
cut 8 Q

Rr Strip Set Rr
10 cut 2¼"
8 cut 2¼"
7 cut 2¼"
cut 4"
make 4 strip sets
cut 8 Rr

Sr Strip Set Sr
8 cut 2¼"
7 cut 2¼"
6 cut 2¼"
5 cut 2¼"
cut 2¼"
make 2 strip sets
cut 8 Sr

T Strip Set T
4 cut 2¼"
5 cut 2¼"
6 cut 2¼"
7 cut 2¼"
8 cut 2¼"
cut 2¼"
make 2 strip sets
cut 8 T

Note the Q in the center
T Sr
Q
Rr
Z **N O P Block Z**
make 8

45° line
strip set
ruler
< 2¼" ruling
Cutting Rows from Strip Sets

trim
short side (top)
long side of row
long side of row
short side (bottom)
Point Trims for Rows

trim
short side
long side of strip
angled end
Point Trim for Strips

trim
short side
long side of row
long side of row
short side
Point Trims for Reversed Rows

trim
short side
angled end
long side of strip
Point Trims for Reversed Strips

Strip Piecing Blocks W and Wr

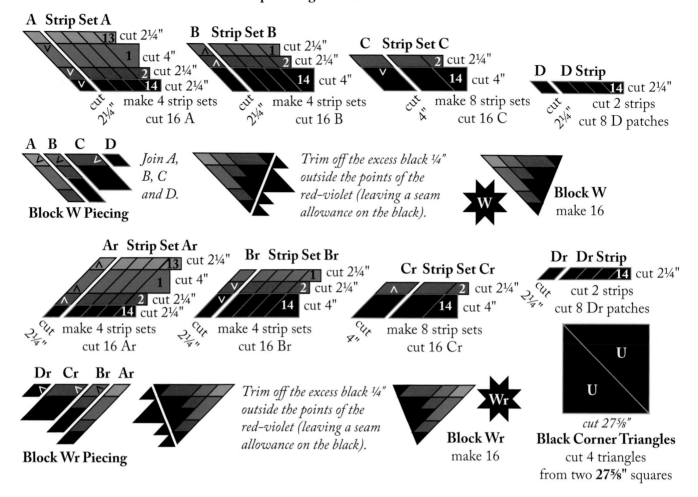

A Strip Set A
13 cut 2¼"
1 cut 4"
2 cut 2¼"
14 cut 2¼"
cut 2¼"
make 4 strip sets
cut 16 A

B Strip Set B
1 cut 2¼"
2 cut 2¼"
14 cut 4"
cut 2¼"
make 4 strip sets
cut 16 B

C Strip Set C
2 cut 2¼"
14 cut 4"
cut 4"
make 8 strip sets
cut 16 C

D D Strip
14 cut 2¼"
cut 2¼"
cut 2 strips
cut 8 D patches

A B C D
Block W Piecing

Join A, B, C and D.

Trim off the excess black ¼" outside the points of the red-violet (leaving a seam allowance on the black).

W   **Block W**
make 16

Ar Strip Set Ar
13 cut 2¼"
1 cut 4"
2 cut 2¼"
14 cut 2¼"
cut 2¼"
make 4 strip sets
cut 16 Ar

Br Strip Set Br
1 cut 2¼"
2 cut 2¼"
14 cut 4"
cut 2¼"
make 4 strip sets
cut 16 Br

Cr Strip Set Cr
2 cut 2¼"
14 cut 4"
cut 4"
make 8 strip sets
cut 16 Cr

Dr Dr Strip
14 cut 2¼"
cut 2¼"
cut 2 strips
cut 8 Dr patches

Dr Cr Br Ar
Block Wr Piecing

Trim off the excess black ¼" outside the points of the red-violet (leaving a seam allowance on the black).

Wr   **Block Wr**
make 16

U
U
cut 27⅝"
Black Corner Triangles
cut 4 triangles
from two **27⅝"** squares

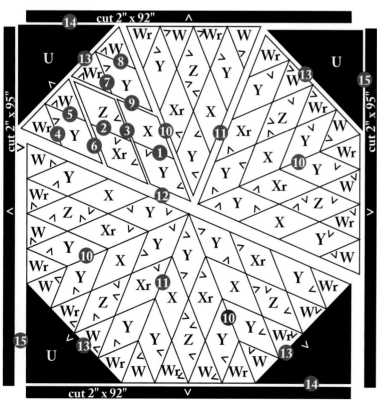

Quilt Assembly with No Y-Seams

Numbers indicate piecing sequence; arrows show pressing direction.

Assembling the Quilt

Play further with block placement and orientation, if you like. When you are sure of a favorite arrangement, sew blocks to make a wedge as shown on page 106. Note that your arrangement may turn the blocks or place them in different positions. Make 8 wedges.

Cut out 4 black U triangles as shown above. Referring to the assembly diagram at left, stitch together the wedges, 4 black U triangles, and black border strips in numerical order. Press the seams to one side after each seam, as indicated by the arrows in the quilt assembly diagram.

Finishing the Quilt

Lana Corcoran quilted in the ditch between the star and the background. She outline quilted the yellow through red areas in the quilt center. She quilted parallel lines in the red-violet, violet, and blue-violet areas and quilted concentric arcs in blue, blue-green and green areas. At the tips of the star, she quilted radiating lines. In the pieced area outside the Lone Star, she quilted curls to suggest wisps of smoke or flickering flames.

I bound my quilt in red-violet. You will find complete binding directions on page 22.

Supernova Setting Variations
USING THE SAME BLOCK QUANTITIES AND YARDAGE

Arrangement 2: quilt center: 8 Y blocks; middle ring: 8 X and 8 Xr blocks; outer tips: 8 Z blocks; starburst blocks: 16 Y, 16 W, and 16 Wr blocks.

Arrangement 3: quilt center: 8 Z blocks; middle ring: 8 X and 8 Xr blocks; outer tips: 8 Y blocks; starburst blocks: 16 Y, 16 W, and 16 Wr blocks.

Arrangement 4: quilt center: 8 Z blocks; middle ring: 16 Y blocks; outer tips: 8 Y blocks; starburst blocks: 8 X, 8 Xr, 16 W, and 16 Wr blocks.

Arrangement 5: quilt center: 8 Z blocks; middle ring: 8 X and 8 Xr blocks; outer tips: 8 Y blocks; starburst blocks: 16 Y, 16 W, and 16 Wr blocks.

Arrangement 6: quilt center: 8 Y blocks; middle ring: 8 X and 8 Xr blocks; outer tips: 8 Z blocks; starburst blocks: 16 Y, 16 W, and 16 Wr blocks.

Arrangement 7: quilt center: 8 Z blocks; middle ring: 16 Y blocks; outer tips: 8 Y blocks; starburst blocks: 8 X, 8 Xr, 16 W, and 16 Wr blocks.

Arrangement 8: quilt center: 8 Z blocks; middle ring: 8 X and 8 Xr blocks; outer tips: 8 Y blocks; starburst blocks: 16 Y, 16 W, and 16 Wr blocks.

Arrangement 9: quilt center: 8 Y blocks; middle ring: 8 X and 8 Xr blocks; outer tips: 8 Z blocks; starburst blocks: 16 Y, 16 W, and 16 Wr blocks.

Arrangement 10: quilt center: 8 Y blocks; middle ring: 8 X and 8 Xr blocks; outer tips: 8 Z blocks; starburst blocks: 16 Y, 16 W, and 16 Wr blocks.

Arrangement 11: quilt center: 4 X and 4 Xr blocks; middle ring: 16 Y blocks; outer tips: 8 Z blocks; starburst blocks: 4 X, 4 Xr, 8 Y, 16 W, and 16 Wr blocks.

Arrangement 12: quilt center: 8 Z blocks; middle ring: 4 X, 4 Xr, and 8 Y blocks; outer tips: 8 Y blocks; starburst blocks: 8 Y, 4 X, 4 Xr, 16 W, and 16 Wr blocks.

Arrangement 13: quilt center: 8 Z blocks; middle ring: 8 X and 8 Xr blocks; outer tips: 8 Y blocks; starburst blocks: 16 Y, 16 W, and 16 Wr blocks.

Simple Little Lone Stars

Any of the sets (block arrangements) in the book that list 8¾"-wide blocks will work with these blocks to make large quilts. See the Broken Star, Unfolding Star, and Grand Lone Star on pages 86–89. These show background patches, background yardages, and quilt assembly diagrams and instructions. The Radiant Star set is on pages 62–65, with background patches and yardage plus quilt assembly diagrams and instructions. These arrangements use blocks in sets of 4 and 4 reversed or sets of 8, 16, 24 or 32. You can use the yardages listed in this chapter and simply multiply by 2, 3, or 4. You can also mix and match these blocks to make Grand Lone Star quilts or any of the suggested sets for large quilts. For example, make 8 of one block and 16 of another for a Radiant Star; or make 8 of 2 different blocks and 16 of a third block for a Grand Lone Star.

Refer to the strip piecing diagrams on page 107 of the Supernova pattern, substituting the block quantities listed in this chapter. The instructions on page 106 will also be helpful. Read the basic Lone Star directions on pages 7–22 to learn tips for cutting, pinning, stitching, and pressing your quilt.

To make simple little Lone Stars just as they appear in this chapter, use the background patches and assembly diagrams and instructions that follow.

The border and binding yardages are for lengthwise borders and binding strips, and they may include extra for cutting any strips of the same value you might need for the quilt. Choose background patches to assemble your quilt with or without Y-seams. Cut them in the dimensions and quantities shown below.

Assemble your blocks, background, and borders in numerical order, as shown in the diagrams below. Press seam allowances to one side after each seam, as indicated by the arrows in the diagrams.

Quilt as desired. You will find a variety of Lone Star quilting ideas on pages 19–21. Photos throughout the book offer additional quilting ideas. Complete binding instructions are presented on page 22.

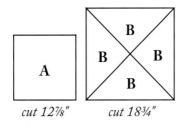 OR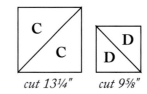

cut 12⅞" *cut 18¾"* *cut 13¼"* *cut 9⅝"*

Background Patches (Y-Seams)
cut 4 A squares **12⅞"**
cut 4 B triangles from one **18¾"** square

Background Patches (No Y-Seams)
cut 8 C triangles from four **13¼"** squares
cut 8 D triangles from four **9⅝"** squares

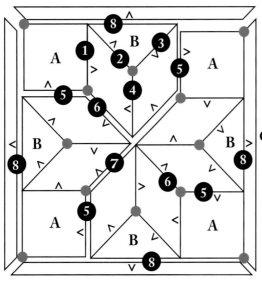 OR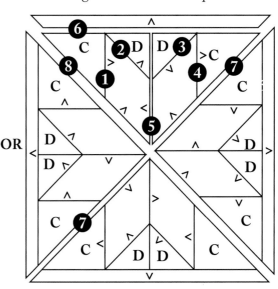

Quilt Assembly with Y-Seams   **Quilt Assembly with No Y-Seams**

112

Portland Lone Star

Quilt Size: 45¾" x 45¾" **Star Size:** 42¼" sq.
Requires: 8 Z blocks **Block Width:** 8¾"

Color		Yardage & Cutting			Strip End
		Yardage	#Strips	Cut Size	
12		1 fat qtr.	2	2¼" x 18"	
11		1 fat qtr.	4	2¼" x 18"	
10		½ yd.	6	2¼" x 18"	
			4	2¼" x 18"	
8		½ yd.	6	2¼" x 18"	
			6	2¼" x 18"	
7		leftovers*	4	2¼" x 18"	
			6	2¼" x 18"	
6		1 fat qtr.	4	2¼" x 18"	
			2	2¼" x 18"	
5		leftovers**	2	2¼" x 18"	
			2	2¼" x 18"	
4		1 fat qtr.	2	2¼" x 18"	
15		1¼ yds.	background *(see page 112)*		
7		1½ yds.*	borders: 4 @ 2¼" x 47"		
		3¼ yds.	backing: 2 pcs. 27¼" x 54"		
5		½ yd.**	binding: 14 strips 2" x 18"		

Strip sets, point trims, and instructions are on pages 106–107. Make strip sets in the following quantities: 4 N, 2 O, 2 P, 2 Q, 4 Rr, 2 Sr, and 2 T. Quilt assembly is on page 112.

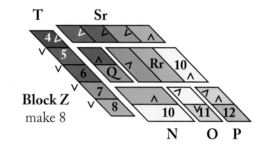

Block Z
make 8

Same Blocks, Different Orientation

Same Blocks, Different Orientation

Boston Lone Star

Quilt Size: 45¾" x 45¾" **Star Size:** 42¼" sq.
Requires: 8 X blocks **Block Width:** 8¾"

Color	Yardage	#Strips	Cut Size	Strip End
1	leftovers*	4	2¼" x 18"	◹
2	leftovers**	8	2¼" x 18"	(all)
3	½ yd.	10	2¼" x 18"	
4	½ yd.	10	2¼" x 18"	
5	½ yd.	10	2¼" x 18"	
6	1 fat qtr.	6	2¼" x 18"	
7	1 fat qtr.	2	2¼" x 18"	
15	1¼ yds.	background (see page 112)		
2	1½ yds.**	borders: 4 @ 2¼" x 47"		
	3¼ yds.	backing: 2 pcs. 27¼" x 54"		
1	½ yd.*	binding: 14 strips 2" x 18"		

Instructions for making strip sets and blocks are on page 106. Point trims and strip sets are shown on page 107. Make strip sets in the following quantities: 4 E, 4 F, and 2 G strip sets. The quilt assembly is presented on page 112.

E F G

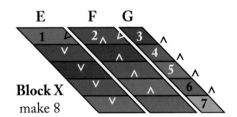

Block X
make 8

Same Blocks, Different Orientation

Same Blocks, Different Orientation

Chicago Lone Star

Quilt Size: 45¾" x 45¾" **Star Size:** 42¼" sq.
Requires: 4 X, 4 Xr **Block Width:** 8¾"

Yardage & Cutting

Color	Yardage	#Strips	Cut Size	Strip End
1	leftovers*	2	2¼" x 18"	
		2	2¼" x 18"	
2	leftovers**	4	2¼" x 18"	
		4	2¼" x 18"	
3	½ yd.	5	2¼" x 18"	
		5	2¼" x 18"	
4	½ yd.	5	2¼" x 18"	
		5	2¼" x 18"	
5	½ yd.	5	2¼" x 18"	
		5	2¼" x 18"	
6	1 fat qtr.	3	2¼" x 18"	
		3	2¼" x 18"	
7	1 fat qtr.	1	2¼" x 18"	
		1	2¼" x 18"	
15	1¼ yds.		background (see page 112)	
2	1½ yds.**		borders: 4 @ 2¼" x 47"	
	3¼ yds.		backing: 2 pcs. 27¼" x 54"	
1	½ yd.*		binding: 14 strips 2" x 18"	

See the strip sets on page 107. Make strip sets in the following quantities: 2 E, 2 F, 1 G, 2 Er, 2 Fr, and 1 Gr.

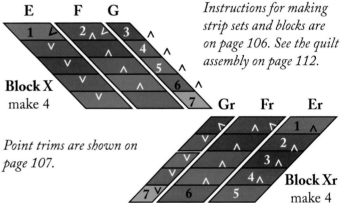

E F G

Block X
make 4

Point trims are shown on page 107.

Gr Fr Er

Block Xr
make 4

Instructions for making strip sets and blocks are on page 106. See the quilt assembly on page 112.

Same Blocks, Different Orientation

Same Blocks, Different Orientation

Albuquerque Lone Star

Quilt Size: 45¾" x 45¾"	**Star Size:** 42¼" sq.
Requires: 8 Y blocks	**Block Width:** 8¾"

Yardage & Cutting

Color	Yardage	#Strips	Cut Size	Strip End
9	1 fat qtr.	2	2¼" x 18"	
10	leftovers*	4	2¼" x 18"	
		2	2¼" x 18"	
11	1 fat qtr.	4	2¼" x 18"	
		4	2¼" x 18"	
12	½ yd.	4	2¼" x 18"	
		6	2¼" x 18"	
13	leftovers**	8	2¼" x 18"	
		6	2¼" x 18"	
1	1 fat qtr.	2	4" x 18"	
		4	2¼" x 18"	
2	1 fat qtr.	2	2¼" x 18"	
	1¼ yds.		background *(see page 112)*	
13	1½ yds.**		borders: 4 @ 2¼" x 47"	
	3¼ yds.		backing: 2 pcs. 27¼" x 54"	
10	1 yd.		binding: 14 strips 2" x 18"	

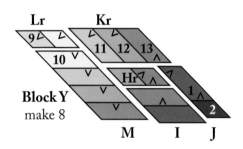

Lr
Kr
9
10
11 12 13
Hr
1
2
Block Y
make 8
M   I   J

Instructions for strip sets and blocks are on page 106.
Point trims and strip sets are shown on page 107.
Make strip sets in the following quantities: 2 Hr, 4 I, 2 J, 4 Kr, 2 Lr, and 4 M. Quilt assembly is on page 112.

Same Blocks, Different Orientation

Same Blocks, Different Orientation

Midnight Lone Star

Color		Yardage	#Strips	Cut Size	Strip End
2	⬛	1 fat qtr.	4	2¼" x 18"	
			2	2¼" x 18"	
3	⬛	leftovers*	4	2¼" x 18"	
			4	2¼" x 18"	
4	⬛	½ yd.	4	2¼" x 18"	
			6	2¼" x 18"	
5	⬜	1 yd.	10	2¼" x 18"	
			8	2¼" x 18"	
6	⬜	1 fat qtr.	2	4" x 18"	
			4	2¼" x 18"	
1	⬛	1¼ yds.	bkgd. 4 A, 4 B or 8 C, 8 D		
			(see page 118)		
		3 yds.	backing: 2 pcs. 25⅝" x 50¾"		
3	⬛	1 yd.*	binding: 13 strips 2" x 18"		

Quilt Size: 42¼" x 42¼" **Star Size:** 42¼" sq.
Requires: 8 Y blocks **Block Width:** 8¾"

Yardage & Cutting

Midnight Lone Star, 42¼" x 42¼", was made from 8 Supernova Y blocks that were recolored. Designed and pieced by Judy Martin. Quilted by Lana Corcoran. The quilt is made from 8 diamond blocks in an 8¾" finished width. They are arranged to form a Lone Star that you can make with or without Y-seamed background patches.

I fussy cut the 8 diamonds in the quilt center. My yardage and directions substitute fabric #5 for the fussy-cut diamonds to allow you to strip piece the blocks in their entirety. If you want to fussy cut, buy enough yardage for 8 repeats of the motif you will be featuring. You will need only 1 fat quarter of fabric #5, as you will be cutting 2 fewer strips. You will need to cut the last 2 strips of fabric #2 into 2¼" wide diamonds. Instead of making 2 Lr strip sets, sew 8 pairs of diamonds (one fussy cut and one cut from fabric #2) to replace Lr at the tip of the block.

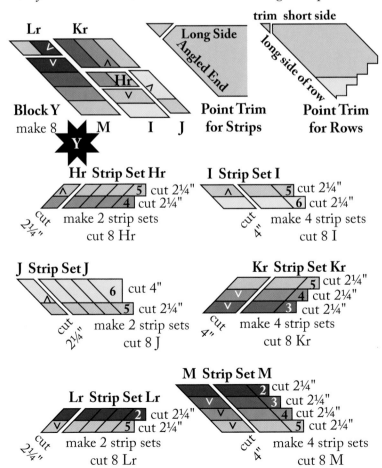

Strip Set and Block Construction

Review pages 7–22. Cut strips for a strip set. Cut off one end of each strip at a 45° angle, as shown in the yardage chart. Trim points of strips. If you don't have a Point Trimmer, download a file at judymartin.com/LSPT.cfm to make one. It will help you align strips and rows for sewing.

Join strips to make a strip set as shown at left, pressing in the direction of the arrows. If necessary, trim a sliver off the angled end of the strip set at a 45° angle. See row cutting on pages 14–15. Lay the listed ruler line on the angled end of the strip, align the 45° line with one long edge, and cut along the ruler's edge to make a row. Cut rows in the sizes and quantities listed. Trim points of rows as shown at left. See the block diagram at left. Sew Lr to M. Sew Hr to I; add J; add Kr. Finally, sew Lr-M to Hr-I-J-Kr to make a block. Press seams as indicated. Make 8 Y blocks.

Quilt Assembly

Cut out 4 A and 4 B or 8 C and 8 D background patches as shown below. Arrange blocks and background patches following the appropriate quilt assembly diagram on this page. Turn the blocks to match the photograph or one of the variations shown below.

Sew the blocks and background patches together in numerical order to make quarters of stars, pressing in the direction of the arrows. Join quarters to make half stars. Join halves to complete the quilt top.

Lana quilted a rope motif in the concentric rings of the star. She repeated this motif in concentric squares (interrupted by the star) in the background.

Read the binding instructions on page 22. Trim the batting and backing even with the quilt top. Sew binding strips together to make 1 long strip, and bind to finish.

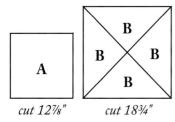

cut 12⅞"   *cut 18¾"*

Background Patches (Y-Seams)
cut 4 A squares **12⅞"**
cut 4 B triangles from one **18¾"** square

OR

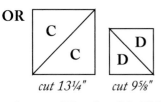

cut 13¼"   *cut 9⅝"*

Background Patches (No Y-Seams)
cut 8 C triangles from four **13¼"** squares
cut 8 D triangles from four **9⅝"** squares

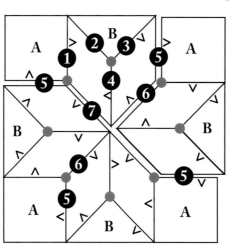

Quilt Assembly with Y-Seams

OR

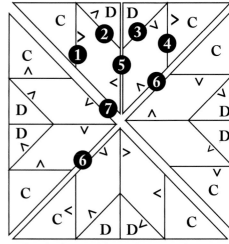

Quilt Assembly with No Y-Seams

Midnight Lone Star Setting Variations
USING THE SAME BLOCK QUANTITIES AND YARDAGE

Arrangement 2: 8 Y blocks with all blocks turned 180° from the blocks in the photographed quilt.

Arrangement 3: 8 Y blocks with 4 blocks turned as in the block at left and 4 blocks arranged like the quilt in the photo.

118

Star of Wonder

Star of Wonder, 90½" x 90½". Designed and pieced by Judy Martin. Quilted by Lana Corcoran. The quilt is made from 32 blocks in an 8¾" finished width. The quilt requires 8 each of blocks X, Xr (reversed), Y, and Z. They are arranged 4 to a star arm to form an 84½" square Lone Star.

This quilt will have you thinking about Lone Stars in a whole new way. I divided the 8 arms of the star into blocks of 4 types, with each block having two different tips. This allows you to achieve completely different looks for your Lone Star simply with the rotation and placement of the blocks. I show 13 versions of the quilt that use the same block quantities and yardage. Play with block placement before you assemble the quilt to come up with even more. Photograph the arrangements as you play to review what you have done and choose your favorite one to sew. It's also a good idea to photograph your star to check for placement errors before you quilt.

Color	Yardage	#Strips	Cut Size	Strip End
1 ■	1½ yds.	2	4¼" x 18"	
		2	4¼" x 18"	
		4	3" x 18"	
		4	3" x 18"	
		18	1¾" x 18"	
		4	1¾" x 18"	
2 ■	1½ yds.	4	4¼" x 18"	
		4	4¼" x 18"	
		4	3" x 18"	
		4	3" x 18"	
		13	1¾" x 18"	
		2	1¾" x 18"	
3 ■	1 yd.	2	4¼" x 18"	
		2	4¼" x 18"	
		6	3" x 18"	
		4	3" x 18"	
		13	1¾" x 18"	
4 ■	1 yd.	6	3" x 18"	
		2	3" x 18"	
		16	1¾" x 18"	
		2	1¾" x 18"	
5 ■	1 yd	4	3" x 18"	
		2	3" x 18"	
		15	1¾" x 18"	
6 ■	1 yd.	8	3" x 18"	
		4	3" x 18"	
		18	1¾" x 18"	
7 ■	1 yd.	2	4¼" x 18"	
		2	4¼" x 18"	
		6	3" x 18"	
		4	3" x 18"	
		11	1¾" x 18"	
8 □	1 yd.	2	4¼" x 18"	
		2	4¼" x 18"	
		4	3" x 18"	
		4	3" x 18"	
		12	1¾" x 18"	
9 □	½ yd.	2	3" x 18"	
		15	1¾" x 18"	
		2	1¾" x 18"	
10 ■	1 yd.	26	1¾" x 18"	

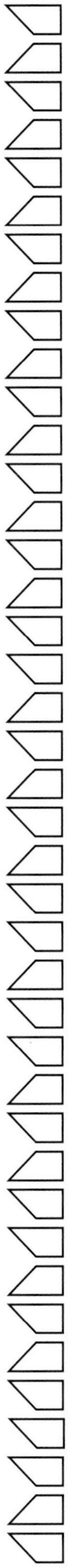

Quilt Size: 90½" x 90½" **Star Size:** 84½" sq.
Requires: 8 X, 8 Xr, **Block Width:** 8¾"
8 Y, 8 Z blocks

Yardage & Cutting

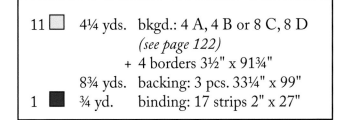

11 □	4¼ yds.	bkgd.: 4 A, 4 B or 8 C, 8 D *(see page 122)*	
		+ 4 borders 3½" x 91¾"	
	8¾ yds.	backing: 3 pcs. 33¼" x 99"	
1 ■	¾ yd.	binding: 17 strips 2" x 27"	

Making Strip Sets and Cutting Rows

Start by reading the glossary, "Pattern Pointers," and "How to Make a Lone Star" chapters on pages 7–22. Note that this quilt has long bias edges on the rows. I suggest blocking the blocks to an outline, as I describe on page 12.

Cut the strips for a strip set, cutting off one end as indicated in the "strip end" column of the yardage chart. If you folded the fabric, unfold it before you cut off the strip ends unless you are cutting X and Xr strips at the same time. Trimming the points of the strips as described on page 14 will help you align strips for sewing. Appropriate trims are shown on page 121 for regular strips and on page 122 for reversed strips. The point should be trimmed at a right angle to the angled end of the strip. Don't trim the point on the top strip of a regular strip set or the bottom strip of a reversed strip set. If you don't have my Point Trimmer tool, download a file to make one at judymartin.com/LSPT.cfm

Lay out strips for a strip set A as shown on the next page. Align the wide angle of the first strip with the trimmed point of the second strip. Finger press and steam press the seam, following the "v" pressing arrows in the strip set diagrams.

Pin and stitch subsequent strips in a similar fashion, finger pressing and steam pressing after each seam. Continue adding strips until the strip set is complete. Measure your strip set A down the middle from the raw edge at the top to the raw edge at the bottom. It should measure 9¼". If it does not, correct your seams before proceeding.

When you have your seam allowance right, trim a sliver off the angled end of the strip set, if necessary, at a precise 45° angle. Read about cutting rows from strip sets on pages 14–15. Cut the strip sets for blocks X, Xr, and most of Y and Z into rows 1¾" wide. That is, lay the 1¾" ruling of your rotary cutting ruler over the angled end of the strip and cut along the ruler's edge. Make a duplicate strip set to allow you to cut 4 more rows like the first 4. The exceptions in the Y and Z blocks are I, N, and U. For I and U strip sets and the N strip, cut rows in the same manner, but with a width of 3". You will need 3 strip sets alike for I and 3 strip sets alike for U; you will need 3 strips for N.

Continue making strip sets and cutting rows in this fashion. When you have all the rows needed for a block, trim both points of each row as shown on page 122 for both regular and reversed rows.

Strip Piecing Block X

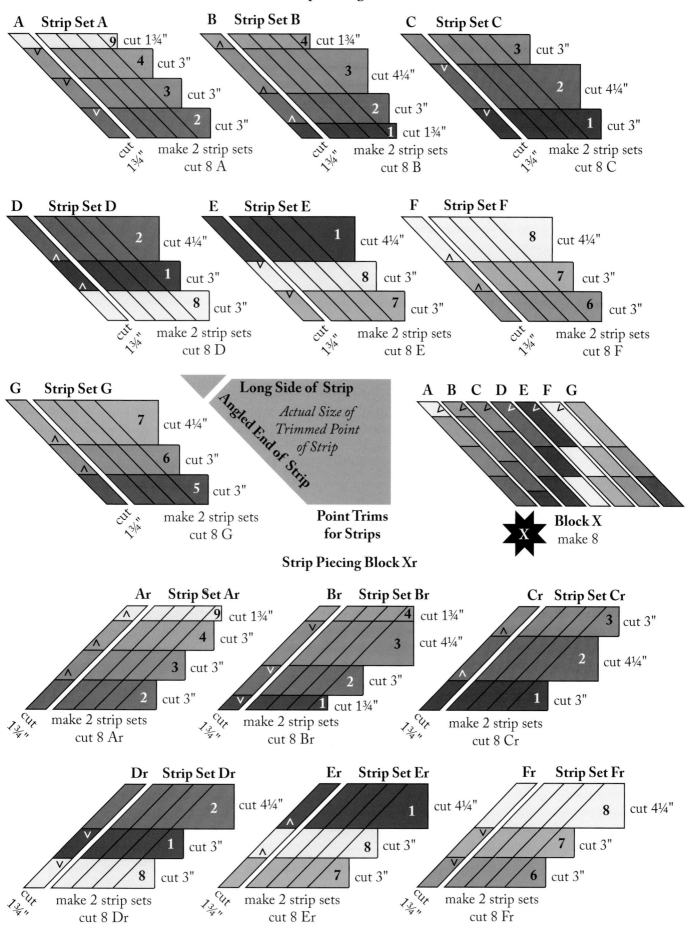

A Strip Set A
9 cut 1¾"
4 cut 3"
3 cut 3"
2 cut 3"
cut 1¾"
make 2 strip sets
cut 8 A

B Strip Set B
4 cut 1¾"
3 cut 4¼"
2 cut 3"
1 cut 1¾"
cut 1¾"
make 2 strip sets
cut 8 B

C Strip Set C
3 cut 3"
2 cut 4¼"
1 cut 3"
cut 1¾"
make 2 strip sets
cut 8 C

D Strip Set D
2 cut 4¼"
1 cut 3"
8 cut 3"
cut 1¾"
make 2 strip sets
cut 8 D

E Strip Set E
1 cut 4¼"
8 cut 3"
7 cut 3"
cut 1¾"
make 2 strip sets
cut 8 E

F Strip Set F
8 cut 4¼"
7 cut 3"
6 cut 3"
cut 1¾"
make 2 strip sets
cut 8 F

G Strip Set G
7 cut 4¼"
6 cut 3"
5 cut 3"
cut 1¾"
make 2 strip sets
cut 8 G

Long Side of Strip
Angled End of Strip
Actual Size of Trimmed Point of Strip
Point Trims for Strips

A B C D E F G
Block X make 8

Strip Piecing Block Xr

Ar Strip Set Ar
9 cut 1¾"
4 cut 3"
3 cut 3"
2 cut 3"
cut 1¾"
make 2 strip sets
cut 8 Ar

Br Strip Set Br
4 cut 1¾"
3 cut 4¼"
2 cut 3"
1 cut 1¾"
cut 1¾"
make 2 strip sets
cut 8 Br

Cr Strip Set Cr
3 cut 3"
2 cut 4¼"
1 cut 3"
cut 1¾"
make 2 strip sets
cut 8 Cr

Dr Strip Set Dr
2 cut 4¼"
1 cut 3"
8 cut 3"
cut 1¾"
make 2 strip sets
cut 8 Dr

Er Strip Set Er
1 cut 4¼"
8 cut 3"
7 cut 3"
cut 1¾"
make 2 strip sets
cut 8 Er

Fr Strip Set Fr
8 cut 4¼"
7 cut 3"
6 cut 3"
cut 1¾"
make 2 strip sets
cut 8 Fr

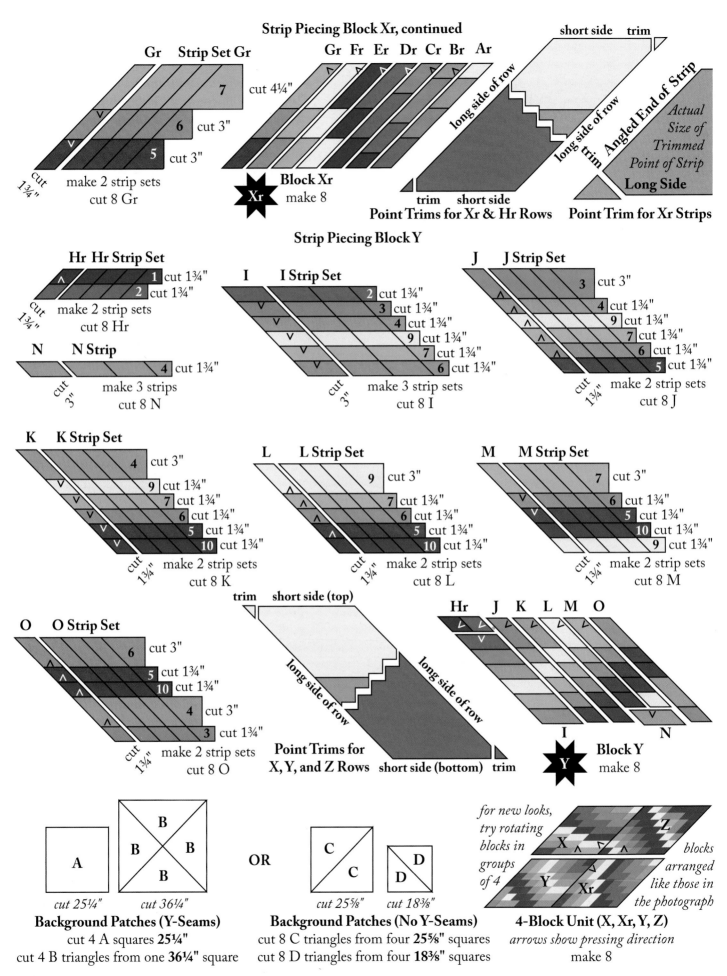

Strip Piecing Block Xr, continued

Gr **Strip Set Gr**

7
6 cut 3"
5 cut 3"

cut 1¾"
make 2 strip sets
cut 8 Gr

Gr Fr Er Dr Cr Br Ar

cut 4¼"

Block Xr
Xr make 8

short side · trim

long side of row

long side of row

trim

Angled End of Strip

Actual Size of Trimmed Point of Strip

Long Side

trim · short side

Point Trims for Xr & Hr Rows

Point Trim for Xr Strips

Strip Piecing Block Y

Hr **Hr Strip Set**

1 cut 1¾"
2 cut 1¾"

cut 1¾"
make 2 strip sets
cut 8 Hr

N **N Strip**

4 cut 1¾"

cut 3"
make 3 strips
cut 8 N

I **I Strip Set**

2 cut 1¾"
3 cut 1¾"
4 cut 1¾"
9 cut 1¾"
7 cut 1¾"
6 cut 1¾"

cut 3"
make 3 strip sets
cut 8 I

J **J Strip Set**

3 cut 3"
4 cut 1¾"
9 cut 1¾"
7 cut 1¾"
6 cut 1¾"
5 cut 1¾"

cut 1¾"
make 2 strip sets
cut 8 J

K **K Strip Set**

4 cut 3"
9 cut 1¾"
7 cut 1¾"
6 cut 1¾"
5 cut 1¾"
10 cut 1¾"

cut 1¾"
make 2 strip sets
cut 8 K

L **L Strip Set**

9 cut 3"
7 cut 1¾"
6 cut 1¾"
5 cut 1¾"
10 cut 1¾"

cut 1¾"
make 2 strip sets
cut 8 L

M **M Strip Set**

7 cut 3"
6 cut 1¾"
5 cut 1¾"
10 cut 1¾"
9 cut 1¾"

cut 1¾"
make 2 strip sets
cut 8 M

O **O Strip Set**

6 cut 3"
5 cut 1¾"
10 cut 1¾"
4 cut 3"
3 cut 1¾"

cut 1¾"
make 2 strip sets
cut 8 O

trim · short side (top)

long side of row

long side of row

Point Trims for X, Y, and Z Rows
short side (bottom) · trim

Hr J K L M O

I

Block Y
Y make 8

N

Background Patches (Y-Seams)

A

B
B B
B

cut 25¼"   cut 36¼"

cut 4 A squares **25¼"**
cut 4 B triangles from one **36¼"** square

OR

C
C

cut 25⅝"

D
D

cut 18⅜"

Background Patches (No Y-Seams)

cut 8 C triangles from four **25⅝"** squares
cut 8 D triangles from four **18⅜"** squares

for new looks, try rotating blocks in groups of 4

X   Z

Y   Xr

blocks arranged like those in the photograph

4-Block Unit (X, Xr, Y, Z)
arrows show pressing direction
make 8

Strip Piecing Block Z

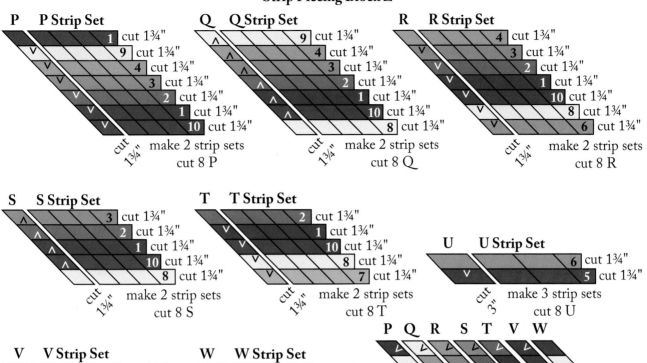

P — P Strip Set
1 cut 1¾"
9 cut 1¾"
4 cut 1¾"
3 cut 1¾"
2 cut 1¾"
1 cut 1¾"
10 cut 1¾"
cut 1¾"
make 2 strip sets
cut 8 P

Q — Q Strip Set
9 cut 1¾"
4 cut 1¾"
3 cut 1¾"
2 cut 1¾"
1 cut 1¾"
10 cut 1¾"
8 cut 1¾"
cut 1¾"
make 2 strip sets
cut 8 Q

R — R Strip Set
4 cut 1¾"
3 cut 1¾"
2 cut 1¾"
1 cut 1¾"
10 cut 1¾"
8 cut 1¾"
6 cut 1¾"
cut 1¾"
make 2 strip sets
cut 8 R

S — S Strip Set
3 cut 1¾"
2 cut 1¾"
1 cut 1¾"
10 cut 1¾"
8 cut 1¾"
cut 1¾"
make 2 strip sets
cut 8 S

T — T Strip Set
2 cut 1¾"
1 cut 1¾"
10 cut 1¾"
8 cut 1¾"
7 cut 1¾"
cut 1¾"
make 2 strip sets
cut 8 T

U — U Strip Set
6 cut 1¾"
5 cut 1¾"
cut 3"
make 3 strip sets
cut 8 U

V — V Strip Set
1 cut 1¾"
10 cut 1¾"
8 cut 1¾"
6 cut 3"
5 cut 1¾"
10 cut 1¾"
cut 1¾"
make 2 strip sets
cut 8 V

W — W Strip Set
10 cut 1¾"
8 cut 1¾"
6 cut 1¾"
5 cut 3"
10 cut 1¾"
1 cut 1¾"
cut 1¾"
make 2 strip sets
cut 8 W

P Q R S T V W

U

Z Block Z
make 8

Making Blocks

Lay out the rows for a block as shown in the block diagrams above or on pages 121 and 122. Pin rows at both ends, aligning the point trim of one row with the wide angle of the other. Also pin at each joint. Strategies for matching joints are on page 15. Stitch all rows together, pressing after each seam. Make 8 blocks of each type.

Assembling the Quilt

Cut out the background patches shown on page 122. Choose patches for use with or without Y-seams.

View the setting variations on the next 3 pages. Arrange blocks as shown in the photograph on page 119 or the setting variation of your choice on pages 124–126. Make 8 4-block units as shown at the bottom of page 122. Make sure your block orientation matches your quilt setting. Referring to the appropriate assembly diagram at left, stitch together the blocks and background patches in numerical order. Press the seams to one side after each seam, as indicated by the arrows in the quilt assembly diagram. The red lines in the quilt assembly diagrams indicate the last seam of each 4-block unit.

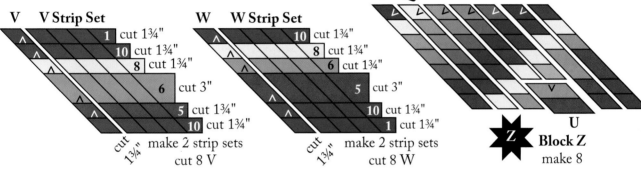

Quilt Assembly with Y-Seams OR **Quilt Assembly with No Y-Seams**

Star of Wonder Setting Variations
USING THE SAME BLOCK QUANTITIES AND YARDAGE

Arrangement 2: 8 Y blocks in the star center; 8 X and 8 Xr blocks in the next ring; and 8 Z blocks at the outer tips.

Arrangement 3: 8 Y blocks in the star center; 8 X and 8 Xr blocks in the next ring; and 8 Z blocks at the outer tips.

Arrangement 4: 8 Z blocks in the star center; 8 X and 8 Xr blocks in the next ring; and 8 Y blocks at the outer tips.

Arrangement 5: 8 X blocks in the star center; 8 Y and 8 Z blocks in the next ring; and 8 Xr blocks at the outer tips.

Finishing the Quilt

Lana Corcoran quilted in the ditch between the star and the background. She quilted arcs, feathers, feathered hearts, and diagonal lines in the background squares and triangles.

She quilted a half-feather serpentine motif in the plain outer border. You can find other suitable quilting ideas in any of the large Lone Stars photographed in the book. Binding directions are on page 22.

Arrangement 6: 8 Z blocks in the star center; 8 X and 8 Xr blocks in the next ring; and 8 Y blocks at the outer tips.

Arrangement 7: 4X and 4 Xr blocks in the star center; 8 Y and 8 Z blocks in the next ring; and 4 X and 4 Xr blocks at the outer tips.

Arrangement 8: 4X and 4 Xr blocks in the star center; 8 Y and 8 Z blocks in the next ring; and 4 X and 4 Xr blocks at the outer tips.

Arrangement 9: 4X and 4 Xr blocks in the star center; 8 Y and 8 Z blocks in the next ring; and 4 X and 4 Xr blocks at the outer tips.

Arrangement 10: 8 Z blocks in the star center; 8 X and 8 Xr blocks in the next ring; and 8 Y blocks at the outer tips.

Arrangement 11: 8 Y blocks in the star center; 8 X and 8 Xr blocks in the next ring; and 8 Z blocks at the outer tips.

Arrangement 12: 8 Y blocks in the star center; 8 X and 8 Xr blocks in the next ring; and 8 Z blocks at the outer tips.

Arrangement 13: 8 Z blocks in the star center; 8 X and 8 Xr blocks in the next ring; and 8 Y blocks at the outer tips.

More Simple Little Lone Stars

These patterns use the blocks and strip sets from the Star of Wonder pattern. Refer to the strip piecing diagrams on pages 121–123, substituting the block quantities listed in this chapter. The instructions on pages 120–123 will also be helpful. Read the basic Lone Star information on pages 7–22 to learn tips for cutting, pinning, stitching, and pressing your quilt.

To make simple little Lone Stars just as they appear in this chapter, use the background patches and assembly diagrams and instructions that follow.

The border and binding yardages are for lengthwise borders and binding strips, and they may include extra for cutting any strips of the same fabric you might need for the quilt. Choose background patches to assemble your quilt with or without Y-seams. Cut them in the dimensions and quantities shown below.

Assemble your blocks, background, and borders in numerical order, as shown in the diagrams below. Press seam allowances to one side after each seam, as indicated by the arrows in the diagrams.

Quilt as desired. You will find a variety of Lone Star quilting ideas on pages 19–21. Photos throughout the book offer additional quilting ideas. Complete binding instructions are presented on page 22.

If you are feeling adventurous, any of the sets (block arrangements) in the book that list 8¾"-wide blocks will work with these blocks to make large quilts. See the Unfolding Star, Broken Star, 4-Lone Star and Grand Lone Star sets on pages 86–89. These show background patches, background yardages, and quilt assembly diagrams and instructions. The Radiant Star set is on pages 62–66, with background patches and yardage plus quilt assembly diagrams and instructions. All of the arrangements I mentioned use blocks in sets of 4 and 4 reversed or sets of 8, 16, 24 or 32. You can use the yardages listed in this chapter and simply multiply by 2, 3, or 4. You can also mix and match the X, Xr, Y, and Z blocks to make large quilts. For example, make 8 Y blocks and 16 Z blocks for a Radiant Star, or make 8 Y and 24 Z blocks for a Broken Star.

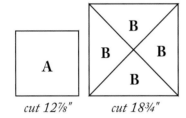

cut 12⅞" *cut 18¾"*

Background Patches (Y-Seams)
cut 4 A squares **12⅞"**
cut 4 B triangles from one **18¾"** square

OR

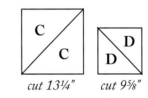

cut 13¼" *cut 9⅝"*

Background Patches (No Y-Seams)
cut 8 C triangles from four **13¼"** squares
cut 8 D triangles from four **9⅝"** squares

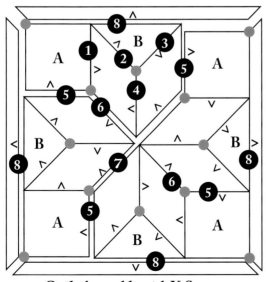

Quilt Assembly with Y-Seams

OR

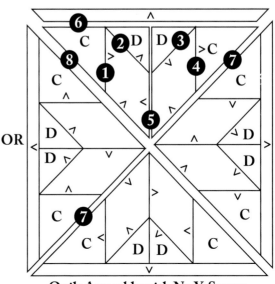

Quilt Assembly with No Y-Seams

Stockholm Lone Star

Quilt Size: 47¼" x 47¼" **Star Size:** 42¼" sq.
Requires: 8 X blocks **Block Width:** 8¾"

Yardage & Cutting

Color	Yardage	#Strips	Cut Size	Strip End
1 ■	leftovers*	2	4¼" x 18"	⟋
		4	3" x 18"	(all)
		2	1¾" x 18"	
2 ■	½ yd.	4	4¼" x 18"	
		4	3" x 18"	
3 ■	leftovers**	2	4¼" x 18"	
		4	3" x 18"	
4 □	1 fat qtr.	2	3" x 18"	
		2	1¾" x 18"	
5 ■	1 fat qtr.	2	3" x 18"	
6 ■	1 fat qtr.	4	3" x 18"	
7 □	½ yd.	2	4¼" x 18"	
		4	3" x 18"	
8 □	½ yd.	2	4¼" x 18"	
		4	3" x 18"	
9 □	1 fat qtr.	2	1¾" x 18"	
10/11 ■/□	1¼ yds.		background (see pg. 127)	
3 ■	1½ yds.**		4 borders cut 3" x 48½"	
	3⅜ yds.		backing: 2 pcs. 28" x 56"	
1 ■	1 yd.*		binding: 7 strips 2" x 36"	

Instructions for making strip sets and blocks are on pages 120–123. Point trims and strip sets are shown there, as well. Make 2 each of strip sets A–G. The quilt assembly is presented on page 127.

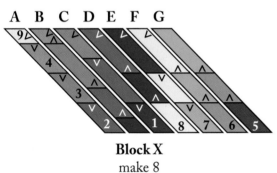

Block X
make 8

Same Blocks, Different Orientation

Barcelona Lone Star

Quilt Size: 47¼" x 47¼" **Star Size:** 42¼" sq.
Requires: 8 X blocks **Block Width:** 8¾"

Color		Yardage	#Strips	Cut Size	Strip End
		Yardage & Cutting			**Strip End**
1	■	leftovers*	2	4¼" x 18"	◹
			4	3" x 18"	(all)
			2	1¾" x 18"	
2	■	½ yd.	4	4¼" x 18"	
			4	3" x 18"	
3	■	leftovers**	2	4¼" x 18"	
			4	3" x 18"	
4	■	1 fat qtr.	2	3" x 18"	
			2	1¾" x 18"	
5	■	1 fat qtr.	2	3" x 18"	
6	■	1 fat qtr.	4	3" x 18"	
7	■	½ yd.	2	4¼" x 18"	
			4	3" x 18"	
8	□	½ yd.	2	4¼" x 18"	
			4	3" x 18"	
9	□	1 fat qtr.	2	1¾" x 18"	
10	■	1¼ yds.	background *(see pg. 127)*		
3	■	1½ yds.**	4 borders cut 3" x 48½"		
		3⅜ yds.	backing: 2 pcs. 28" x 56"		
1	■	1 yd.*	binding: 7 strips 2" x 36"		

Instructions for making strip sets and blocks are on pages 120–123. Point trims and strip sets are shown there, as well. Make 2 each of strip sets A–G. The quilt assembly is presented on page 127.

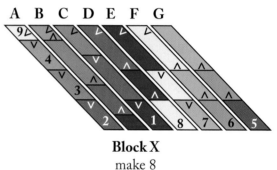

Block X
make 8

Same Blocks, Different Orientation

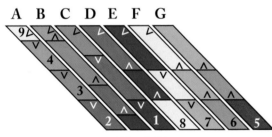

A B C D E F G

Block X
make 4
also make 4 Xr from the next page

Edinburgh Lone Star

Quilt Size: 47¼" x 47¼" **Star Size:** 42¼" sq.
Requires: 4 X, 4 Xr **Block Width:** 8¾"

Yardage & Cutting

Color	Yardage	#Strips	Cut Size	Strip End
1 ▪	leftovers*	1	4¼" x 18"	
		1	4¼" x 18"	
		2	3" x 18"	
		2	3" x 18"	
		1	1¾" x 18"	
		1	1¾" 18"	
2 ▪	½ yd.	2	4¼" x 18"	
		2	4¼" x 18"	
		2	3" x 18"	
		2	3" x 18"	
3 ▪	leftovers**	1	4¼" x 18"	
		1	4¼" x 18"	
		2	3" x 18"	
		2	3" x 18"	
4 ▪	1 fat qtr.	1	3" x 18"	
		1	3" x 18"	
		1	1¾" x 18"	
		1	1¾" x 18"	
5 ▪	1 fat qtr.	1	3" x 18"	
		1	3" x 18"	
6 ▪	1 fat qtr.	2	3" x 18"	
		2	3" x 18"	
7 ▪	½ yd.	1	4¼" x 18"	
		1	4¼" x 18"	
		2	3" x 18"	
		2	3" x 18"	
8 ▪	½ yd .	1	4¼" x 18"	
		1	4¼" x 18"	
		2	3" x 18"	
		2	3" x 18"	
9 ▪	1 fat qtr.	1	1¾" x 18"	
		1	1¾" x 18"	
11 ▪	1¼ yds.	background *(see pg. 127)*		
3 ▪	1½ yds.**	4 borders cut 3" x 48½"		
	3⅜ yds.	backing: 2 pcs. 28" x 56"		
1 ▪	1 yd.*	binding: 7 strips 2" x 36"		

Instructions and strip set diagrams are on pages
120–123. Make 1 each of strip sets A–G and Ar–Gr.
The quilt assembly is presented on page 127.

Same Blocks, Different Orientation

New York Lone Star

Quilt Size: 47¼" x 47¼"   **Star Size:** 42¼" sq.
Requires: 4 X, 4 Xr   **Block Width:** 8¾"

Color		Yardage	#Strips	Cut Size	Strip End
			Yardage & Cutting		
1		leftovers*	1	4¼" x 18"	
			1	4¼" x 18"	
			2	3" x 18"	
			2	3" x 18"	
			1	1¾" x 18"	
			1	1¾" x 18"	
2		½ yd.	2	4¼" x 18"	
			2	4¼" x 18"	
			2	3" x 18"	
			2	3" x 18"	
3		leftovers**	1	4¼" x 18"	
			1	4¼" x 18"	
			2	3" x 18"	
			2	3" x 18"	
4		1 fat qtr.	1	3" x 18"	
			1	3" x 18"	
			1	1¾" x 18"	
			1	1¾" x 18"	
5		1 fat qtr.	1	3" x 18"	
			1	3" x 18"	
6		1 fat qtr.	2	3" x 18"	
			2	3" x 18"	
7		½ yd.	1	4¼" x 18"	
			1	4¼" x 18"	
			2	3" x 18"	
			2	3" x 18"	
8		½ yd.	1	4¼" x 18"	
			1	4¼" x 18"	
			2	3" x 18"	
			2	3" x 18"	
9		1 fat qtr.	1	1¾" x 18"	
			1	1¾" x 18"	
10		1¼ yds.	background *(see pg. 127)*		
3		1½ yds.**	4 borders cut 3" x 48½"		
		3⅜ yds.	backing: 2 pcs. 28" x 56"		
1		1 yd.*	binding: 7 strips 2" x 36"		

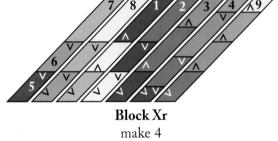

Block Xr
make 4
also make 4 X from the previous page

Instructions and strip set diagrams are on pages 120–123. Make 1 each of strip sets A–G and Ar–Gr. The quilt assembly is presented on page 127.

Same Blocks, Different Orientation

Dublin Lone Star

Quilt Size: 47¼" x 47¼" **Star Size:** 42¼" sq.
Requires: 8 Y blocks **Block Width:** 8¾"

Color		Yardage	#Strips	Cut Size	Strip End
		Yardage & Cutting			**Strip End**
1	■	leftovers*	2	1¾" x 18"	
2	■	1 fat qtr.	3	1¾" x 18"	
			2	1¾" x 18"	
3	■	leftovers**	2	3" x 18"	
			5	1¾" x 18"	
4	■	½ yd.	4	3" x 18"	
			8	1¾" x 18"	
5	■	1 fat qtr.	10	1¾" x 18"	
6	■	½ yd.	2	3" x 18"	
			11	1¾" x 18"	
7	■	½ yd.	2	3" x 18"	
			9	1¾" x 18"	
9	□	1 fat qtr.	2	3" x 18"	
			9	1¾" x 18"	
10	■	1 fat qtr.	8	1¾" x 18"	
11	□	1¼ yds.	background (see pg. 127)		
3	■	1½ yds.**	4 borders cut 3" x 48½"		
		3⅜ yds.	backing: 2 pcs. 28" x 56"		
1	■	½ yd.*	binding: 14 strips 2" x 18"		

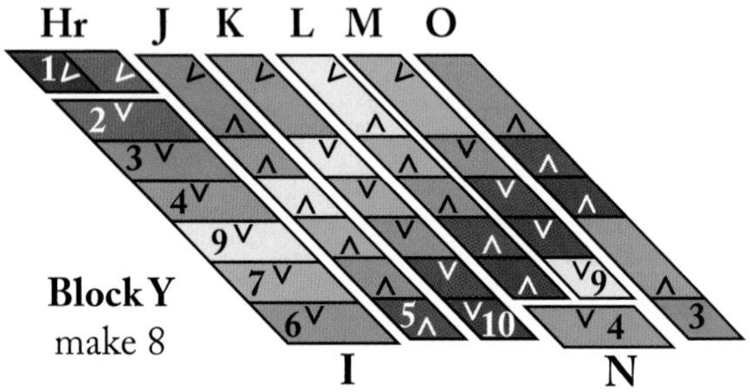

Hr J K L M O

Block Y make 8

I   N

Instructions and strip set diagrams are on pages 120–123. Make 3 of strip sets I and N; make 2 each of the remaining strip sets. Quilt assembly is on page 127.

Same Blocks, Different Orientation

Same Blocks, Different Orientation

London Lone Star

Quilt Size: 47¼" x 47¼"   **Star Size:** 42¼" sq.
Requires: 8 Z blocks   **Block Width:** 8¾"

Color		Yardage	#Strips	Cut Size	Strip End
		Yardage & Cutting			**Strip End**
1		leftovers*	16	1¾" x 18"	
2		1 fat qtr.	10	1¾" x 18"	
3		leftovers**	8	1¾" x 18"	
4		1 fat qtr.	6	1¾" x 18"	
5		1 fat qtr.	2	3" x 18"	
			5	1¾" x 18"	
6		1 fat qtr.	2	3" x 18"	
			7	1¾" x 18"	
7		1 fat qtr.	2	1¾" x 18"	
8		½ yd.	12	1¾" x 18"	
9		1 fat qtr.	4	1¾" x 18"	
10		½ yd.	18	1¾" x 18"	
11		1¼ yds.	background *(see pg. 127)*		
3		1½ yds.**	4 borders cut 3" x 48½"		
		3⅜ yds.	backing: 2 pcs. 28" x 56"		
1		1 yd.*	binding: 7 strips 2" x 36"		

Instructions and strip set diagrams are on pages 120–123. Make 3 of strip set U; make 2 each of the remaining strip sets. The quilt assembly is presented on page 127.

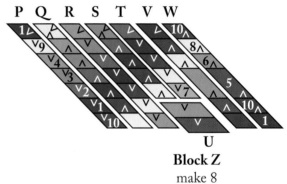

Block Z
make 8

Same Blocks, Different Orientation

Same Blocks, Different Orientation

133

Colorado Lone Star

Quilt Size: 42¼" x 42¼" **Star Size:** 42¼" sq.
Requires: 8 Xr blocks **Block Width:** 8¾"

Color	Yardage	#Strips	Cut Size	Strip End
		Yardage & Cutting		**Strip**
Color	**Yardage**	**#Strips**	**Cut Size**	**End**
2 ■	½ yd.*	2	3" x 18"	⬎
		2	1¾" x 18"	⬎
3 ■	½ yd.	2	4¼" x 18"	⬎
		8	3" x 18"	⬎
4 ■	½ yd.	4	4¼" x 18"	⬎
		6	3" x 18"	⬎
5 ■	½ yd.	2	4¼" x 18"	⬎
		4	3" x 18"	⬎
		2	1¾" x 18"	⬎
6 ■	½ yd.	2	4¼" x 18"	⬎
		4	3" x 18"	⬎
7 ■	½ yd.	2	4¼" x 18"	⬎
		4	3" x 18"	⬎
		2	1¾" x 18"	⬎
1 ■	1¼ yds.	background *(see page 136)*		
	3⅛ yds.	backing: 2 pcs. 25⅝" x 50¾"		
2 ■	leftovers*	binding: 13 strips 2" x 18"		

Cut the binding strips from the leftovers after cutting strips from color #2.

The X block on page 136 is used only for the last 2 setting variations on page 137.

Colorado Lone Star, 42¼" x 42¼". Designed by Judy Martin, pieced and quilted by Chris Hulin. This quilt is made from 8 of the Xr blocks from Star of Wonder that have been recolored.

Note that you use the same yardage and strips for all examples shown on page 137. However, if you are making one of the quilts that requires 4 X and 4 Xr blocks, you need to cut strip ends of two types: Cut half of the strips of each color and width with the strip end shown in the yardage chart and the other half with the strip end shown here: ⬏ *. You can cut strips from folded fabric and get equal quantities of each type.*

Making Strip Sets and Cutting Rows

Start by reading the glossary, "Pattern Pointers," and "How to Make a Lone Star" chapters on pages 7–22. Study the setting variations on page 137 and compare them to the block arrangement in the photo above. Choose a setting that uses 8 Xr blocks (as in the photo) or 4 Xr and 4 X blocks (as in some variations on page 137) before you begin cutting.

Cut the strips for a strip set, cutting off one end at a 45° angle as indicated in the "strip end" column of the yardage chart. If you folded the fabric, unfold it before you cut off the strip ends unless you are making one of the setting variations that requires 4 Xr and 4 X blocks.

Trim the points as described on page 14 and shown on pages 135–136 to help you align patches for sewing. The point should be trimmed at a right angle to the angled end of the strip. Don't trim the point on the top strip of a regular strip set or the bottom strip of a reversed strip set. If you don't have my Point Trimmer tool, download a file to make one at judymartin.com/LSPT.cfm

Align the trimmed point of one strip with the wide angle of the neighboring strip. Pin and stitch strips together. Press after each seam, following the "v" pressing arrows in the strip set diagrams. Continue stitching strips to each other to complete a strip set as shown. Measure your strip set from the raw edge at the top straight down to the raw edge at the bottom. It should be 9¼". If it is not, correct your seams before proceeding.

When you have your seam allowance right, trim a sliver off the angled end of the strip set, if necessary, at a precise 45° angle. See the row cutting diagram on page 135. Cut the strip set into rows 1¾" wide. That is, lay the 1¾" ruling of your rotary cutting ruler over the angled end of the strip; also align the 45° line with one of the raw edges or seamlines. Cut along the ruler's edge. If your set requires 8 Xr blocks, make a duplicate strip set to allow you to cut 4 more rows like the first 4.

Continue making strip sets and cutting rows in this fashion. When you have all the rows needed for a block, trim both points of each row as shown on page 135.

Strip Piecing the Xr Block

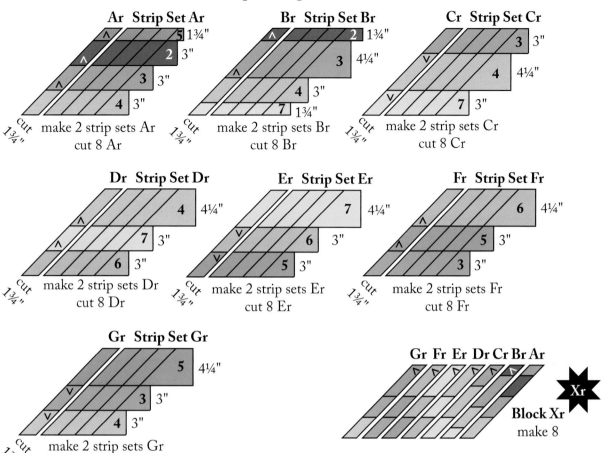

Ar Strip Set Ar
5 — 1¾"
2 — 3"
3 — 3"
4 — 3"
cut 1¾"
make 2 strip sets Ar
cut 8 Ar

Br Strip Set Br
2 — 1¾"
3 — 4¼"
4 — 3"
7 — 1¾"
cut 1¾"
make 2 strip sets Br
cut 8 Br

Cr Strip Set Cr
3 — 3"
4 — 4¼"
7 — 3"
cut 1¾"
make 2 strip sets Cr
cut 8 Cr

Dr Strip Set Dr
4 — 4¼"
7 — 3"
6 — 3"
cut 1¾"
make 2 strip sets Dr
cut 8 Dr

Er Strip Set Er
7 — 4¼"
6 — 3"
5 — 3"
cut 1¾"
make 2 strip sets Er
cut 8 Er

Fr Strip Set Fr
6 — 4¼"
5 — 3"
3 — 3"
cut 1¾"
make 2 strip sets Fr
cut 8 Fr

Gr Strip Set Gr
5 — 4¼"
3 — 3"
4 — 3"
cut 1¾"
make 2 strip sets Gr
cut 8 Gr

Gr Fr Er Dr Cr Br Ar
Block Xr
make 8

Making Blocks

These rows have long bias edges. I suggest stay stitching within the seam allowances of the long edges and/or blocking the blocks to an outline (page 12). On a table, lay out the rows for a block as shown in the block diagrams above and on the next page. Pin rows at both ends, aligning the trimmed point of one row with the wide angle of the other. Also pin at each joint. Strategies for matching joints are on page 15. Stitch all rows together, pressing after each seam in the direction indicated with an arrow. Make 8 Xr blocks or 4 Xr and 4 X blocks.

Assembling the Quilt

Cut out your choice of background patches on the next page. Choose patches for use with or without Y-seams. See page 17 for helpful tips about cutting patches larger than your ruler.

Arrange blocks and background patches as shown in the photograph on page 134 or the setting variation of your choice on page 137. Referring to the appropriate assembly diagram on the next page, stitch together the blocks and patches in numerical order. Press the seam allowances to one side after each seam, as indicated by the arrows in the quilt assembly diagram.

Finishing the Quilt

Chris quilted in the ditch between rows in the star and between the star and the background. She quilted parallel lines 1¼" apart in the background. Binding directions are on page 22.

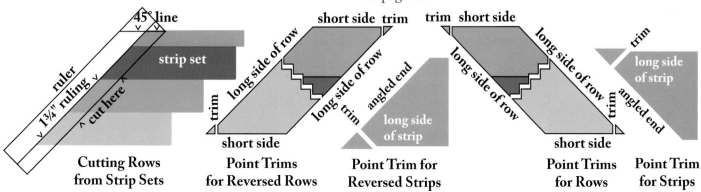

Cutting Rows from Strip Sets

Point Trims for Reversed Rows

Point Trim for Reversed Strips

Point Trims for Rows

Point Trim for Strips

45° line
ruler
1¾" ruling
cut here
strip set
short side trim
long side of row
long side of row
trim
short side
angled end
long side of strip
trim
trim short side
long side of row
long side of row
short side
trim
angled end
trim
long side of strip

Note that you do not need the X blocks to make the quilt as photographed. If you prefer to make one of the last two arrangements on page 137, you will need to make 4 Xr blocks (page 135) and 4 X blocks (below). In that case, you will need just 1 strip set each of Ar–Gr as well as A–G.

Strip Piecing the X Block

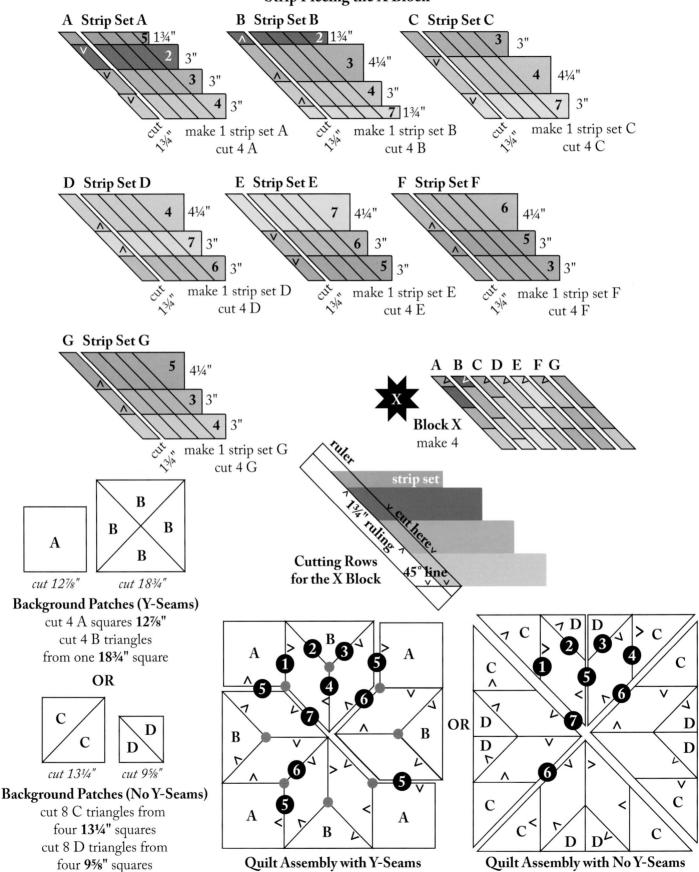

A Strip Set A
5 1¾"
2 3"
3 3"
4 3"
cut 1¾"
make 1 strip set A
cut 4 A

B Strip Set B
2 1¾"
3 4¼"
4 3"
7 1¾"
cut 1¾"
make 1 strip set B
cut 4 B

C Strip Set C
3 3"
4 4¼"
7 3"
cut 1¾"
make 1 strip set C
cut 4 C

D Strip Set D
4 4¼"
7 3"
6 3"
cut 1¾"
make 1 strip set D
cut 4 D

E Strip Set E
7 4¼"
6 3"
5 3"
cut 1¾"
make 1 strip set E
cut 4 E

F Strip Set F
6 4¼"
5 3"
3 3"
cut 1¾"
make 1 strip set F
cut 4 F

G Strip Set G
5 4¼"
3 3"
4 3"
cut 1¾"
make 1 strip set G
cut 4 G

X
A B C D E F G
Block X
make 4

ruler
strip set
1¾" ruling
cut here
45° line
Cutting Rows for the X Block

Background Patches (Y-Seams)
cut 4 A squares **12⅞"**
cut 4 B triangles from one **18¾"** square
A cut 12⅞"
B B B B cut 18¾"

OR

Background Patches (No Y-Seams)
cut 8 C triangles from four **13¼"** squares
cut 8 D triangles from four **9⅝"** squares
C C cut 13¼"
D D cut 9⅝"

Quilt Assembly with Y-Seams

OR

Quilt Assembly with No Y-Seams

136

Colorado Lone Star Setting Variations
USING THE SAME YARDAGE

Arrangement 2: 8 Xr blocks in a Lone Star, with 4 blocks turned with the orange tip on the outer point. This example requires 2 strip sets of each kind from Ar–Gr.

Arrangement 3: 8 Xr blocks in a Lone Star, with all 8 blocks turned with the orange tip on the outer point. This example requires 2 strip sets of each kind from Ar–Gr.

Arrangement 4: 4 X and 4 Xr (reversed) blocks with orange tips at the center. Note that you need just one strip set of each kind from A–G and Ar–Gr.

Arrangement 5: 4 X and 4 Xr (reversed) blocks with all blocks turned with the orange tip on the outer point. You need just one strip set of each kind from A–G and Ar–Gr.

Appalachian Spring

Appalachian Spring, 102" x 102". Pieced by Judy Martin from her original design. Quilted by Deb Treusch. The quilt is made from 8 diamond blocks in a 17½" finished width set in an 84½" square star. The strip and row widths vary, with the smallest dimensions at the block center and the largest ones at the tips of the blocks. This progression results in scalloped rings rather than the usual octagonal rings. Colored and white diamonds alternate for an airy look.

This pattern is no more difficult to sew than other Lone Stars, but the many strip and row widths will require you to keep your head screwed on straight. I suggest sorting strips by width and draping strips of the same width over a coat hanger or a clothes drying rack. Note that all strip sets are made using the same size order. Strips were chosen to repeat the colors of the background fabric. The border print provides a simple, yet intriguing, finish for the quilt.

Quilt Size: 102" x 102" **Star Size:** 84½" sq.
Requires: 8 blocks **Block Width:** 17½"

Color	Yardage	#Strips	Cut Size	Strip End
	Yardage & Cutting			**Strip End**
1 ◻	1 yd.	5	2½" x 18"	⬭
		2	2¼" x 18"	(all)
		5	2" x 18"	
		4	1¾" x 18"	
		4	1½" x 18"	
		4	1⅜" x 18"	
		2	1¼" x 18"	
2 ◻	1 yd.	4	2½" x 18"	
		4	2¼" x 18"	
		5	2" x 18"	
		2	1¾" x 18"	
		5	1½" x 18"	
		4	1⅜" x 18"	
		2	1¼" x 18"	
3 ◻	1 yd.	4	2½" x 18"	
		4	2¼" x 18"	
		4	2" x 18"	
		4	1¾" x 18"	
		5	1½" x 18"	
		2	1⅜" x 18"	
		3	1¼" x 18"	
4 ◻	leftovers*	10	2½" x 18"	
		8	2¼" x 18"	
		8	2" x 18"	
		8	1¾" x 18"	
		9	1½" x 18"	
		6	1⅜" x 18"	
		5	1¼" x 18"	

Color	Yardage	#Strips	Cut Size	Strip End
5 ◻	1 yd.	4	2½" x 18"	⬭
		4	2¼" x 18"	(all)
		5	2" x 18"	
		2	1¾" x 18"	
		5	1½" x 18"	
		4	1⅜" x 18"	
		2	1¼" x 18"	
6 ◻	1 yd.	5	2½" x 18"	
		2	2¼" x 18"	
		5	2" x 18"	
		4	1¾" x 18"	
		4	1½" x 18"	
		4	1⅜" x 18"	
		2	1¼" x 18"	
7 ◻	4½ yds.	24	2½" x 18"	
		32	2¼" x 18"	
		24	2" x 18"	
		32	1¾" x 18"	
		24	1½" x 18"	
		32	1⅜" x 18"	
		12	1¼" x 18"	
	9¾ yds.		back: 3 pcs. 37¼" x 110½"	
4 ◻	2¼ yds.*		6 binding strips 2" x 81"	

* see below for bkgd. and border options

*Yardage for Background (Border Print)

6¾ yds. border print *with borders on 2 edges*

OR

12½ yds. border print *with border on 1 edge only*

*Yardage for Background & Separate Borders

4¼ yds. for standard background from page 94
3⅛ yds.: 4 borders cut 9¼" x 103¼" (102" quilt)

*Choose a border print for a combined background and border or choose the standard background option with a separate border. Background patches and cutting layouts for the border print are on page 143.

I had to allow for shrinkage in case readers prewash their fabric, as I do mine. If you do not prewash, you may find that you can cut more rows from your strip sets than I list. I suggest that you cut strips for just 1 strip set at a time. You may find you don't need a second one.

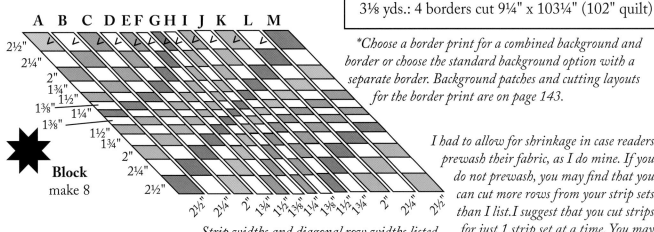

A B C D E F G H I J K L M

2½" 2¼" 2" 1¾" 1½" 1⅜" 1¼" 1⅜" 1½" 1¾" 2" 2¼" 2½"

Block
make 8

2½" 2¼" 2" 1¾" 1½" 1⅜" 1¼" 1⅜" 1½" 1¾" 2" 2¼" 2½"

Strip widths and diagonal row widths listed are cut sizes, including seam allowances.

Strip Piecing

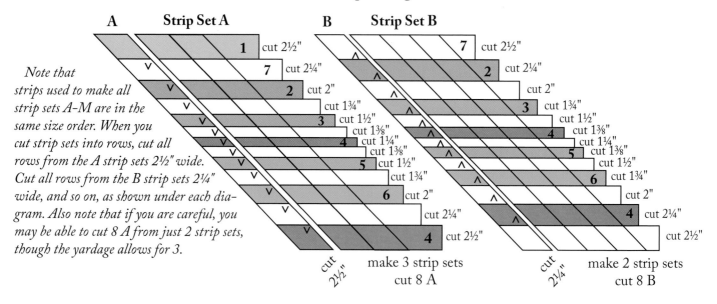

A   Strip Set A

Note that strips used to make all strip sets A–M are in the same size order. When you cut strip sets into rows, cut all rows from the A strip sets 2½" wide. Cut all rows from the B strip sets 2¼" wide, and so on, as shown under each diagram. Also note that if you are careful, you may be able to cut 8 A from just 2 strip sets, though the yardage allows for 3.

1 cut 2½"
7 cut 2¼"
2 cut 2"
3 cut 1¾"
   cut 1½"
4 cut 1⅜"
   cut 1¼"
5 cut 1⅜"
   cut 1½"
6 cut 1¾"
   cut 2"
   cut 2¼"
4 cut 2½"

cut 2½"
make 3 strip sets
cut 8 A

B   Strip Set B

7 cut 2½"
2 cut 2¼"
3 cut 2"
   cut 1¾"
4 cut 1½"
   cut 1⅜"
5 cut 1¼"
   cut 1⅜"
6 cut 1½"
   cut 1¾"
   cut 2"
4 cut 2¼"
   cut 2½"

cut 2¼"
make 2 strip sets
cut 8 B

C   Strip Set C

You need to make a second strip set of B–F and H–L. The extra strip set will allow you to cut the 8 rows needed for the quilt.

2 cut 2½"
7 cut 2¼"
3 cut 2"
   cut 1¾"
4 cut 1½"
   cut 1⅜"
5 cut 1¼"
   cut 1⅜"
6 cut 1½"
   cut 1¾"
4 cut 2"
   cut 2¼"
1 cut 2½"

cut 2"
make 2 strip sets
cut 8 C

D   Strip Set D

7 cut 2½"
3 cut 2¼"
   cut 2"
4 cut 1¾"
   cut 1½"
5 cut 1⅜"
   cut 1¼"
6 cut 1⅜"
   cut 1½"
4 cut 1¾"
   cut 2"
1 cut 2¼"
   cut 2½"

cut 1¾"
make 2 strip sets
cut 8 D

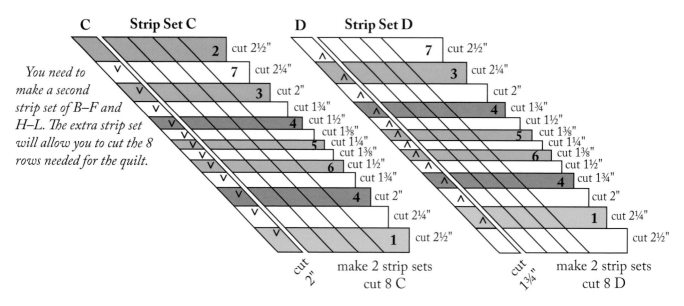

E   Strip Set E

3 cut 2½"
7 cut 2¼"
4 cut 2"
   cut 1¾"
5 cut 1½"
   cut 1⅜"
6 cut 1¼"
   cut 1⅜"
4 cut 1½"
   cut 1¾"
1 cut 2"
   cut 2¼"
2 cut 2½"

cut 1½"
make 2 strip sets
cut 8 E

F   Strip Set F

7 cut 2½"
4 cut 2¼"
   cut 2"
5 cut 1¾"
   cut 1½"
6 cut 1⅜"
   cut 1¼"
4 cut 1⅜"
   cut 1½"
1 cut 1¾"
   cut 2"
2 cut 2¼"
   cut 2½"

Note that if you are careful and your yardage was cut generously, you may be able to cut all 8 F rows from a single strip set. The yardage allows for 2.

cut 1⅜"
make 2 strip sets
cut 8 F

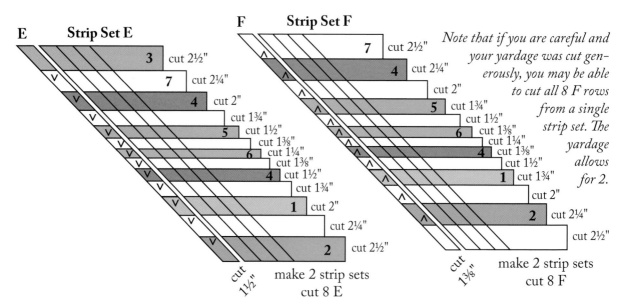

140

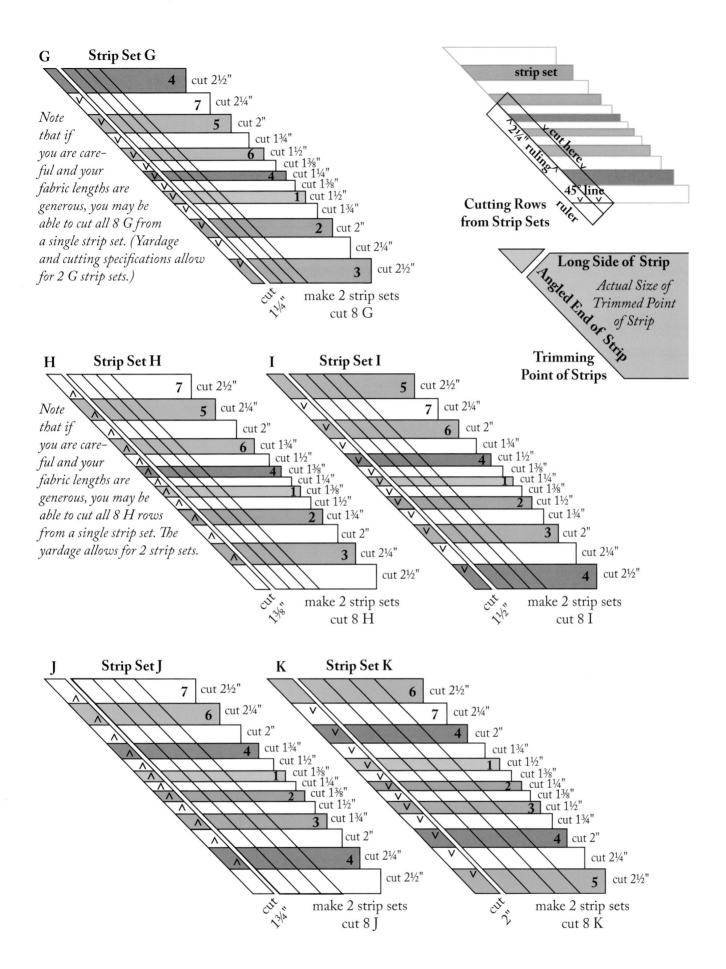

G   **Strip Set G**

4   cut 2½"
7   cut 2¼"
5   cut 2"
   cut 1¾"
6   cut 1½"
   cut 1⅜"
4   cut 1¼"
   cut 1⅜"
1   cut 1½"
   cut 1¾"
2   cut 2"
   cut 2¼"
3   cut 2½"

Note that if you are careful and your fabric lengths are generous, you may be able to cut all 8 G from a single strip set. (Yardage and cutting specifications allow for 2 G strip sets.)

cut 1¼"

make 2 strip sets
cut 8 G

Cutting Rows from Strip Sets

strip set
2¼" ruling
cut here
45° line
ruler

Long Side of Strip
Actual Size of Trimmed Point of Strip

Angled End of Strip

Trimming Point of Strips

H   **Strip Set H**

7   cut 2½"
5   cut 2¼"
   cut 2"
6   cut 1¾"
   cut 1½"
4   cut 1⅜"
   cut 1¼"
1   cut 1⅜"
   cut 1½"
2   cut 1¾"
   cut 2"
3   cut 2¼"
   cut 2½"

Note that if you are careful and your fabric lengths are generous, you may be able to cut all 8 H rows from a single strip set. The yardage allows for 2 strip sets.

cut 1⅜"

make 2 strip sets
cut 8 H

I   **Strip Set I**

5   cut 2½"
7   cut 2¼"
6   cut 2"
   cut 1¾"
4   cut 1½"
   cut 1⅜"
1   cut 1¼"
   cut 1⅜"
2   cut 1½"
   cut 1¾"
3   cut 2"
   cut 2¼"
4   cut 2½"

cut 1½"

make 2 strip sets
cut 8 I

J   **Strip Set J**

7   cut 2½"
6   cut 2¼"
   cut 2"
4   cut 1¾"
   cut 1½"
1   cut 1⅜"
   cut 1¼"
2   cut 1⅜"
   cut 1½"
3   cut 1¾"
   cut 2"
4   cut 2¼"
   cut 2½"

cut 1¾"

make 2 strip sets
cut 8 J

K   **Strip Set K**

6   cut 2½"
7   cut 2¼"
4   cut 2"
   cut 1¾"
1   cut 1½"
   cut 1⅜"
2   cut 1¼"
   cut 1⅜"
3   cut 1½"
   cut 1¾"
4   cut 2"
   cut 2¼"
5   cut 2½"

cut 2"

make 2 strip sets
cut 8 K

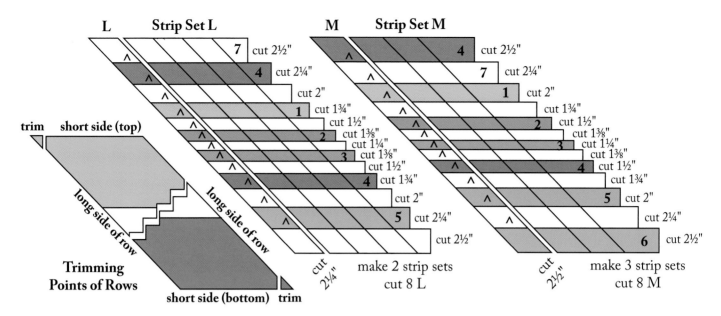

L	Strip Set L			M	Strip Set M	
		7 cut 2½"		4		cut 2½"
		4 cut 2¼"			7	cut 2¼"
		cut 2"			1	cut 2"
		1 cut 1¾"				cut 1¾"
		2 cut 1½"			2	cut 1½"
		cut 1⅜"				cut 1⅜"
		3 cut 1¼"			3	cut 1¼"
		cut 1⅜"				cut 1⅜"
		cut 1½"			4	cut 1½"
		4 cut 1¾"				cut 1¾"
		cut 2"			5	cut 2"
		5 cut 2¼"				cut 2¼"
					6	cut 2½"

cut 2¼" make 2 strip sets cut 8 L

cut 2½" make 3 strip sets cut 8 M

trim **short side (top)**

long side of row **long side of row**

Trimming Points of Rows

short side (bottom) **trim**

Making Strip Sets and Cutting Rows

Read the glossary, "Pattern Pointers," and "How to Make a Lone Star" chapters on pages 7–22.

Referring to the yardage chart and the strip set diagrams on pages 139–142, cut strips in the widths and colors needed for a strip set. Cut off one end of each strip as shown in the yardage chart. Trim the point as shown on page 141. If you don't have a Point Trimmer, download a file at judymartin.com/LSPT.cfm and make one. Stitch strips together. After each seam, press the seam allowances in the direction indicated in the diagram.

Below each strip set diagram I indicate the number of strip sets of that type you need to make. As you complete each strip set, trim a sliver off the angled end at precisely 45° if it is necessary to even it. The quantity and width of the rows that you need to cut from each strip set is listed under each strip set. For example, the L strip set (above) is cut into 2¼" rows. See the diagram at the top right of page 141. Lay the 2¼" ruling of your rotary ruler on the angled end of the strip and cut along the edge of the ruler. For these long rows, you will need to slide your ruler up and realign the 45° line with the raw edge at the top or one of the seamlines within the strip set to cut the rest of the row. The rows are outlined in the strip set diagram, with the first row separated slightly. Make the listed number of strip sets of each type, and cut the total number of rows listed.

Sewing Rows to Make Blocks

Trim the points of each row with a Point Trimmer as described on page 15 and shown above.

Lay out rows for a block. Place the first two rows face to face, aligning the ends of the point trims with the wide angles of the neighboring row. Pin ends and joints as described on page 16; stitch. Continue adding rows. Press after each seam, being careful not to stretch the bias. Continue pinning, stitching, and pressing to complete the 8 blocks required for the quilt.

Assembling the Quilt

Make cloth templates and rotary cut the background patches according to the directions on the next page.

Read about Y-seams on page 18. Refer to the Assembly diagram on the next page. 1) Pin and stitch a diamond block to a B with a Y-seam: Starting precisely ¼" in from the raw edge as indicated by the red dot, stitch forward 2 stitches and backward 2 stitches before proceeding to stitch to the raw edge at the opposite end of the seamline. Remove the work from the machine. 2) Pin and stitch a second diamond to the same B patch using a Y-seam. Start precisely where you started the last seam, and remove the work from the machine at the raw edge. 3) Stitch the 2 diamonds to each other, again starting at the precise point you started the previous 2 seams. 4–5) Stitch an A to the left end and an Ar to the right end of the unit, stitching from raw edge to raw edge. Press in the direction of the arrows in the diagram. This complete ¼ of the quilt.

Repeat to make four quarters of the quilt. 6) Pin and stitch two quarters to make a half block, sewing from raw edge to raw edge. Press seams in the direction shown. Repeat to make a second half block. 7) Pin and stitch from raw edge to raw edge to join the two halves together to complete the quilt top. Press well.

Quilting and Finishing

Deb Treusch quilted in the ditch between the star and the background. She quilted in the ditch between the white and the colored diamonds and parallelograms. She also quilted diagonally down the length of the white parallelograms. She quilted large concentric quarter-circles in the background between the star arms to define areas for further quilting. She filled these areas with feathers and radiating lines. Serpentine feathers grace the area outside the arcs, and parallel lines extend outward from the feathers to the edges of the quilt. Bind the quilt as described on page 22.

Rotary Cutting the Large Background Patches

The idea is to easily and accurately rotary cut patches that are likely larger than your rotary ruler. You can cut with confidence by making a template out of inexpensive stabilizer, an ugly remnant or never-used piece from your stash, or bargain-basement fabric. Simply lay the cloth template in position on your fabric, align your ruler with the template's edge, and cut along the ruler's edge.

To make the fabric template for patch A, use your rotary ruler and a sharp pencil to mark the right angle onto template fabric; slide your ruler over to extend these lines to precisely 34⅜" from the corner. Lay the 45° angle on one line at the 34⅜" mark. Mark the angle. Repeat at the other corner. Connect the angle lines. Double check measurements and rotary cut on the lines.

Make the B template in a similar fashion, stacking or sliding rulers to measure and mark the triangle shown in green and the rectangle shown in red. Check angles and

measurements, and cut them out. To complete the green triangle, lay the ½" line of your ruler over the long side of the triangle and trim off ½" along the ruler's edge. You will use this trimmed green triangle as a guide for cutting off the corners of the red rectangle. Align the trimmed green triangle's square corner with one corner of the rectangle shown in red. Align your ruler with the long edge of the green triangle, and cut off the corner of the red rectangle. Repeat at the adjacent corner of the rectangle, as shown, to complete the red B template.

To cut your A and B patches from border print or other fabric, place the template over your fabric and pat it down. (If you like, press the template in place over the fabric.) Align your ruler with the edge of the template, and cut your fabric along the ruler's edge. Slide your ruler down the length of the template, as needed. Cut around all sides of the template.

Making a Cloth Template for Rotary Cutting A

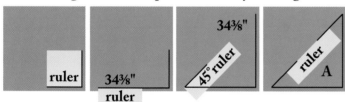

Mark 90° angle; extend lines to 34⅜"; mark 45° angles; check measurements and angles; cut template.

Making A Cloth Template for Rotary Cutting B

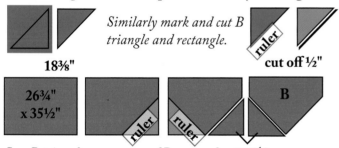

Similarly mark and cut B triangle and rectangle.

Lay B triangle over corner of B rectangle; align ruler with template; cut; repeat in other corner, as shown.

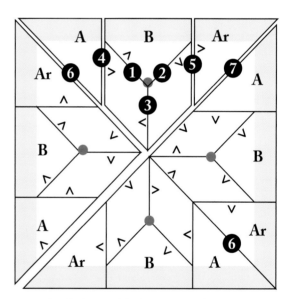

Quilt Assembly Using Border Print

Aqua band indicates border print. Red dots indicate Y-seams. Arrows indicate pressing direction.

Use the layout at right for cutting background patches from fabric with borders on both selvages. The gaps between patches are wasted fabric.

Use the layout below if you are cutting background patches from border print with a border on only one selvage. The fabric above the patches is left over for your stash.

Cutting Layouts for Border Prints

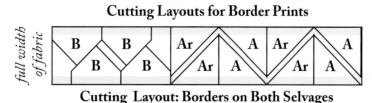

Cutting Layout: Borders on Both Selvages

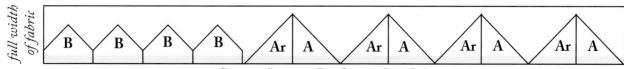

Cutting Layout: Border on One Selvage

Coloring 2: 8 blocks the same as the photographed quilt, but with the orange tips in the center.

Coloring 3: 8 blocks; same as arrangement 2, but with dark gray substituted for fabric #7 and light gray substituted for the off-white border print.

Coloring 4: 8 blocks; same as the photographed quilt, but with deep blue substituted for fabric #7.

Coloring 5: 8 blocks; same as the photographed quilt, but with deep blue substituted for both fabric #7 and for the off-white border print in the background.

Queen of Diamonds

Queen of Diamonds, 103" x 103". Pieced by Judy Martin from her original design. Quilted by Lana Corcoran. The quilt is made from 8 diamond blocks in a 17½" finished width. The Lone Star set for an 84½" square finished star has satellite stars and half stars in the background squares and triangles. A Singular Diamonds border completes the quilt.

If you plan to make the quilt as shown, with the satellite stars in the background and the pieced border, be sure to use the total

yardage figures at the top of the yardage chart on the left of page 146 These yardage totals have less waste and are slightly less than the sum of the parts. Below that I separate yardage figures for satellite blocks, borders, backing and binding. Doing so makes it easy for you to use these elements in other quilts or to substitute the border from another quilt here. The combination of plain and Singular Diamonds pieced borders here will fit any 84½" stars in the book, as will the satellite stars.

Quilt Size: 103" x 103" **Star Size:** 84½" sq.
Requires: 8 W, 48 X, **Block Width:** 17½"
4 Y, 4 Z blocks

Total Yardage for Quilt as Photographed

Red: 26 fat qtrs. or 6¼ yds. (includes binding),
cream: 11¼ yds., backing: 9⅞ yds.

Yardage & Cutting for W

Color	Yardage	#Strips	Cut Size	Strip End
■	15 fat qtrs.	12	2¼" x 18"	◹
	or 3½ yds.	20	2⅛" x 18"	(all)
		24	2" x 18"	
		20	1⅞" x 18"	
		24	1¾" x 18"	
		20	1⅝" x 18"	
		24	1½" x 18"	
□	5 yds.	4 borders	4" x 92¾"	◹
		10	2¼" x 18"	
		24	2⅛" x 18"	(all)
		20	2" x 18"	
		24	1⅞" x 18"	
		20	1¾" x 18"	
		24	1⅝" x 18"	
		20	1½" x 18"	

*Yardage & Cutting for X, Y, Z

Color	Yardage	#Strips	Cut Size	Strip End
■	4 fat qtrs.	10	1⅞" x 18"	◹
	or 1 yd.	32	1⅝" x 18"	◹
		#Patches	**Cut Size**	
□	4⅛ yds.	16 strips	1⅞" x 18"	◹
		20 strips	1⅝" x 18"	◹
		20 L	2 L per 13¼"	◻
		8 N	4 N per 13⅝"	⊠
		20 K	4 K per 8½"	⊠
		24 J	5⅝" square	☐
		8 M	2 M per 4½"	☐

**Yardage & Cutting for Borders

Color	Yardage	#Strips	Cut Size	Strip End
■	4 fat qtrs.	27 (108 O)	2⅛" x 18"	◺
	or 1 yd.			
		#Patches	**Cut Size**	
□	3⅛ yds.	4 borders	2" x 104¼"	
		108 P	see pg. 149	
		216 Q	see pg. 149	
		4 R	2 R per 3⅜"	◹

Yardage & Cutting for Backing

Color	Yardage	#Panels	Cut Size
	9⅞ yds.	3 panels	37½" x 111½"

Yardage & Cutting for Binding

Color	Yardage	#Strips	Cut Size
■	¾ yd.	19	2" x 27"

*If you prefer a plain background to the pieced star blocks in the background of this quilt, use the yardage and cutting instructions for the large (84½") Lone Star background on pages 91 and 94. Delete the yardage and cutting for X, Y, and Z blocks listed at left.

**If you prefer simply a plain border, use the yardage listed at left for cutting W. It includes a cream border to make a 91½" quilt. Pair it with satellite stars or plain background patches, as listed at left or in the paragraph above. Delete the yardage and cutting for borders listed above. If you make the 91½" version having no pieced border, you will need just 8⅞ yds. of backing fabric cut into 3 panels 33½" x 100".

I made my Queen of Diamonds quilt from red fat quarters and a single cream solid. Use a single red fabric if you prefer.

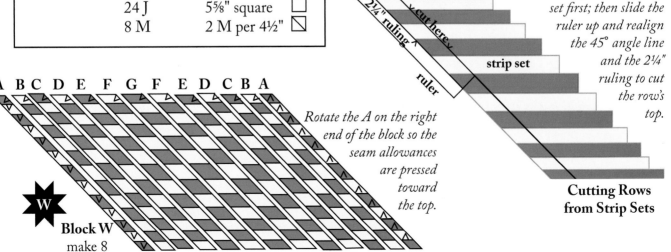

A B C D E F G F E D C B A

Rotate the A on the right end of the block so the seam allowances are pressed toward the top.

W
Block W
make 8

45° line
2¼" ruling
cut here
ruler
strip set

Cut the bottom of the G-A strip set first; then slide the ruler up and realign the 45° angle line and the 2¼" ruling to cut the row's top.

Cutting Rows from Strip Sets

Strip Sets for Block W

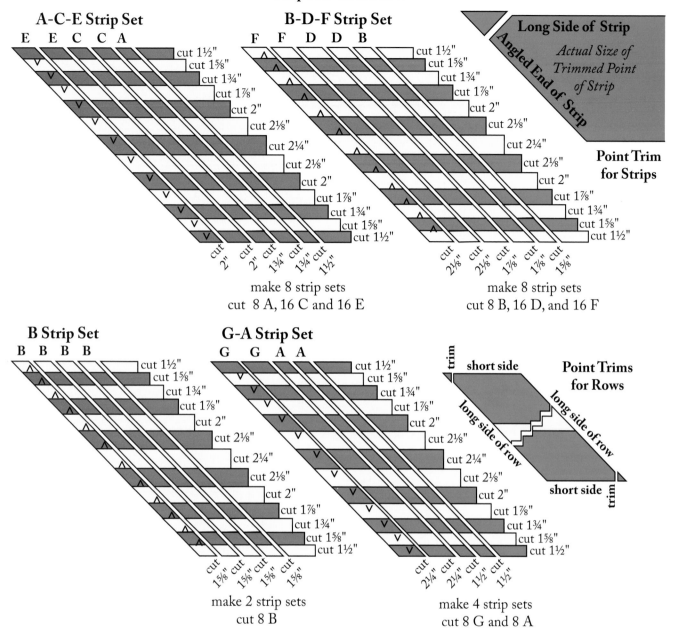

A-C-E Strip Set
E   E   C   C   A

cut 1½"
cut 1⅝"
cut 1¾"
cut 1⅞"
cut 2"
cut 2⅛"
cut 2¼"
cut 2⅛"
cut 2"
cut 1⅞"
cut 1¾"
cut 1⅝"
cut 1½"

cut 2" cut 2" cut 1¾" cut 1¾" cut 1½"

make 8 strip sets
cut 8 A, 16 C and 16 E

B-D-F Strip Set
F   F   D   D   B

cut 1½"
cut 1⅝"
cut 1¾"
cut 1⅞"
cut 2"
cut 2⅛"
cut 2¼"
cut 2⅛"
cut 2"
cut 1⅞"
cut 1¾"
cut 1⅝"
cut 1½"

cut 2⅛" cut 2⅛" cut 1⅞" cut 1⅞" cut 1⅝"

make 8 strip sets
cut 8 B, 16 D, and 16 F

Long Side of Strip
Actual Size of Trimmed Point of Strip

Angled End of Strip

Point Trim for Strips

B Strip Set
B   B   B   B

cut 1½"
cut 1⅝"
cut 1¾"
cut 1⅞"
cut 2"
cut 2⅛"
cut 2¼"
cut 2⅛"
cut 2"
cut 1⅞"
cut 1¾"
cut 1⅝"
cut 1½"

cut 1⅝" cut 1⅝" cut 1⅝" cut 1⅝"

make 2 strip sets
cut 8 B

G-A Strip Set
G   G   A   A

cut 1½"
cut 1⅝"
cut 1¾"
cut 1⅞"
cut 2"
cut 2⅛"
cut 2¼"
cut 2⅛"
cut 2"
cut 1⅞"
cut 1¾"
cut 1⅝"
cut 1½"

cut 2¼" cut 2¼" cut 1½" cut 1½"

make 4 strip sets
cut 8 G and 8 A

Point Trims for Rows
trim   short side
long side of row
long side of row
short side   trim

Making Strip Sets and W Blocks

Begin by reading pages 7-22 to learn every detail of using this pattern and making Lone Star quilts.

Cut 4 borders 4" x 92¾" and 4 borders 2" x 104¼" from cream; set aside for later. Cut off 7 pieces 18" long x the full width of the cream fabric. From these pieces, cut 18" lengthwise strips of cream in the widths listed in the yardage chart on page 146. From assorted reds, cut the red strips listed in the yardage chart. Pin a label listing the width to each cream and red strip. Cut off one end of each strip at a 45° angle and trim its point as shown above right. Read about making your own Point Trimmer on page 14.

All strip sets, shown above, use the same sequence of strip widths, but some strips start with a red strip and some start with a cream strip. Join strips in the order shown to make strip sets. Make them in the quantities listed below each strip set.

Cut strip sets into rows as shown on page 146, sliding the ruler up and realigning the 45° line with a seamline to cut the top of the row. You may be cutting rows of different widths from some of the strip sets. Trim points of rows as shown above. Pin lettered labels to the rows.

Referring to the block diagram on page 146, lay out the rows in order. Pin and stitch rows together to complete a block. (I join the first 2 rows for each block, then add the third row to each block, and so on.) Make 8 W blocks.

Making X, Y, and Z Blocks

See the H and I strip set diagrams on the next page. These are for the small stars in the background of the quilt. Make 16 H and 10 I strip sets.

Strip Sets for Satellite Stars Y and Z

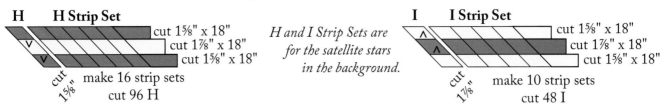

H Strip Set

cut 1⅝" x 18"
cut 1⅞" x 18"
cut 1⅝" x 18"

cut 1⅝"
make 16 strip sets
cut 96 H

H and I Strip Sets are for the satellite stars in the background.

I Strip Set

cut 1⅝" x 18"
cut 1⅞" x 18"
cut 1⅝" x 18"

cut 1⅞"
make 10 strip sets
cut 48 I

Patches and Blocks for Satellite Stars X, Y, and Z

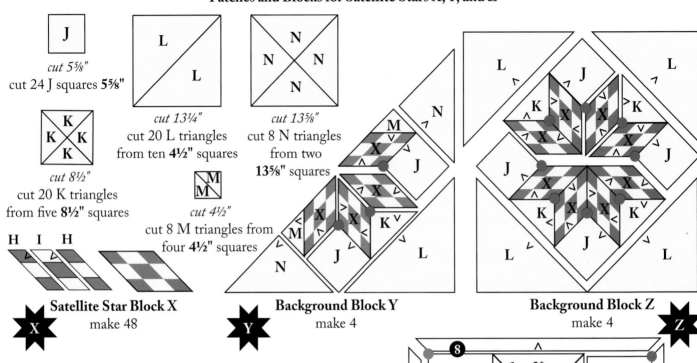

J
cut 5⅝"
cut 24 J squares **5⅝"**

L L
cut 13¼"
cut 20 L triangles from ten **4½"** squares

N N N N
cut 13⅝"
cut 8 N triangles from two **13⅝"** squares

K K K K
cut 8½"
cut 20 K triangles from five **8½"** squares

M M
cut 4½"
cut 8 M triangles from four **4½"** squares

Satellite Star Block X
make 48

Background Block Y
make 4

Background Block Z
make 4

Cut H strip sets into 1⅝"-wide rows; cut I strip sets into 1⅞"-wide rows, as shown. Sew 2 H rows to either side of an I row to make an X block. Make 48 X blocks.

Cut out background patches J–N as shown above. Arrange X blocks and patches to form Y and Z blocks. See the Y and Z blocks above right. Pin and stitch the Z stars in the same sewing sequence as shown in the quilt assembly diagram at right. Add an L triangle to each side of the star. Pin and stitch the Y half stars as shown above. Add the L and N triangles last. Make 4 Y and 4 Z blocks.

Assembling the Quilt Center

Arrange the 8 W blocks with the Y and Z blocks as shown in the quilt diagram at the right. Pin and stitch these together in numerical order. The red dots are Y-seams. Read about them on page 18. Press after each seam, following the arrows in the diagram to see which way to press seam allowances. Add the wider, shorter cream border and miter its corners.

Making Cloth Rotary Cutting Templates

See the figures at the top of the next page. From an unwanted scrap of fabric, cut a strip 2⅛" x 6" or so. Cut off one end at a 45° angle. Cut off a diamond by laying the 2⅛" ruling on the angled end of the strip and cutting along the ruler's edge. This diamond should be the same size as

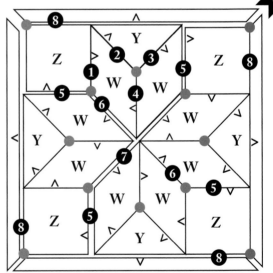

Quilt Assembly with Y-Seams

the red O patches shown on page 149. Lay the ¼" rule line of your rotary ruler over the short diagonal of the diamond. Cut on the ruler's edge; the smaller piece is waste; the larger piece is your Q template.

Make a P template in a similar fashion: Cut a strip 3¾" x 9" or so. Cut off the end at a 45° angle. Cut off a diamond 3¾" wide, measured from the angled end. Lay the ¼" rule line of your rotary ruler from corner to corner on the diamond's short diagonal. Cut on the ruler's edge to complete a cloth template for P.

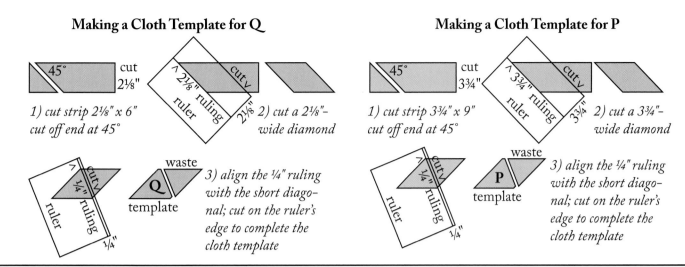

Making a Cloth Template for Q

1) cut strip 2⅛" x 6" cut off end at 45°

2) cut a 2⅛"-wide diamond

3) align the ¼" ruling with the short diagonal; cut on the ruler's edge to complete the cloth template

Making a Cloth Template for P

1) cut strip 3¾" x 9" cut off end at 45°

2) cut a 3¾"-wide diamond

3) align the ¼" ruling with the short diagonal; cut on the ruler's edge to complete the cloth template

Using Cloth Rotary Cutting Templates

To cut Q's, cut a lengthwise strip of cream fabric 3⅛" x 24". Place the cloth template for Q with its short side even with one long edge of the strip. Align your rotary ruler with one long edge of the cloth Q; cut. Align your ruler with the other long edge of the cloth Q; cut. Rotate the template 180° and move it down the strip to cut more Q's. One long side of each subsequent Q patch should align with the edge you just cut. Download a file at judymartin.com/cdef.cfm to learn how to make Point Trimmers for O,

P, Q, and R patches. Trim points of Q's to help you align the patches for sewing.

Cut P patches in the same fashion: Start by cutting a cream strip 5¼" x 24". Place the cloth template for P with its short side even with one long edge of the strip. Align your ruler with one long edge of the cloth template; cut. Repeat for the other long edge of the cloth template. Rotate the cloth template and move it down the strip to cut additional P patches. Trim the points of the P's.

Using the Cloth Template to cut Q Patches

Cut 13 strips 3⅛" x 24" for Q's.

Using the Cloth Template to cut P Patches

Cut 11 strips 5¼" x 24" for P's.

Making the Singular Diamonds Pieced Borders

Cut 108 O diamonds from 27 red strips cut 2⅛" x 18" as shown below; trim their points. Cut 4 cream R's for corners from 2 squares of 3⅜" as shown below; trim points.

Make 104 border units and 4 corner units as shown below. Join 26 border units; add a corner unit to the left end as shown on page 150. Repeat to make 4 borders alike.

Cutting O and R Patches and Making Pieced Borders

O **Strip for O Patch**

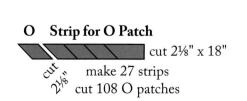

cut 2⅛" x 18"

make 27 strips
cut 108 O patches

cut 3⅜"

Border Corner Triangle R
cut 4 R triangles
from two **3⅜"** squares

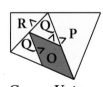

Corner Unit
make 4
sew one to the left
end of each border

Border Unit
make 104
join 26 for
each border

Singular Diamonds Pieced Border

press seam allowances to the right in the pieced borders

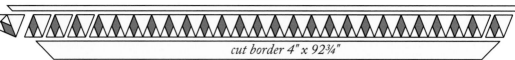

cut border 2" x 104¼"

cut border 4" x 92¾"

Pin and stitch the pieced borders to the inner plain borders already attached to the quilt center; stitch the miters. Pin and stitch the narrow outer borders to the quilt; stitch the miters to complete the quilt top.

Quilting and Finishing

Quilt with feathers in the cream background and outline quilting and echo quilting around diamonds and triangles. Bind as described on page 22 to finish the quilt.

Queen of Diamonds Coloring 2: Same blocks as the photographed quilt, with blue substituted for the cream background and white substituted for the red diamonds in the borders.

Queen of Diamonds Coloring 3: Same blocks and yardage as the phtotographed quilt, with black substituted for red.

Queen of Diamonds Coloring 4: Same blocks and yardage as the photographed quilt, with blue substituted for red.

Queen of Diamonds Coloring 5: Same blocks and yardage as the photographed quilt, with blue substituted for cream and cream substituted for red.

Wave on Wave

Wave on Wave, 92½" x 92½". Pieced by Chris Hulin from an original design by Judy Martin. Quilted by Lana Corcoran. Chris named the quilt after a song. After playing with the curved illusions in Appalachian Spring, I wanted to design a Lone Star with deep, undulating curves. Though the quilt looks very different, the blocks are made much like the scalloped blocks in that quilt. Wave on Wave is made from 8 diamond blocks in a 17½" finished width. They are arranged to form an 84½" square Lone Star. A pieced border of Lazy Diamonds completes the quilt. If you plan to use this border, be sure to stay stitch within the seam allowance along the border's edge so you don't stretch the bias edges of the quilt.

This quilt glows with monochromatic gradations like the quilts on pages 35–53, but does so simply with 4 values.

Quilt Size: 92½" x 92½" **Star Size:** 84½" sq.
Requires: 8 blocks **Block Width:** 17½"

Yardage & Cutting

Color	Yardage	#Strips	Cut Size	Strip End
1 ⬛	leftovers*	13	2½" x 18"	▱
		16	2¼" x 18"	▱
		5	2¼" x 18"	▱
		8	2" x 18"	▱
		8	1¾" x 18"	▱
		11	1½" x 18"	▱
		14	1⅜" x 18"	▱
		10	1¼" x 18"	▱
2 ⬛	3½ yds.	20	2½" x 18"	▱
		22	2¼" x 18"	▱
		5	2¼" x 18"	▱
		15	2" x 18"	▱
		15	1¾" x 18"	▱
		17	1½" x 18"	▱
		20	1⅜" x 18"	▱
		8	1¼" x 18"	▱
		2 E	4⅜" 2 in	◺

Color	Yardage	#Strips	Cut Size	S. End
3 ⬛	3½ yds.	15	2½" x 18"	▱
		22	2¼" x 18"	▱
		5	2¼" x 18"	▱
		20	2" x 18"	▱
		20	1¾" x 18"	▱
		17	1½" x 18"	▱
		14	1⅜" x 18"	▱
		6	1¼" x 18"	▱
4 ⬛	2½ yds.	8	2½" x 18"	▱
		16	2¼" x 18"	▱
		5	2¼" x 18"	▱
		13	2" x 18"	▱
		13	1¾" x 18"	▱
		11	1½" x 18"	▱
		8	1⅜" x 18"	▱
		4	1¼" x 18"	▱
5 ⬜	4¼ yds.	4 borders cut 2¾" x 90¼"		
		+ bkgd.: 4 A, 4 B or 8 C, 8 D		
	9 yds.	backing: 3 pcs. 34" x 101"		
1 ⬛	3 yds.*	binding: 4 strips 2" x 100"		

After cutting binding, cut fabric #1 into 6 lengths of 18".

Strip Piecing

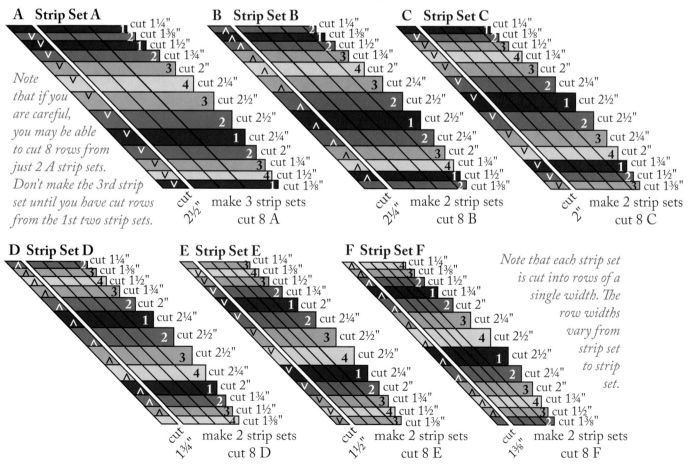

A Strip Set A
cut 1¼" · cut 1⅜" · cut 1½" · cut 1¾" · cut 2" · cut 2¼" · cut 2½" · cut 2½" · cut 2¼" · cut 2" · cut 1¾" · cut 1½" · cut 1⅜"

Note that if you are careful, you may be able to cut 8 rows from just 2 A strip sets. Don't make the 3rd strip set until you have cut rows from the 1st two strip sets.

cut 2½" make 3 strip sets cut 8 A

B Strip Set B
cut 1¼" · cut 1⅜" · cut 1½" · cut 1¾" · cut 2" · cut 2¼" · cut 2½" · cut 2½" · cut 2¼" · cut 2" · cut 1¾" · cut 1½" · cut 1⅜"

cut 2¼" make 2 strip sets cut 8 B

C Strip Set C
cut 1¼" · cut 1⅜" · cut 1½" · cut 1¾" · cut 2" · cut 2¼" · cut 2½" · cut 2½" · cut 2¼" · cut 2" · cut 1¾" · cut 1½" · cut 1⅜"

cut 2" make 2 strip sets cut 8 C

D Strip Set D
cut 1¼" · cut 1⅜" · cut 1½" · cut 1¾" · cut 2" · cut 2¼" · cut 2½" · cut 2½" · cut 2¼" · cut 2" · cut 1¾" · cut 1½" · cut 1⅜"

cut 1¾" make 2 strip sets cut 8 D

E Strip Set E
cut 1¼" · cut 1⅜" · cut 1½" · cut 1¾" · cut 2" · cut 2¼" · cut 2½" · cut 2½" · cut 2¼" · cut 2" · cut 1¾" · cut 1½" · cut 1⅜"

cut 1½" make 2 strip sets cut 8 E

F Strip Set F
cut 1¼" · cut 1⅜" · cut 1½" · cut 1¾" · cut 2" · cut 2¼" · cut 2½" · cut 2½" · cut 2¼" · cut 2" · cut 1¾" · cut 1½" · cut 1⅜"

cut 1⅜" make 2 strip sets cut 8 F

Note that each strip set is cut into rows of a single width. The row widths vary from strip set to strip set.

Make all strip sets using the same sequence of strip widths.

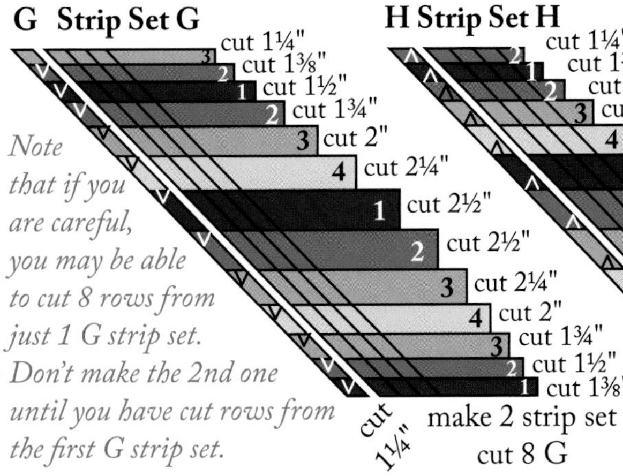
G Strip Set G
3 cut 1¼"
2 cut 1⅜"
1 cut 1½"
2 cut 1¾"
3 cut 2"
4 cut 2¼"
1 cut 2½"
2 cut 2½"
3 cut 2¼"
4 cut 2"
3 cut 1¾"
2 cut 1½"
1 cut 1⅜"
cut 1¼"
make 2 strip set
cut 8 G

Note that if you are careful, you may be able to cut 8 rows from just 1 G strip set. Don't make the 2nd one until you have cut rows from the first G strip set.

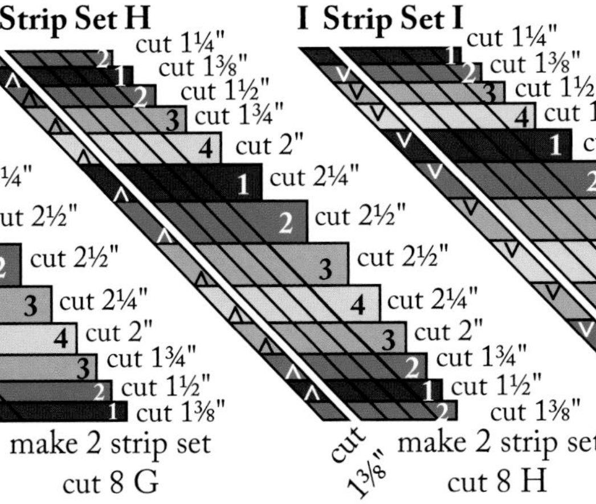
H Strip Set H
2 cut 1¼"
1 cut 1⅜"
2 cut 1½"
3 cut 1¾"
4 cut 2"
1 cut 2¼"
2 cut 2½"
3 cut 2½"
4 cut 2¼"
3 cut 2"
2 cut 1¾"
1 cut 1½"
2 cut 1⅜"
cut 1⅜"
make 2 strip sets
cut 8 H

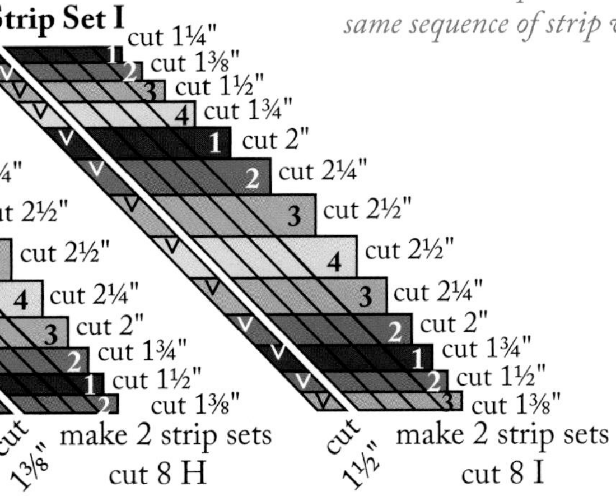
I Strip Set I
1 cut 1¼"
2 cut 1⅜"
3 cut 1½"
4 cut 1¾"
1 cut 2"
2 cut 2¼"
3 cut 2½"
4 cut 2½"
3 cut 2¼"
2 cut 2"
1 cut 1¾"
2 cut 1½"
3 cut 1⅜"
cut 1½"
make 2 strip sets
cut 8 I

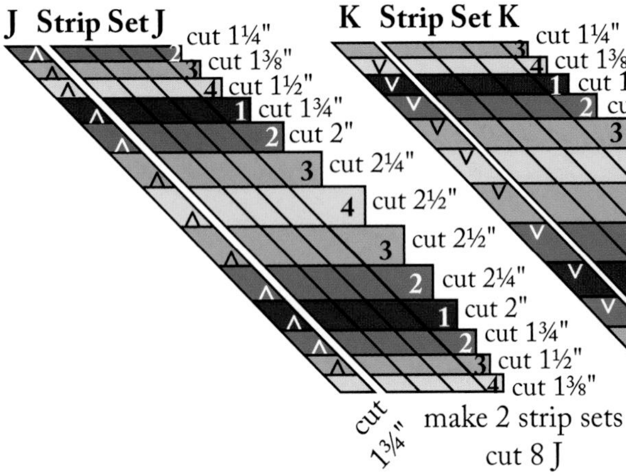
J Strip Set J
2 cut 1¼"
3 cut 1⅜"
4 cut 1½"
1 cut 1¾"
2 cut 2"
3 cut 2¼"
4 cut 2½"
3 cut 2½"
2 cut 2¼"
1 cut 2"
2 cut 1¾"
3 cut 1½"
4 cut 1⅜"
cut 1¾"
make 2 strip sets
cut 8 J

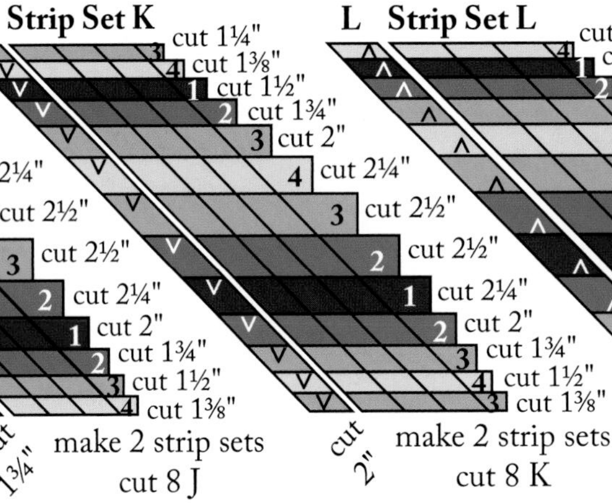
K Strip Set K
3 cut 1¼"
4 cut 1⅜"
1 cut 1½"
2 cut 1¾"
3 cut 2"
4 cut 2¼"
3 cut 2½"
2 cut 2½"
1 cut 2¼"
2 cut 2"
3 cut 1¾"
4 cut 1½"
3 cut 1⅜"
cut 2"
make 2 strip sets
cut 8 K

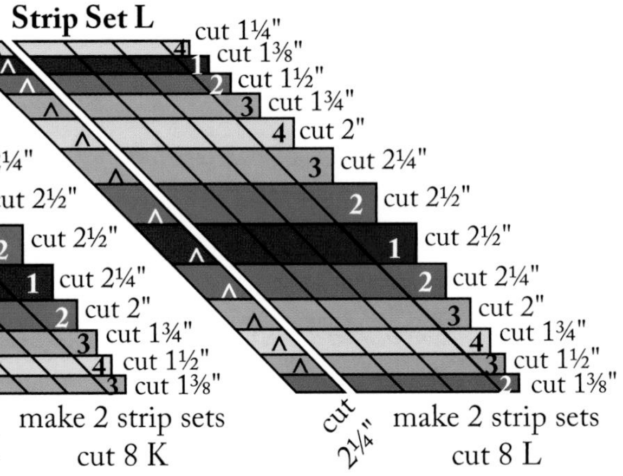
L Strip Set L
4 cut 1¼"
1 cut 1⅜"
2 cut 1½"
3 cut 1¾"
4 cut 2"
3 cut 2¼"
2 cut 2½"
1 cut 2½"
2 cut 2¼"
3 cut 2"
4 cut 1¾"
3 cut 1½"
2 cut 1⅜"
cut 2¼"
make 2 strip sets
cut 8 L

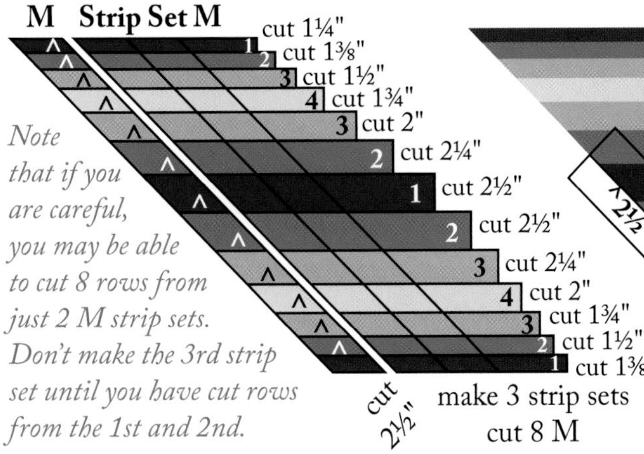
M Strip Set M
1 cut 1¼"
2 cut 1⅜"
3 cut 1½"
4 cut 1¾"
3 cut 2"
2 cut 2¼"
1 cut 2½"
2 cut 2½"
3 cut 2¼"
4 cut 2"
3 cut 1¾"
2 cut 1½"
1 cut 1⅜"
cut 2½"
make 3 strip sets
cut 8 M

Note that if you are careful, you may be able to cut 8 rows from just 2 M strip sets. Don't make the 3rd strip set until you have cut rows from the 1st and 2nd.

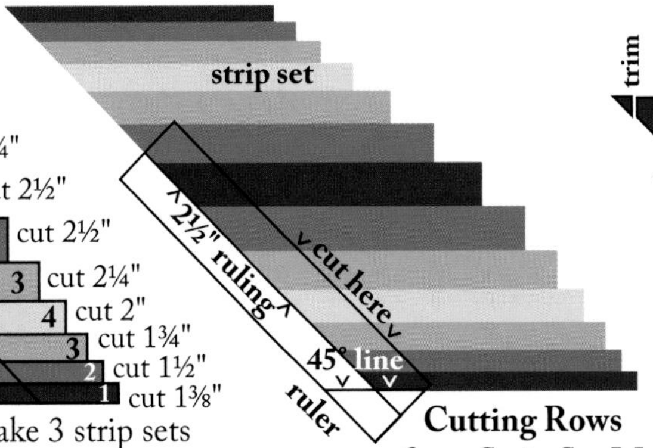
strip set
2½" ruling
cut here
45° line
ruler

Cutting Rows from Strip Set M

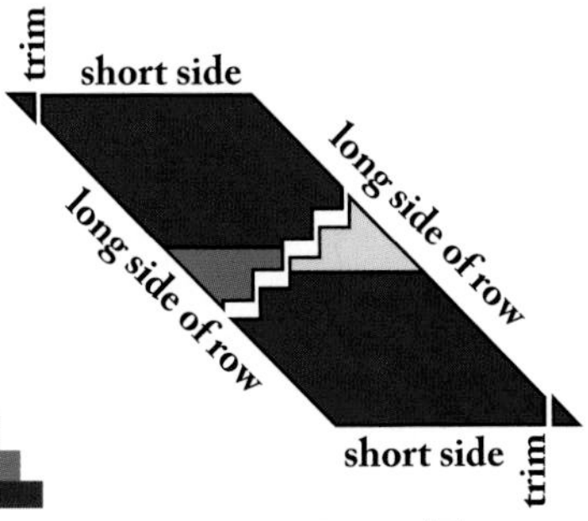
trim
short side
long side of row
long side of row
short side
trim

Point Trims for Rows (Regular)

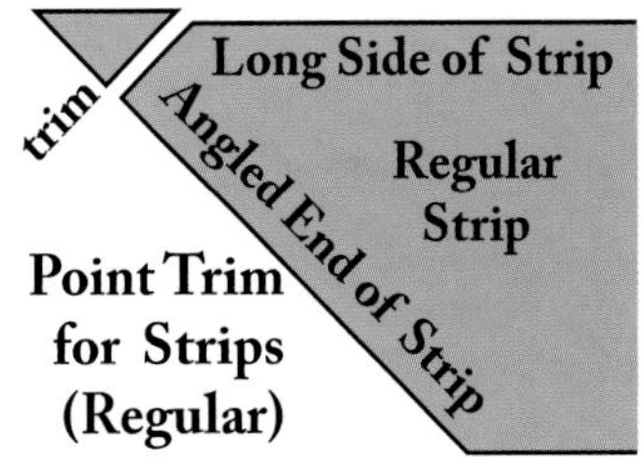
Long Side of Strip
trim
Angled End of Strip
Regular Strip

Point Trim for Strips (Regular)

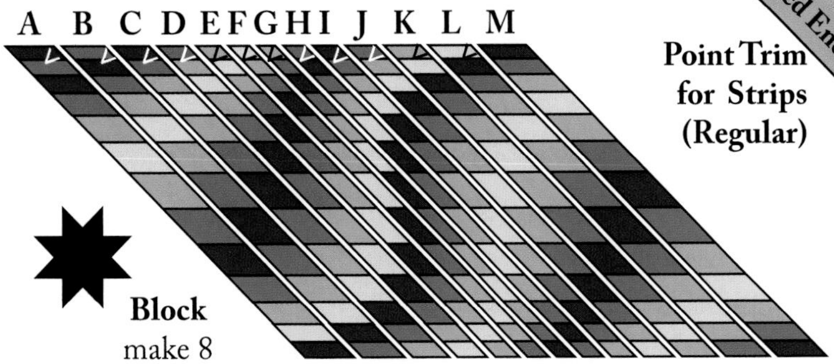
A B C D E F G H I J K L M

Block
make 8

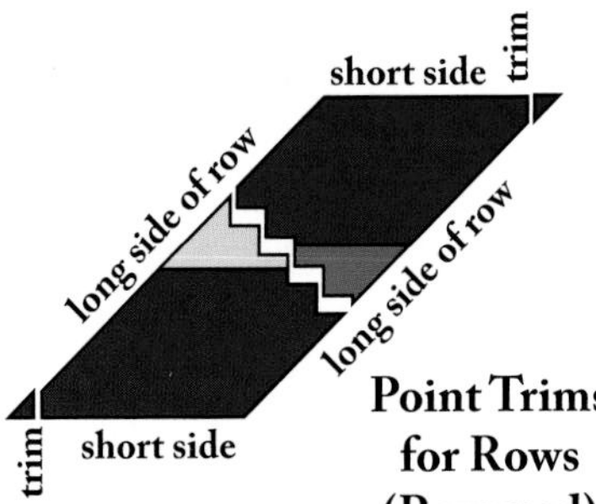
short side
trim
long side of row
long side of row
trim
short side

Point Trims for Rows (Reversed)

Making Strip Sets and Cutting Rows

Start by reading the glossary, "Pattern Pointers," and "How to Make a Lone Star" chapters on pages 7–22. You can cut all the strips before you sew any, or cut a little and sew a little, according to your preference. Cut the strips for a strip set, cutting off one end as indicated in the "strip end" column of the yardage chart. If you folded the fabric, unfold it before you cut off the strip ends unless you are making the N and Nr strips sets for the borders.

Trim the points as described on page 14 and shown on page 154 to help you align patches for sewing. The point should be trimmed at a right angle to the angled end of the strip. If you don't have my Point Trimmer tool, download a file to make one at judymartin.com/LSPT.cfm. Trim the points on all the strips except the top strip of a strip set or the bottom strip of a reversed strip set.

Align the trimmed point of one strip with the wide angle of the neighboring strip. Pin and stitch strips in the order shown. Press after each seam, following the "v" pressing arrows in the strip set diagrams. Continue pinning and stitching strips together to complete a strip set as shown. Trim a sliver off the angled end of the strip set, if necessary, at a precise 45° angle. See the row cutting diagram and instructions on page 154. Cut the strip set into rows of the width listed below the strip set. That is, lay the listed rule line of your rotary ruler over the angled end of the strip, align the 45° line with the top or bottom strip, and cut along the ruler. Make the listed number of strip sets and cut the listed number of rows. Trim both points of each row as shown on page 154.

Making Blocks

Lay out the rows for a block as shown in the block diagram on page 154. Pin rows at both ends, aligning the point trim of one row with the wide angle of the other. Also pin at each joint. Strategies for matching joints are on page 15. Stitch rows together, pressing after each seam in the direction indicated. Make 8 blocks.

Making the Pieced Borders

See the strip piecing diagrams for N and Nr below. Trim points of N and Nr strips as shown below and on page 154. Make 5 N and 5 Nr strip sets. Cut a total of 18 N and 18 Nr rows. Trim the points of N and Nr rows as shown at the bottom of page 154. Join 9 N rows end to end to make a border for the left side of the quilt. Repeat to make a border for the right side. Similarly, make top and bottom borders by sewing 9 Nr rows end to end for each border. Stay stitch within the seam allowances on both long edges of each border to prevent stretching.

Cut out the 2¾" x 90¼" plain borders from the background fabric if you have not yet done so. Also cut two E triangles from a 4⅜" square of blue #2 for the corners.

Assembling the Quilt

Cut out background patches shown below. Choose patches for use with or without Y-seams. See page 17 for tips on cutting patches larger than your ruler. Place blocks

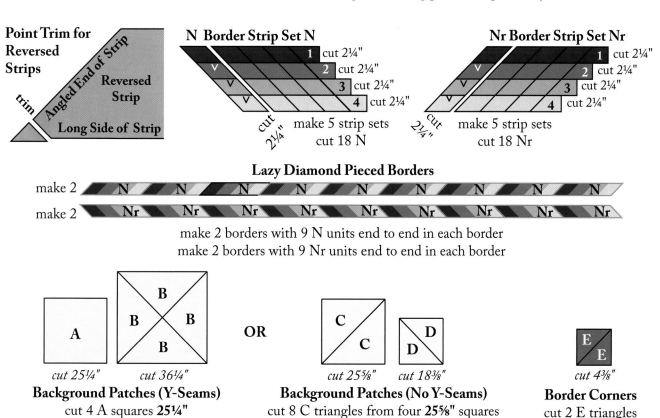

Point Trim for Reversed Strips

trim / Angled End of Strip / Reversed Strip / Long Side of Strip

N Border Strip Set N
1 cut 2¼"
2 cut 2¼"
3 cut 2¼"
4 cut 2¼"
cut 2¼"
make 5 strip sets
cut 18 N

Nr Border Strip Set Nr
1 cut 2¼"
2 cut 2¼"
3 cut 2¼"
4 cut 2¼"
cut 2¼"
make 5 strip sets
cut 18 Nr

Lazy Diamond Pieced Borders

make 2   N N N N N N N N N

make 2   Nr Nr Nr Nr Nr Nr Nr Nr Nr

make 2 borders with 9 N units end to end in each border
make 2 borders with 9 Nr units end to end in each border

A — cut 25¼"
B — cut 36¼"

OR

C — cut 25⅝"
D — cut 18⅜"

E E — cut 4⅜"

Background Patches (Y-Seams)
cut 4 A squares **25¼"**
cut 4 B triangles from one **36¼"** square

Background Patches (No Y-Seams)
cut 8 C triangles from four **25⅝"** squares
cut 8 D triangles from four **18⅜"** squares

Border Corners
cut 2 E triangles from one **4⅜"** square

and background patches as shown in the photo or setting variation of your choice. Be careful to turn the blocks as planned. Referring to the appropriate assembly diagram below, stitch blocks and patches in numerical order. Press after each seam, as indicated by the arrows. The quilt assembly with no Y-seams has you make the star in diagonal quarters, which lets you miter the borders without

Y-seams. Sew the pieced to the plain borders; stitch these to the ¼ blocks before they are joined to make a star. Add an E to upper right and lower left corners.

Finishing the Quilt

Lana Corcoran quilted in the ditch around the star. She quilted feathers in the background and wavy lines in the star. Binding directions are on page 22.

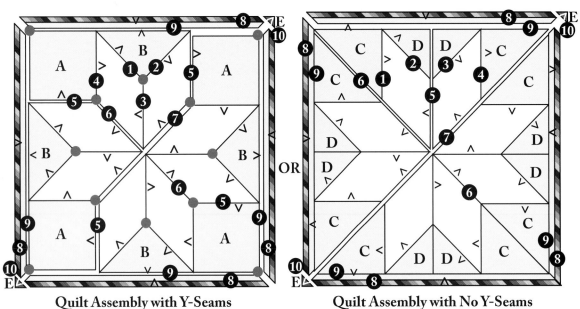

Quilt Assembly with Y-Seams   OR   Quilt Assembly with No Y-Seams

The 9 Nr border strips go on the top and bottom of the quilt. The 9 N border strips go on the right and left sides of the quilt. Turn the borders so that the light ends meet at upper left and lower right miters.

Wave on Wave Setting Variations
USING THE SAME BLOCK QUANTITIES AND YARDAGE

Arrangement 2: 8 blocks with opposite tips at the center.

Arrangement 3: 8 blocks with 4 turned with one tip in alternated with 4 turned with the other tip in.

156

Wave on Wave Color Variations
SUBSTITUTING ONE COLOR FOR ANOTHER IN YARDAGE AND DIAGRAMS

Coloring 2: 8 blocks with navy for #1, bright blue for #2, red for #3, cream for #4, and white for #5 background.

Coloring 3: 8 blocks with red for #1, orange for #2, yellow-orange for #3, bright yellow for #4, and cream for #5.

Coloring 4: 8 blocks with dark brown for #1, medium brown for #2, medium pink for #3, light pink for #4, and cream for #5.

Coloring 5: 8 blocks with navy for #1, turquoise for #2, lime for #3, bright yellow for #4, and white for #5 background.

Coloring 6: 8 blocks with black for #1, dark gray for #2, red for #3, light gray for #4, and white for #5 background.

Coloring 7: 8 blocks with black for #1, gray for #2, bright yellow for #3, pale yellow for #4, and white for #5 background.

Coloring 8: 8 blocks with violet for #1, bright blue for #2, turquoise for #3, green for #4, and white for #5 background.

Coloring 9: 8 blocks with red for #1, dark pink for #2, medium pink for #3, light pink for #4, and cream for #5.

Pattern Index

How-To Index

Judy Martin's Books & Products

Judy Martin has been making quilts since 1969 and writing quilting books since 1980. *Singular Stars* is her 23rd book. She was an editor at *Quilter's Newsletter* and *Quiltmaker* magazines before she and her husband began self-publishing her books in 1988. Judy has curated exhibits of her quilts at The National Quilt Museum and The Iowa Quilt Museum. She hopes to live long enough to use up her fabric stash.

Extraordinary Log Cabin Quilts, 2013, 128 pages. 15 fresh, new patterns presented in multiple sizes, each with 12 or more setting or coloring variations. Expert tips on everything from choosing values to rotary cutting and sewing. "These designs just blow my mind!" –Bonnie K. Hunter, author, quilter

Patchwork Among Friends, 2011, 128 pages. 10 glorious patterns, 12 tasty potluck recipes. Each pattern is presented in two sizes, with color diagrams, pressing instructions, and cutting layouts. Find great ideas for quilt get-togethers. "Go order a copy of *Patchwork Among Friends* - it's really, really good! Gorgeous quilt patterns!"–Tara Darr, Sew Unique Creations, Joliet, IL

Stellar Quilts, 2010, 128 pages. 13 patterns for outstanding star quilts in multiple sizes. Includes additional colorings for each. "Your quilts are fabulous. *Stellar Quilts* took my breath away." –Mary V., Lincoln, NE "Judy designs quilts like no other....complex looking, but not necessarily complex in construction."–*American Quilt Retailer*

Judy Martin's Log Cabin Quilt Book, 2007, 128 pages. 16 Log Cabins and exciting variations are presented in multiple sizes. This lavishly illustrated book has 100 setting plans, charts, and more. "As usual, Judy's instructions are precise, complete, and easy to follow." –Helen Weinman, Hyannis, MA

Star Happy Quilts E-book, 2001, 32 pages. The Star Happy quilt is presented with complete patterns for rotary cutting and machine piecing in 5 sizes. The pattern lends itself to setting variations, and Judy includes illustrations of 27 additional possibilites.

Piece 'n' Play Quilts, 2002, 96 pages. Complete patterns for 12 new and easy Drunkard's Paths, Log Cabins, and more. First you follow the pattern and piece the blocks. Then you play with their arrangement until you find the look YOU want. "*Piece 'n' Play Quilts* is a great book for beginners as well as the more experienced quilter." –Patricia T., Pahoa, HI

Cookies 'n' Quilts, 2001, 80 pages. 8 original quilt patterns feature stars within stars, maple leaves in a Log Cabin, and Snail's Trails made all from logs. The cookies and bars will take your baking to a new level of delicious decadence. "The book is well worth every penny, even if you buy it for the quilt patterns alone." –Sophie Littlefield, QuiltersReview.com

Judy Martin's Ultimate Rotary Cutting Reference, 1997, 80 pages. You'll find charts and instructions for cutting 52 shapes in countless sizes, plus detailed information on tools and techniques. "*Judy Martin's Ultimate Rotary Cutting Reference* will show you how to make the most of the rotary cutting rulers and tools you already own to cut shapes you didn't think were possible to rotary cut." –Liz Porter, "Love of Quilting"

Point Trimmer Tool, 1996. The Point Trimmer is the easiest way to pre-trim points, helping you align neighboring patches and reducing bulk in your quilt. "The Point Trimmer is one of the greatest tools ever." –Barbara L., Lancaster, PA

Shapemaker 45 Ruler, 1996. Save time, fabric, and money with the S45! Now you can easily rotary cut your favorite shapes – octagons, trapezoids, prisms, bow ties, house shapes, and more. "I just converted a very old template pattern into rotary cutting using your very-easy-to-use instructions and the Shapemaker 45." –Karen M., Littleton, CO

Scraps E-book, 2006, 128 pages. 16 original quilts are presented in multiple sizes. Learn all about scrap use, with tips from one of the foremost authorities on the subject. "*Scraps* is wonderful!!! It has wonderful patterns and easy-to-follow instructions." –Martha S., Frankfort, KY

See all of Judy's books and products at judymartin.com and JudyMartinEbooks.com